CADOGAN GUIDES

"Cadogan Guides really need no introduction and are mini-encyclopaedic on the countries covered ... they give the explorer, the intellectual or cultural buff—indeed any visitor—all they need to know to get the very best from their visit ... a good read too by the many inveterate armchair travellers." —*The Book Journal*

"The quality of writing in this British series is exceptional.... From practical facts to history, customs, sightseeing, food and lodging, the Cadogan Series can be counted on for interesting detail and informed recommendations." —*Going Places* (US)

"Standouts these days are the Cadogan Guides ... sophisticated, beautifully written books." —*American Bookseller Magazine*

"Entertaining companions, with sharp insights, local gossip and far more of a feeling of a living author ... The series has received plau~~dits worldwide for intelli~~ nality and a slightly irreverent sense of fun."

Other titles in the Cadogan Guides

AUSTRALIA
BALI
THE CARIBBEAN
ECUADOR, THE
    GALAPAGOS
    & COLOMBIA
GREEK ISLANDS
INDIA
IRELAND
ITALIAN ISLANDS
ITALY
NORTHEAST ITALY
NORTHWEST ITALY
MEXICO
MOROCCO
NEW YORK
PORTUGAL
PRAGUE

R
SCOTLAND
SOUTH ITALY
SPAIN
SOUTHERN SPAIN
THAILAND & BURMA
TURKEY
TUSCANY & UMBRIA
VENICE

Forthcoming:

AMSTERDAM
CENTRAL AMERICA
CZECHOSLOVAKIA
GERMANY
PARIS
SOUTH OF FRANCE
TUNISIA

For Marion

CADOGAN CITY GUIDES

BERLIN

ANDREW GUMBEL

CADOGAN BOOKS
London

THE GLOBE PEQUOT PRESS
Chester, Connecticut

Cadogan Books Ltd
Mercury House, 195 Knightsbridge, London SW7 1RE

The Globe Pequot Press
138 West Main Street, Chester, Connecticut 06412, USA

Cover design by Ralph King
Cover illustration by Amanda Hutt
(Please note: cover illustration on *Cadogan City Guide to Rome* is by Caroline Smith)

Maps © Cadogan Books, drawn by Ruth Hodkinson
Index by Dorothy Groves

Editor: Antony Mason
Series Editors: Rachel Fielding and Paula Levey

First published in 1991

British Library Cataloguing in Publication Data

Gumbel, Andrew
    Berlin.—(Cadogan city guides).
    1. Berlin.
    I. Title
914.315504879
ISBN 0–947754–29–6

Library of Congress Cataloging-in-Publication-Data

Gumbel, Andrew.
    Berlin/Andrew Gumbel.
        p.   cm.—(Cadogan guides)
    Includes index.
    ISBN 0–87106–238–0
    1. Berlin (Germany)—Description—Guide-books.   I. Title.
    II. Series.
    DD859.G95   1991   CIP
    914.31′5504879–dc20   91–15789

Photoset in Ehrhardt on a Linotron 202
Printed on recycled paper and bound in Great Britain by
Redwood Press Ltd, Melksham, Wiltshire

CONTENTS

CONTENTS

LIST OF MAPS

ABOUT THE AUTHOR

Andrew Gumbel went to Berlin for a week's holiday to watch the Wall come down in November 1989. He ended up staying more than a year. As a journalist living in both East and West Berlin, he tracked the collapse of East Germany and the run-up to German unification. Born in London, he graduated in modern languages and spent two years in Italy before going to Berlin. His work has appeared in newspapers around the world including the *Independent*, *Guardian*, *Boston Globe* and *Los Angeles Times*.

ACKNOWLEDGEMENTS

A big thank-you to Bruce Johnston who first put me in touch with Cadogan Books; to Martin, Alex, Mark, Paul, Erdmute, Doug, Andreas, Volker and Christian, my workmates in Berlin who helped more than some of them realized; to Angeli Büttner for sharing many Berlin secrets and to Enzo Vollmer for his historical insights; to Justine Ferchel and Antal Nemeth for help with the nightlife and hotel sections; to my family who fed me, offered various beds and made me laugh just when I needed it most; to my editor Antony Mason for his sound judgement, encouragement and good humour; to Ruth Hodkinson for her great maps; to Paula Levey, who was not only a pleasure to work for, but also gave up a room in her house and made sure I never lacked for chocolate or wine; and finally to the security guard at Tegel airport who, after long deliberation, decided my computer was not a bomb after all and let me (and it) go home to finish this book.

INTRODUCTION

The Brandenburg Gate

Make no mistake, Berlin is still two cities. The Wall may have gone, Germany may be reunified and the Cold War may have been pronounced dead a hundred times, but it will take years before East and West Berlin feel like one and the same place.

Everything continues to reek of division—the buildings, the people, their lifestyles, their culture. Berlin is suffering a giant hangover from the Cold War. If anything, the double nature of the city is more marked now that the borders are open, because everything has become more visible. Like Noah's Ark, Berlin has two of everything—from city halls and transport systems to opera houses, Egyptology museums and zoos. The two sides are not simply mirror images; they are different worlds. Before the Wall came down, crossing Berlin through the corridor-like border at Checkpoint Charlie felt like stepping into C. S. Lewis's wardrobe and emerging in the fantasy world of Narnia, whichever direction you were going in. The lights of the West seemed impossibly bright next to the uncanny grey calm of the East. Nowadays the transition is less mysterious, and certainly less cumbersome, but the sense of wonder persists.

Curiously, the old claustrophobia of Wall-bound West Berlin and the old mistrust between East and West have lived on too; the scar left by the Wall through the heart of the city is still a very real psychological barrier. Berliners do not introduce themselves just as Berliners; they almost always add, with a slightly sheepish awkwardness, the tag East or West.

They still find it difficult to venture into the unfamiliar, other part of the city. Taxi drivers feel a sense of panic when asked to drive through the divide. Friends from *drüben*, 'over there', are introduced at parties like curiosities, creatures from another time and another planet. Why? They speak the same language, don't they? Didn't they yearn, all those years when concrete and barbed wire kept them apart, for the day they could come back together? Didn't they hug, kiss and weep on that magical November night in 1989 when the borders fell? And even if their living standards don't quite match up yet, haven't they at least got used to each other?

Perhaps one should imagine West and East like twins reunited in middle age after decades of enforced separation. Let's call them Horst and Helga. Horst has gone into business and prospered. He has a fine house in a quiet, orderly suburb, drives a Mercedes and plays golf at weekends. His wife, a Rhinelander, can be a bit bossy sometimes but she has been unswervingly loyal to him through thick and thin. Horst has a cellar of fine French wines and a collection of leather-bound classics which he says he will read when he retires. He has aged gracefully and, apart from an ever-expanding waistline, is in robust health. Helga, on the other hand, looks a bit of a wreck. Life has been a constant struggle, what with her disastrous marriage to a vodka-swilling lout who promised her equality but never let her do anything without his permission. He forbade her to visit Horst and flew into a rage whenever her brother sent her a new dress or a box of chocolates. She had a steady job in a textiles factory and had no trouble feeding and clothing her children, but she never really had any fun. She fancied herself as an actress, or perhaps a novelist, travelling the world, dancing with strange men and eating exotic food that she had only ever read about. Finally, incredibly, she managed to run away from her increasingly paranoid husband. With nowhere else to turn, she went to live with Horst and his wife in their dowdy suburb. At first they were delighted to see each other, but now the excitement has definitely worn off. Horst keeps telling Helga how marvellous his French wine is and suggests she becomes an accountant. He thinks her marriage has made her soft in the head and tells her to get serious. Helga fancies taking up the saxophone or flying to Paris. She wishes Horst wouldn't keep telling her what to do.

No wonder they don't get on. The pace of change in Berlin has been so breathtaking that people simply haven't been given the chance to catch up. The West feels its cocooned, privileged lifestyle—propped up by hefty subsidies from Bonn—has been invaded and destroyed. The East

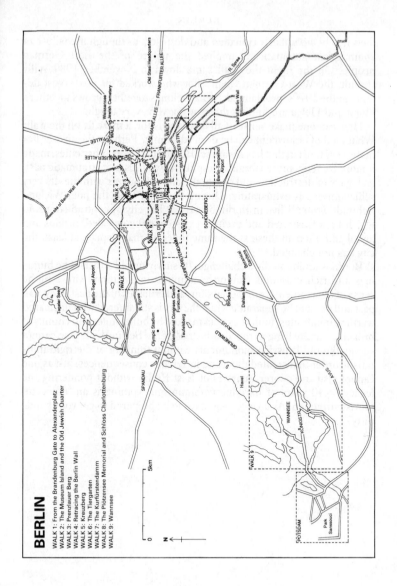

BERLIN

WALK 1: From the Brandenburg Gate to Alexanderplatz
WALK 2: The Museum Island and the Old Jewish Quarter
WALK 3: Prenzlauer Berg
WALK 4: Retracing the Berlin Wall
WALK 5: Kreuzberg
WALK 6: The Tiergarten
WALK 7: The Kurfürstendamm
WALK 8: The Plötzensee Memorial and Schloss Charlottenburg
WALK 9: Wannsee

feels it is being unfairly ridiculed and despised, as though the failure of communism automatically implied the failure of the East German people. On the night the Wall came down in November 1989 Willy Brandt, the West German Chancellor who worked for East–West détente in the 1970s, proclaimed: 'What belongs together, grows together.' Horst and Helga are finding the growing very, very tough.

How can one make sense of all this as a visitor, a mere fly on the wall? What kind of enjoyment can be derived from it? Perhaps the answer lies in the very tension that has always set Berlin apart from other cities, made it more frenetic, more vibrant. Despite the wounds of its traumatic past, its legacy of destruction and death, the city still buzzes with life. Its very schizophrenia is exhilarating. During the Cold War, the poet Wieland Schmidt wrote: 'I live in Berlin because it is a city of contradictions, in which I am frustrated and excited, exposed and concealed, furious and joyful and often all these at the same time.' In that respect, at least, the city has not changed.

Berlin is undoubtedly a challenge. Its surviving old streets, fine buildings and rich museums cannot be admired in isolation, with a blithe sense of detachment from the passions and cruelties of the past. How can past and present be separated when the city is still littered with uncleared wartime bomb sites, buildings pockmarked by bullet holes and chunks of broken concrete lying in the 'death strip' of the Berlin Wall? One cannot survey the old Prussian monuments without thinking of the rigid militaristic order that created them and its terrible consequences, just as one cannot visit the poorer quarters of East Berlin without pondering the legacy of 40 years of hardline communism. Nothing is an 'innocent' tourist attraction. As a visitor you have to be prepared to get your hands dirty.

Travel

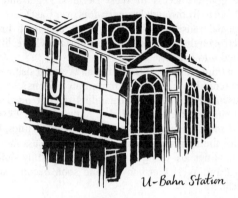

U-Bahn Station

Berlin: Some Facts and Figures

Berlin lies in the middle of a huge plain in north-eastern Germany, just 34 m above sea level, at 52.31 degrees latitude and 13.25 degrees longitude. It is no further east than Naples, and yet it is closer to Poland than to the old West German border. After reunification on 3 October 1990, Berlin became the capital of Germany, as it had been from 1871 to 1945. However, the seat of government has remained in the old West German capital, Bonn. Berlin's city boundaries encompass some 883 sq km, 480 in the West and 403 in the East. The area constitutes one of Germany's 16 federal states. The city's population is roughly the same as it was in 1920 when the present boundaries of Greater Berlin were established: around 4 million, of whom just over 2 million live in the West and just under 2 million in the East. One-sixth of the metropolitan area is woodland, and another sixth is made up of parks or agricultural land. Nearly a fifth of the population is under 20, making Berlin one of the youngest cities in Germany, while another fifth is over 65. The city symbol is the bear.

Arriving in Berlin

Getting to Berlin is a lot easier than it used to be. The East was, of course, subject to visa and currency requirements; there were

1

accommodation difficulties and restriction of movement. But reaching the West was tricky too. You had to pay special surcharges. Only airlines from the United States, Britain and France—the three Western wartime allies—were granted access to West Berlin's Tegel and Tempelhof airports and had to fly through low corridors over East German airspace. Cars used special transit routes and had to take care not to break down or run out of petrol on the way. Now all these obstacles have, like the Berlin Wall, vanished into history.

Visas are a thing of the past for nearly all Western visitors staying less than 90 days (certainly European Community citizens, Americans, Canadians, Australians and New Zealanders do not need one—just a passport or British visitor's card will do). At the end of 1990 the German state carrier Lufthansa, along with countless other airlines, began flying into Berlin for the first time since 1945. Proper access motorways with full service facilities are being built, and the painfully slow train links between East and West Germany should soon become speedier and more practical.

By Air: The main airport for international flights is **Tegel** (known very occasionally as Flughafen Otto Lilienthal) in the West, tel (W) 41011. Originally built in 90 days during the 1948–49 airlift, it was completely revamped in the early 1970s and is now modern, efficient and quick. The airport is shaped like a doughnut with separate customs and passport checks at each gate, making for minimal walking and minimal queues when checking in for the return journey. The bars, duty-free shops and restaurant are expensive and close early. A taxi can get you to the centre of West Berlin in 20 minutes in light traffic and costs around DM 15. Bus no. 9 to Bahnhof Zoo takes a little longer (buy your DM 2.70 ticket from the driver; try to have the right change ready). Central East Berlin is twice as far and costs twice as much by taxi. During business hours heavy traffic can turn the journey from the airport into a nightmare. A good tip is to take the no. 9 bus one stop to Jakob-Kaiser-Platz, then change onto the U-Bahn (see p. 4) using the same ticket. It sounds complicated, especially with luggage, but it can save up to an hour.

The West's second airport, **Tempelhof**, tel (W) 6909433, is in the middle of a built-up area and is used only for a handful of charter flights. It is beside Platz der Luftbrücke U-Bahn station, 10 minutes by public transport from central East Berlin and 20 minutes from central West Berlin.

Ever more charter and scheduled flights are opting for the East's **Schönefeld** airport, tel (E) 6720. From here you can catch an S-Bahn into town (30 minutes to East Berlin, 50 minutes to West). There are also special buses to Bahnhof Zoo and Tegel airport.

Airline offices are sprouting in Berlin like alfalfa. While the former East German carrier Interflug has gone out of business, the likes of Lufthansa and other western companies are flooding in. So this (by no means exhaustive) list is subject to change:

Aeroflot: Budapester Str. 50, tel (W) 2618250 and Unter den Linden 51–53, tel (E) 2291592
Air France: Europa Center, tel (W) 261051
Alitalia: Tauentzienstr. 16, tel (W) 2110129
Austrian Airlines: Frankfurter Tor 8a, tel (E) 5892777
British Airways: Kurfürstendamm 178–79 and Tegel, tel (W) 41012647
Dan Air: Tegel, tel (W) 41012716
Delta Airlines: Kurfürstendamm 209, tel (W) 8824881
KLM: Friedrichstr. 73, tel (E) 2291915
Lufthansa: Kurfürstendamm 220, tel (W) 88755
Pan Am: Europa Center, tel (W) 881011
SAS: Unter den Linden 24, tel (E) 2291880

By Train: This is still long, tedious and expensive and only worth it if you are in Germany already. The main destination from points west is **Bahnhof Zoo**, slap bang in the centre of West Berlin. Trains from the east, north and south tend to wind up at stations a long way out of town like the misleadingly named **Hauptbahnhof** (literally main station) and **Bahnhof Lichtenberg**. Both of these are on the East Berlin S-Bahn system and are roughly 20 minutes from Alexanderplatz in the city centre. Check train timetables carefully for the correct station, or call (W) 19419 for information.

By Car: Approach roads are bumpy and ill-lit. If you see a petrol station, fill up because it could be the last for 100 km. The speed limit on motorways in former East German territory is 100 kph although it is regularly abused in light traffic. When leaving Berlin, you might be interested in *Mitfahrzentralen*, agencies that put drivers with space in their cars in touch with passengers willing to contribute petrol money. Try the Mitfahrzentrale im Kudammeck, Kurfürstendamm 227, tel (W) 8827606, or the Mitfahrzentrale Citykontakt, Marienburger Str. 47, tel (E) 4365447.

Getting Around Berlin

By Underground: Berlin has an extensive urban railway network, which provides the quickest transport around the city. Trains come in two varieties: the **S-Bahn**, short for *Stadtbahn* or city train, which tends to cover more outlying areas and stops less often; and the **U-Bahn**, *Untergrundbahn* or underground train, which concentrates on inner-city routes. Despite the names, both sorts go above and below ground at various points. You can pick up a free map of the network at most stations. East and West have reconnected and integrated all their old links. A straightforward adult ticket costs DM 2.70 and lasts 2 hours (valid on buses too). A multiple ticket, good for four or five trips, will save you a mark or two. A one-day pass costs DM 9. A week's pass (requiring a passport photo) is DM 26. The network is closed from around midnight to 4 am. Get your tickets from coin-operated dispensers or from manned counters, and punch them in special machines as you walk on the platform. There are no barriers and few spot-checks on passengers—not necessary because nearly every Berliner displays model Prussian obedience and unfailingly buys a ticket. The fine for travelling without, should you be caught, is DM 60.

By Bus: East and West are only slowly joining up their bus systems, so there are still two separate networks. The driver announces each stop in advance. Berlin buses used to run right on schedule, but chronic traffic problems have changed all that and you do better to keep off them for long journeys during business hours. Tickets are interchangeable for bus and underground and cost the same. Something to remember is that jaunts along the Kurfürstendamm come at the knockdown price of DM 1. Night buses operate only in West Berlin; see Entertainment and Nightlife section for more details.

By Tram: These are confined to the East of the city. Tickets are the same as for buses. Trams have nostalgia value but tend to be slow.

By Car: Be prepared for jams, frustration and lots and lots of parking tickets. Berlin has turned into a traffic nightmare. Cars are only useful to get home late at night or to get out of town. Be careful, too, of the drink-driving laws which are strictly enforced. In East Berlin you can't drink at all; in West Berlin the limit is 0.8 parts per 1000 (two glasses of wine or a large beer). Watch out for the appalling road surfaces in the East, especially the 'shudder effect' when approaching traffic lights.

4

Addresses for out-of-hours petrol include Kantstr. 126, Uhland-str. 187 (both Charlottenburg), Reichpietschufer 16–18 (Schöneberg) and Hohenzollerndamm 41–42 (Zehlendorf). If you break down, call ADAC, the German equivalent of the Automobile Association, on (W) 19211.

The cheapest and best **car rental** agency is TAR, tel (E) 5416017. It is based out in the backwoods of East Berlin, but a car can be delivered to your address free of charge. Otherwise check out the usual names:

Avis: Budapester Str. 43 and Tegel airport, tel (W) 2611881

Hertz: Budapester Str. 39 and Tegel airport, tel (W) 2611053

InterRent Europcar: Kurfürstendamm 178–79 and Tegel, tel (W) 8818093

By Taxi: Easy and quite cheap (around DM 15 for an average journey). Flag one down, or tel (W) 240024, 6902, 261026 or 240202.

By Bicycle: This is a pleasure, and practical too, with plentiful cycle lanes and intelligently laid-out traffic junctions to minimize the danger of being flattened by an angry Mercedes. Be extra careful of thieves, who are more ruthless in Berlin than most places; there is a roaring second-hand trade in stolen bicycles. You can hire bikes for around DM 10 per day, leaving your passport as a deposit, from:

Fahrradverleih Rad Lust: Waldemarstr. 42 (Kreuzberg), tel (W) 651925

Fahrradbüro Berlin: Hauptstr. 146 (Schöneberg), tel (W) 7845562

Grunewald S-Bahn station (summer only): Schmetterlingsplatz, tel (W) 8115829

On Foot: Just two pieces of commonly neglected advice. Don't walk on the cycle paths, which are red and hug the kerb: you are liable to be shouted at, abused or even run down. Think twice, too, about jaywalking. It's not that it's dangerous or even particularly illegal, although you can be fined if you are very unlucky. It's just that you will invariably get a 5-minute lecture from tut-tutting fellow pedestrians—even if there isn't a car in sight.

Travellers with Disabilities

Despite good intentions, Berlin presents several problems for travellers with disabilities. The Wall was never meant to provide easy access for anyone, and links between the two sides of the city are still tricky for anyone of limited mobility. Paths and pavements near the site of the Wall are virtually impassable in a wheelchair. The same goes for the tumbledown streets beyond the centre of East Berlin. But Berlin's main problem is its size: there is inevitably a lot of ground to cover, especially as several interesting sights are out of doors. On the bright side, roughly half Berlin's museums and half its underground stations have wheelchair facilities. A number of organizations might be of help. The Interessengemeinschaft von Geburt an Behinderter (lobby group for those disabled from birth) at Otto-Suhr-Allee 131, tel (W) 3411797, lends out free wheelchairs to anyone in need. The Behindertendienst (disabled service) at Joachimstaler Str. 15, tel (W) 880033, organizes special bus tours. For more general information try the Landesbeauftragte für Behinderte (regional authority for the disabled) in Sächsische Str. 28–30, tel (W) 8676114. The British organization RADAR has information on specialized holidays. Contact them at 25 Mortimer St, London W1M 8AB, tel (071) 637 5400.

Maps

The demise of the Berlin Wall was a map-maker's nightmare. No sooner had publishers rushed to produce new editions showing the newly opened border crossings than the border disappeared altogether. With roads still being reconnected, even the most recent editions are not entirely up to the minute. An out-of-date map is nonetheless intriguing as it confronts you with the astonishingly rapid physical changes that Berlin has undergone. Far and away the most respected publisher is Falk. Their tourist map costs about DM 4 and covers all but the very outskirts of the city. Their fuller city map is twice as expensive, covers Potsdam as well as all of greater Berlin, and is intricately cut and folded to help you consult a section without having to spread out the entire thing. Both are available at airports and at all newsagents and bookshops.

Practical A–Z

Alexanderplatz

Best Time to Go, Climate, Packing

Don't go to Berlin for the weather. In the summer it is often sunny but rarely hot. In the winter it can get piercingly cold and rains or snows much of the time; the stars of all those old spy films did not wear thickly lined coats, gloves and hats for nothing. The famous Berlin air, much praised by the cabaret songwriters of the 1920s, is now fouled by traffic fumes and industrial smog. Nevertheless, the summer months can be delightful, with parks and lakes looking resplendent and pavement cafés bursting with life. Autumn mists and changing colours can be irresistibly atmospheric. This is how average temperatures look month by month:

Jan	−1° (29° F)	July	20° (69° F)
Feb	0° (32° F)	Aug	20° (68° F)
Mar	4° (41° F)	Sept	16° (60° F)
Apr	10° (50° F)	Oct	10° (50° F)
May	15° (59° F)	Nov	4° (40° F)
June	18° (65° F)	Dec	0° (32° F)

These are only averages; temperature variation is startling, especially in winter when it can get as cold as −10 or −15°. Bring your woollies and sturdy waterproof shoes most of the year round. Otherwise dress as outlandishly as you please. See the Entertainment and Nightlife section for some idea of varying fashions; you can't go too far wrong with black leather.

Voltage is 220 AC; outlets take plugs with two round prongs. Clothes, camera film and anything else you might have forgotten are reasonably priced and easy to find.

Children

'It is extremely unlikely that a society with few children will be friendly towards children,' German Interior Minister Wolfgang Schäuble once commented about his country. Before unification West Germany had the lowest birth rate in Europe, and West Berlin had fewer children than any other city. Families were not attracted to the claustrophobic life of an enclave city, so the population had a disproportionate number of students and pensioners. East Berlin was very different. People tended to marry young and have large families; crèches, playgrounds and schools were plentiful and free. Unfortunately things now seem to be going the West's way. Mothers who used to take their children to shops or offices without a care now get cold, disapproving stares; the East's crèches will soon have to pay their own way instead of relying on large state subsidies.

So Berlin is probably even less accommodating for children than other big cities. However, there is no reason why older ones, at least, should not be as interested as adults in many of the sights. Walk IV (retracing the Wall) and Walk IX (the fairy-tale castles, parks and forests around Wannsee) will probably have the widest appeal. One 'must', if it snows, is the **Teufelsberg** (see Walk IX), a long, gentle hill in the Grunewald forest justly famous for its toboggan runs. The tourist office will try to fob you off with a number of 'special' children's attractions. These tend to be a long way out of the centre, or cringingly awful, or both. After all, if the West Berlin zoo is a disappointment for adults (see Walk VI), why should children like it any better?

There are a handful of sights not mentioned in the tours that travellers with children should know about. The Kurfürstendamm has two entertaining museums: the **Panoptikum** (wax museum) on the third floor of the Ku'damm Eck (corner of Joachimstaler Str., open 10 am–11 pm daily, adm), and the **Teddy Museum Berlin** on the first floor of the Kurfürstendamm Karree (corner of Uhlandstr., open 3–10 pm except Tues, free), which has an enchanting collection of Paddington, Winnie-the-Pooh and Rupert bears spanning the 20th century.

Look out for **circuses**, which are advertised all over the city and generally of a very high standard. Common sites for companies such as Roncalli, Busch and Berolina are Stüler Str. in the Tiergarten, Potsdamer Platz and Volkspark Friedrichshain (off Artur-Becker-Str.) In the summer there are often **outdoor puppet shows** on Kollwitzplatz in Prenzlauer Berg. For German-speaking children, **Grips** on Altonaer Str. 22 (tel (W) 3914004) in the Tiergarten is an excellent and versatile theatre. Finally, if you want to go to a zoo, East Berlin's **Tierpark** in Friedrichsfelde is more varied, more interesting and cheaper than its counterpart in the West. It has its own U-Bahn station on line 6 from Alexanderplatz. Its resources are being cut, so call the tourist office, tel (W) 2626031, for latest details of opening hours and admission fees.

If you want to be rid of your children for the day or the evening, try one of these baby-sitting agencies. They cost around DM 12–15 per hour:
Heinzelmännchen: Unter den Eichen 96 (Dahlem), tel (W) 8316071
TUSMA: Hardenbergstr. 35 (Charlottenburg), tel (W) 3134054

Consulates

Unification spelled the end for countless foreign embassies in East Berlin. Although Berlin is officially the new German capital, ambassadors and most of their staff have stayed put in Bonn. Consulates in West Berlin have, however, remained open:

Canada: Europe Center, tel (W) 2611161
Great Britain: Uhlandstr. 7, tel (W) 3095292
Ireland: Ernst-Reuter-Platz 10, tel (W) 34800822
United States: Clayallee 170, tel (W) 8324087

Crime

Berlin never used to have a crime problem. The East was kept in check by the pervasive power of the Stasi security police and the West only suffered from the odd riot and a few addicts stealing for dope money. All that, alas, has changed. The opening of the Wall has brought all sorts of social upheaval and unwanted side-effects, from muggings to car break-ins to bank robberies. Women say that for the first time they feel unsafe in the streets at night, especially in ill-lit East Berlin. However, anyone used to London or New York should still find it relatively friendly. The usual warnings apply: hold on to your handbags and wallets, and don't lurk around quiet suburbs after dark. Watch out, too, for gangs of skinheads who have recently diverted their attention from fighting each other to attacking unsuspecting passengers on the U-Bahn. Their favourite technique is to grab your purse while the train is at a station, then toss you out onto the platform as the train moves off again.

If you are unlucky enough to be robbed, or have your car bashed, or suffer misfortune of any kind, get in touch with the **police** immediately. Their number is (W) 6990 or, in emergencies, (W) 110. You will need them for any insurance claims and risk hostile treatment if you try to sidestep them. The police tend to be gruff, pedantic and unsympathetic to foreigners. If they think you have hesitated so much as a moment before contacting them, they will be no help at all. If the police start messing you around, the best way to deal with them is to shout. Don't be rude, just shout authoritatively and they will usually do what you want. Should you end up on the wrong side of the law, insist on speaking to your consulate (see above for numbers) straight away. As long as your alleged offence is not too heinous you should be well treated.

Festivals and a Calendar of Events

West Berlin never offered much in the way of festivals; East Berlin has now lost all its official Communist Party parades and heavily subsidized cultural programmes. It remains to be seen how the city will celebrate the momentous events of 1989–90. For the moment the list of annual shindigs is short and a bit glum:

15 January	March in Volkspark Friedrichshain to mark the anniversary of the murders of revolutionaries Rosa Luxemburg and Karl Liebknecht in 1919 (see Walk VI)
February	Berlin Film Festival
	International Tourism Fair
May	The Peace Race, involving cyclists from all over eastern Europe; usually has a stage beginning or ending in
	Berlin Theatre Festival, bringing talent from all Germany
1 May	Annual riot in Kreuzberg
10 May	Writers gather in Bebelplatz on anniversary of the Nazi book burning which took place here in 1933
July	Jazz in July festival
September	Berlin Arts Festival (*Festwochen*). Includes exhibitions, plays and special events

October	Berlin Marathon (on the first Sunday of the month)
	Berlin Motor Show (at the International Congress
	Centre)
3 October	Day of German Unity
9 November	Anniversary of the Wall opening in 1989, and of the
	Nazis' 1938 anti-Jewish pogrom. City officials and
	Jewish leaders vie for attention with upbeat speeches
	on the one hand and sober synagogue services on the
	other
December	Open-air Christmas markets appear on
	Wittenbergplatz, Alexanderplatz and elsewhere selling
	toys, knick-knacks and hot food and drink
31 December	New Year celebrations at the Brandenburg Gate

Lavatories

These are a German speciality, impeccably clean and never short of loo paper. Perhaps the most impressive are to be found in the Curator Hotel in Charlottenburg, where the bathrooms are kitted out with telephone, stereo sound system, air conditioning, central heating and electronically activated flush. There aren't too many public toilets in Berlin, but bars, restaurants and hotels will be happy to grant free use of their facilities. There are just two possible pitfalls. One is the Communist-era paper still being used up in some amenities in East Berlin, which is grey, crinkly and about as absorbent as a lump of rock. The other is the highly disconcerting platform most toilets have beneath the occupant's bottom. This ingeniously avoids splashing, but also means you are virtually forced to inspect, and worse still smell, your business before flushing it away. Erica Jong became quite obsessed with this 'wash out' style of plumbing in her novel *Fear of Flying*, and suspected the Germans rather enjoyed examining their stools. She wrote: 'Anyone who can build toilets like this is capable of anything.'

Medical Emergencies, Insurance, Doctors and Pharmacies

For an **ambulance**, tel (W) 3871 or (E) 115.

The **emergency numbers** for a doctor, day or night, are (W) 310031 or (E) 1259. Ask for one who speaks English if you need it—most in the West do. The doctor can get you into a hospital if necessary. Berlin's

11

health system, now unified, is somewhat bureaucratic but quite good. Hospitals are clean and usually have spare beds. Doctors and nurses in the East tend to have a more human approach and are as unused to the complicated form-filling as any foreigner. You can get hold of a dentist out of hours on tel (W) 1141 between 9 pm and 2 am, or (W) 8920379 at the following times: Fridays 4–6 pm; Saturdays, Sundays and holidays 10 am–12 pm and 4–6 pm.

National medical insurance covers UK and Canadian citizens (in Britain, pick up form E111 from the Department of Social Security at least 2 weeks before you leave). Other nationals may want to take out travel insurance (check your current policy to see if it covers you while abroad), available from most travel agents. Most travel policies cover not only health, but stolen or lost baggage, cancelled or delayed flights too.

Go to any pharmacy (*Apotheke*) and you will see, in the window, a list of those staying open late. Otherwise call (W) 1141 or (E) 160 to find out where your nearest dispensary is.

Money

There is a single currency, the deutschmark or *deutsche Mark* (DM), made up of 100 pfennigs. If you ever get old East German small change you are not being diddled, but it is only accepted in the East. There are very roughly 3 DM to the pound, rather less than two of them to the US dollar. Germany is very much a cash society, so expect to pay for most things with notes and coins. Shops, hotels and restaurants will accept Eurocheques; the poshest (for hotels, three stars and over), plus petrol stations, take credit cards. If you don't have Eurocheques, bring traveller's cheques and change them regularly. **Banks** are open 8.15–12.30 weekday mornings and begin afternoon business at 1.30. On Mon–Wed they close at 4.00, Thurs at 6.00 and Fri at 3.30. They are shut Saturdays and Sundays. If you have any dealings with a bank, bring every document you possess: they are bureaucratic in the extreme and painfully slow. Head offices of the main banks are:

Berliner Bank: Hardenbergstr. 32, tel (W) 31090
Berliner Commerzbank: Potsdamer Str. 125, tel (W) 26971
Berliner Volksbank: Kurfürstendamm 46, tel (W) 8841930
BfG:Bank: Am Schillertheater 2, tel (W) 31140
Deutsche Bank: Otto-Suhr-Allee 6, tel (W) 34070
Dresdner Bank: Uhlandstr. 9–11, tel (W) 31961

The best **out-of-hours banking** is with the currency changers near Bahnhof Zoo. Try:

AGW: Joachimstaler Str. 1–3 (open Mon–Fri 8–8, Sat 9–3), tel (W) 8821086
Wechselstube Bahnhof Zoo: in the station (open Mon–Fri 8–9 and Sat 9–6), tel (W) 8817117

There is only one **credit card office** in Berlin:
American Express: Kurfürstendamm 11, tel (W) 8827585

Museums

Berlin is a storehouse of museums of all kinds, from the great collections of antiquities in the Pergamon Museum and other treasures of Museum Island to the modern art collection of the National Gallery, from the Checkpoint Charlie Museum (devoted to the Wall) to a museum of hairdressing (see Berlin by Theme, p. 51–2). What's more, many of Berlin's museums are free, or at least comparatively inexpensive. In West Berlin admission to state-owned museums (run by the *Staatliche Museen Preussischer Kulturbesitz*, or state museums of Prussian heritage) is free. Elsewhere prices rise only to about DM 6, or half that for pensioners, students and groups. East Berlin museums used to be the cheapest of all, with a standard charge of 1 mark and 5 pfennigs.

Since unification, all the city's museums have been under review. Plans are under way to move artefacts from one side of the city to the other (for example the Egyptian collection at Schloss Charlottenburg is due to move on to the Museum Island with the Bodemuseum's Egyptian section by the year 2000). So expect some surprises.

Post Offices

East and West still have separate postal systems. The East has cheaper telegrams but is otherwise hopelessly inefficient. If you don't want post to get held up or lost, keep to the West. Letters take only 3 or 4 days to reach other European countries from there; about twice as long to get across the Atlantic. West Berlin's main post office at Bahnhof Zoo has one counter open 24 hours a day. Regular hours are Mon–Fri 8–6 and Sat 8–noon. Here are a few key branches:

Goethestr. 2 (Charlottenburg), tel (W) 34090
Geisbergstr. 9 (Schöneberg), tel (W) 21281

Hallesches Ufer 60 (Kreuzberg), tel (W) 2680
Französische Str. 9–12 (Mitte), tel (E) 22050
Bahnhof Friedrichstr. (Mitte), tel (E) 2071992
Wörtherstr. 30 (Prenzlauer Berg), tel (E) 4484536

Public Holidays

Shops, banks, offices and schools are shut on: 1 January, Good Friday,
1 May (Labour Day), Ascension Day, Whit Monday, 3 October
(German Unity Day), 1 November (All Saints), Day of Repentance and
Prayer (*Buss- und Bettag*, a moveable feast in November), Christmas Day,
26 December.

Religious Affairs

The church played a crucial role in the peaceful East German revolution
of 1989, largely because it was the only institution where free discussion
and free association were tolerated. Dissidents met in churches as the
revolution gathered pace, and street demonstrators sought refuge there
from the Stasi security police. The old passions have not entirely
dimmed and church-going in East Berlin can still be absorbing: for a
taste of this, try the Gethsemane Church in Prenzlauer Berg (Geth-
semanestr. 9, tel (E) 4484235) or the more central Marienkirche (Karl-
Liebknecht-Str. 8, tel (E) 2124467). Both have Sunday services starting
at 10.30 am.

Both halves of the city are predominantly Protestant, with many more
practising Christians in the East than the West. Catholics make up about
8 per cent of the city's population. Interestingly the Vatican never
recognized the division of Berlin and its bishop was always responsible
for both halves. The main Roman Catholic church is St Hedwig's
Cathedral in Bebelplatz in East Berlin, which holds four masses each
Sunday. Services in English are sporadic and change location for each
service. For details call one of the consulates (see above).

The city also has a small but very active Jewish community which
pricks the conscience of modern Germany and fights to maintain its
traditions. For details of synagogue services and community events,
contact the Jüdisches Gemeindehaus in Fasanenstr. 79–80, tel (W)
8842030.

West Berlin's large Turkish population has spawned a few makeshift
mosques, all in deserted warehouses or front rooms of private homes.

14

The main ones are at Eisenbahnstr. 16 and Skalitzerstr. 135 (both in Kreuzberg).

Senior Citizens and Students

Anyone with a valid senior citizen or student ID is eligible for half-price admission to museums. There are also reductions for public transport—ask at the relevant counter as these concessions are all under review at the time of writing. Students and young people under 26 are eligible for Eurorail discount fares on trains. Look out for the free book *Berlin für junge Leute*, available in English as *Berlin for Young People* from the Informationszentrum, Hardenbergstr. 20, tel (W) 310040.

Telephones

Berlin will only begin to be a truly unified city the day it has a single telephone system. The government has tentatively pencilled in 1997 as the target date. Until then communication across the city will continue to be frustrating in the extreme. Although you are charged only local rates (30 pfennigs in phone boxes) to call one side of Berlin from the other, in practice you can hardly ever get through because there are so few lines. Expect to redial *at least* 20 times to get through from East to West; you should have a little more luck in the other direction. East Berlin businesses, hotels and restaurants have bribed and twisted the post office for Western lines. As a result you can never be quite sure if the side of town you happen to be in corresponds with the phone system you are using. The code for East Berlin numbers from the West is 0372. The code for West Berlin numbers from the East is 849. They are indicated in this book by the prefixes (E) and (W).

You will have great difficulty calling other parts of eastern Germany from either half of Berlin; dialling abroad from the East (international code 06) only stands any chance of success in the middle of the night. Don't bother trying to call the operator or 'information' in the East. They will tell you ever so politely that they are quite unable to help with your particular query. Directory enquiries have been known to suggest to callers—in deadly earnest—to look up the number they wanted in the phone book. Phoning East Berlin from abroad (code 37 2) is, happily, quite easy; if, that is, the person or establishment you wish to speak to has a phone at all—only about 20 per cent of East Germans do, although the number is rising fast. The surest way to make advance bookings is by telex. You can consult telex directories at major post offices around the world.

Life is much easier in West Berlin. The code from abroad is 49 30. Phones at city government offices are often engaged, but otherwise the system works with standard German efficiency. The operator's number is 03; directory enquiries for Germany are on 1188; the international code is 00; for international enquiries dial 001188. Calls are cheapest after 10 pm and all day Sunday; they are most expensive on weekday mornings.

Tourist Information

Because of West Berlin's ideological importance during the Cold War, the city tirelessly produced free leaflets, information folders and books about itself to remind everyone it was still there. Despite unification, the **Informationszentrum Berlin** (Hardenbergstr. 20, open Mon–Fri 8–7 and Sat 8–4, tel (W) 310040) is still going strong and, although not strictly speaking a tourist facility, is a goldmine for visitors, with publications in several languages and details of lectures and special tours.

The tourist office proper is the **Verkehrsamt Berlin,** with branches in the Europa Center (open 7.30 am–10.30 pm daily, tel (W) 2626031), Bahnhof Zoo (open 8 am–11 pm daily, tel (W) 3139063) and Tegel airport (same hours as Bahnhof Zoo, tel (W) 41013145). These hand out information leaflets and maps, and find last-minute accommodation where possible. The offices tend to be besieged by visitors, so go only if absolutely necessary. There are tourist offices in the East at the television tower (tel (E) 2124675) and off Alexanderplatz in the Haus des Reisens (tel (E) 2154402). At the time of writing they are in a state of confusion and can offer little in the way of information or anything else.

Topics

The Trabant

A Snout for Humour

'A German must have a sense of humour, and most of them do indeed have it,' wrote Johannes Gross in a study of his fellow-countrymen, 'but it is humour of a kind which does not exclude the suggestion that the Germans do not have any sense of humour after all.' There can be few things more galling than a reputation, as the Germans have, for incurable humourlessness. Folk wisdom would have us believe they are an earnest bunch who can't laugh at themselves, and whose idea of fun is to drink several litres of beer and slap their knees a lot. Can they really be that awful? Whatever the truth behind such a cruel stereotype, it certainly does not apply to Berlin.

Berliners take the view that most of the horrors visited upon them through history have been the work of despotic outsiders; the best they can do is to try to see the funny side. Ever since Frederick the Great (himself an acerbic wit) subjected them to war after war in the 18th century, they have developed a distinctive brand of humour known as *Berliner Schnauze*, literally Berlin snout, a kind of cheeky irreverence combined with a talent for quick-witted one-liners. When Frederick was on his deathbed he asked if his doctor had seen many people off to the next world. 'Not as many as Your Majesty,' came the tart reply.

17

The more miserable the political situation, the more spirited the Berliners appear to be. One popular joke during the Nazi period went: 'Why is the Third Reich like a tram?' 'Because a *Führer* stands at the front of both, the people are constantly paying and nobody can jump off.' Much of the humour is rather inscrutable to the foreigner because it relies heavily on wordplay and puns. At the end of the Second World War Berliners renamed the city districts that had been reduced to rubble by allied bombing. Charlottenburg became Klamottenburg (ragsville), Lichterfelde was called Trichterfelde (crater fields) and Steglitz was known as Steht nix (there's nothing there).

This self-deprecating tone came into its own with the arrival of the Communists in East Berlin. One story has it that when East German leader Erich Honecker returned from his state visit to Bonn in September 1987, the politburo asked him what the West was like. 'Oh, just the same as here,' he replied. 'For hard currency you can get everything.'

Another tale is of a young man on Alexanderplatz who shouts at the top of his voice: '*Scheissrepublik!*' (which translates, rather badly, as 'shit republic'). Immediately two Stasi security policemen run out of the shadows to arrest him, but he protests: 'I never specified which country I was talking about and, of course, I would never besmirch the good name of East Germany.' The two Stasi men look at each other, shrug their shoulders and let him go. The next day the young man is back on Alexanderplatz shouting: '*Scheissrepublik!*' The same two Stasi men run out of the shadows to arrest him. 'What's going on?' he says. 'I thought we sorted this out yesterday.' 'We've checked up,' the Stasi men reply. 'There is only one *Scheissrepublik.*'

As problems mount following unification, there are sure to be plenty of jokes about the yawning gaps between East and West. Some have surfaced already. Soon after the Berlin Wall opened, one East Berliner placed a small ad in a Western newspaper saying: 'Will exchange one Communist Party handbook for used car.'

Oh Lord, Won't You Buy Me a Mercedes–Benz?

Used cars are all the rage in East Berlin. Times may be bad and money may be short, but nothing will stop East Berliners from shelling out thousands of marks for a second-hand Volkswagen or Audi (or Mercedes or BMW). More than a million more cars were registered in Berlin in the first six months after the introduction of the deutschmark in East Germany in July 1990. As a result traffic has come to a standstill. City officials have begun issuing pollution alarms. Soon there will be nearly as many cars as people.

To explain this craze you need look no further than the chugging little cars East Germans used to drive in the old days. When box-like Trabants and Wartburgs began spilling through the newly opened Berlin Wall in November 1989, many observers found them rather endearing. One West German magazine even suggested nominating the Trabant as Car of the Year, seeing it as a triumphant symbol of freedom. But these first impressions were of the cars in their best light—at a safe, long distance. Struggling to own one, let alone drive it, was quite a different story.

The average waiting time for delivery of a new Trabant or Wartburg was 15 years. To explain what that felt like, East Berliners like to dig out an old East German 10-mark note. On one side is a young woman laboratory assistant showing off the wonders of communist technology. On the other is a portrait of a prominent socialist educator, Clara Zetkin, in the twilight of her years. The first picture, the East Berliners say, is what you looked like when you ordered your Trabi. The second picture is what you looked like when it arrived. Because of the outrageous delay, second-hand Trabis did swift business on the black market and often cost more than new models. Anyone wanting to sell a car (which was illegal) simply left the back window slightly open. Potential buyers popped their offers in on slips of paper. The owner would then drive to the address of the highest bidder and sell it on the spot.

The Trabant itself is no wonder machine. It has a speedometer, but no rev counter or fuel or oil gauge. The body is a mixture of PVC, cotton waste and sawdust. The engine design was out of date when it was introduced in the 1950s and has barely changed since. On a good day the car might reach 80 kph. On a bad day it will just choke and splutter. As one foreign journalist put it after a test spin round East Berlin: 'Driving one sounds and feels a bit like mowing the lawn, only your feet don't touch the ground.'

The one plus point about Trabis is that they are hardy beasts, and most of the 2.5 million that rolled off the production line are still put-putting around somewhere. German television excitedly reports Trabi sightings as far away as London or Athens. There is even a rumour that Princess Gloria von Thurn und Taxis, the nearest thing Germany has to Princess Diana, bought one. But the initial chorus of enthusiasm has turned to general moaning about Trabis slowing down motorway traffic or belching fumes onto pedestrians at traffic lights. The moaning won't need to last much longer: an attempt to build a new Trabant with a Volkswagen engine was deemed a waste of time and the model has been scrapped.

Remember, Remember the 9th of November

How should the Germans commemorate 9 November 1989, the night the Berlin Wall fell? Perhaps make it a public holiday, or organize annual firework parties, or rename a street Strasse des 9. November, like Strasse des 17. Juni (which pays tribute to the 1953 workers' uprising in East Berlin). The Germans would love to do all these things, but they can't. The happiest event in their history happens to fall on the most embarrassing date in their calendar. *Reichskristallnacht*, the Nazis' orgy of anti-Jewish violence and destruction, occurred on 9 November 1938. Since 1945 German synagogues have held sober memorial services every year, urging the country never to forget the past—scarcely the right occasion to sing and dance in the streets. As if that were not enough, 9 November was also the day in 1923 on which Hitler staged his beer hall *putsch* in Munich. And on 9 November 1918, anarchy broke out in Berlin when Communists and Social Democrats announced the founding of rival German republics following the abdication of Kaiser Wilhelm II.

This unhappy series of coincidences is particularly ironic because the Germans are fascinated by dates and attach great importance to them. Usually they make a great fuss of birthdays and anniversaries, both in private and in public. Every day newspapers will pick on some past event for a weighty anniversary piece. Parliament will stop its business for several minutes to wish a deputy many happy returns of the day, and television news bulletins will add their congratulations in their reports on the proceedings. When the Swiss author Friedrich Dürrenmatt died in December 1990, most German obituaries pointed out the 70th birthday he had missed by two weeks before making any reference to his merits as a writer.

Given this fascination, it is perhaps not surprising that picking a date for the reunification of Germany in 1990 was an agonizing affair. Public debate lasted months, and came within a whisker of bringing down the East German government as it was preparing to vote itself out of existence. The anniversary of the Wall opening was, of course, a non-starter. Nobody wanted it on or after 7 October, the day East Germany was founded in 1949; the discredited state could not, after all, be allowed the privilege of another birthday. Other possible dates had to be carefully vetted to ensure they did not coincide with some past atrocity. Fingers crossed that the final choice, 3 October, remains as unsullied as it is.

Making Money out of the Wall

One of the first acts of the East German government after it opened the Berlin Wall was to set up a company selling segments of graffiti-sprayed concrete for hard currency. In the first six months of trading, the company, called Limex Bau, earned more than DM 2 million thanks to an apparently insatiable demand for Cold War memorabilia. US universities and Japanese banks bought unwieldy 2.7-tonne slabs, complete with certificate of authenticity, for a cool DM 50,000 apiece. The Wall became one of the dying Communist state's few lucrative exports.

That may seem an extraordinarily cynical way to behave after 28 years of tension, intimidation and border shootings, but the truth is that the Wall was a perverse moneyspinner from the moment it was built. West Germans and foreigners crossing into the East after 1961 had to pay an entrance fee and exchange a minimum daily quantity of hard currency at the extortionate official rate of one to one. By 1989 the price of a day trip was DM 30 per visitor. The Communist government also persuaded Bonn to put up money for a number of public works projects, notably transit motorways from Hamburg, Hanover and Nuremberg to West Berlin. The West also paid annual tributes for use of railway and underground train links running through East Berlin or East German territory. Most lucrative of all, East Germany sold political prisoners— prominent dissidents or citizens caught trying to flee across the fortified border—for between DM 40,000 and 100,000 marks each. By the 1980s they were handing over as many as 2000 people each year. Bonn branded its neighbour a callous trader in human beings, but continued to come up with the readies.

West Germans cashed in too. As security at the Wall tightened, the business of fleeing to the West became more tricky—and more lucrative for a small band of professional escape-organizers. Most of them were ex-soldiers with extensive intelligence contacts as well as expertise in digging tunnels or adapting the back seats of cars to conceal bodies without risk of detection. The going rate for their services ran from DM 50,000 to 100,000. The risks were high—imprisonment or death—and satisfaction could not be guaranteed, even at that price.

After the Wall came down, it was not just the East German government that spotted an easy way of earning a little pocket money. Hundreds of street traders joined the throngs of tourists bashing away at the concrete with blunt instruments, flogging small pieces at stalls for DM 5 or 10. Some smart hawkers even rented out hammers and chisels by the hour. Soon hoardings advertising Western cigarettes appeared, where not so long before guards had patrolled with orders to shoot to kill. Large companies, notably Daimler–Benz, began bidding for pieces of the grassy strip running through the city, once no man's land but now prime real estate.

In its own curious way, the Berlin Wall has undergone a transition to the market economy. As a leaflet frequently handed out by artists at Checkpoint Charlie says: 'If you think communism was crazy, just take a look at this.'

Four Infuriating Things about Berlin

Sooner or later something gets on your nerves about any city. Here is a personal list of Berlin bugbears:

Alles verboten: The Prussian Kaisers may be long gone, but Prussian values such as discipline, order and cleanliness are as strong as ever. Notices abound telling you not to smoke, not to lie on the grass, not to walk the dog. Playgrounds in West Berlin offer this intimidating welcome: 'Only for children up to the age of 15. Persons over 15 years old allowed only to look after children entrusted to them. Playing equipment may only be used with the agreement or under the supervision of a parent or authorized guardian. No liability admitted for damage of any kind. Dogs must be kept away.' The extraordinary thing is that on the whole Berliners scrupulously obey every sign they see. They do not dare cross the road at a red pedestrian light even if it is 2 am and there isn't a car in sight. Even at the height of summer, vast tracts of the Tiergarten park stay empty while all the sunbathers cram onto *Liegewiesen*, fields specially designated for lying in.

Minding other people's business: Some people are not content just to obey the rules; they feel compelled to dictate them too. Businessmen on underground trains tell mothers to keep their crying babies quiet. Old ladies on buses tell students to stop talking and have some respect for their elders. Pedestrians tell complete strangers on the street to keep a safe distance from the kerb, or straighten their tie, or put their hand in front of their mouth when they yawn.

22

No left turn: It's almost impossible to turn left on major avenues in East Berlin. Tramlines and metal barriers run down the middle of the road, except at major junctions where a large sign usually tells you to drive straight on. U-turns are out of the question for the same reason, so if you miss the chance to turn left when offered, you're stuck. On one stretch of Greifswalder Strasse you cannot turn left for nearly 5 km.

Early closing: Germany's *Ladenschlussgesetz* (shop closing-time law) forces shops to shut just when they might be most useful (see Shopping).

Five Famous Berlin Sights You Can't See

Vacant lots, bomb-damaged houses, scorch marks and bullet holes confront you on nearly every street in Berlin. Many hundreds of buildings have been extensively rebuilt since 1945; many hundreds more were too badly damaged and are gone forever. Some of the destruction was self-inflicted, the obliteration of discredited ideologies and disturbing memories. Here are five of the most famous sights you will *not* be able to see. Given the current backlash against the Communist era in East Germany, quite a few more monuments could soon be joining the list.

The Berlin Wall: For 28 years this barrier of concrete and barbed wire dividing the city seemed impenetrable. Immediately after its surprise opening in November 1989 thousands of 'wall woodpeckers' began chipping away at it with hammers. The bulldozers soon followed and within a year it had all but disappeared. Two stretches, next to Potsdamer Platz and on Bernauer Strasse, remain as protected monuments. Art exhibits in the former death strip, the prohibited patrol area behind the Wall, include the odd watchtower or slab of concrete. Small souvenir lumps adorn countless mantelpieces around the world. But the armed guards, border posts, sniffer dogs, glaring lights and scatter guns are gone for good.

Checkpoint Charlie: A prefabricated wooden hut erected by the Western Allies shortly after the Wall went up to monitor rights of access between West and East Berlin, Checkpoint Charlie became part of the mythology of the divided city and the scene of many a movie spy-swap. It was hoisted into history by a giant crane on 22 June 1990.

The Kaiser's Palace: This multi-layered architectural wonder, begun in the 17th century and refashioned in neo-classical style by Karl Friedrich Schinkel 200 years later, was bombed repeatedly, but not irreparably, during the Second World War. However, East Berlin's

Communist leaders decided the building embodied the worst of Germany's imperialistic past and blew it up in 1950. The gleaming orange Palace of the Republic which Erich Honecker built to replace the old *Schloss* in the 1970s has not fared so well itself. Lined with asbestos, it was deemed a cancer risk in September 1990 and closed.

Hitler's Chancellery: The *Reichskanzlei* became such an object of hate by the end of the war that occupying Soviet soldiers ripped up its bombed-out remains stone by stone. Some of the marble was later used in Berlin's two Soviet war memorials. The Chancellery bunker, where Hitler spent the final phase of the war and committed suicide, is only slightly more visible. With its entrance sealed and buried, it appears as a mere bump along the former death strip of the Berlin Wall.

Spandau Prison: Rudolf Hess, Hitler's deputy and one the great mystery men of the 20th century, spent the last 41 years of his life in this stern red-brick jail on the outskirts of West Berlin. From 1966 until his appropriately enigmatic death in 1987 he was the only inmate in its 600 cells, the world's loneliest prisoner. Given a life sentence at the Nuremberg trials, Hess had been captured in Scotland in 1941 after a mysterious solo flight, apparently on some kind of peace mission. It has never been clear if he was following Hitler's orders or acting alone, if the trip might have been a set-up to get rid of him or if he was insane. Hess took the mystery to his grave. In 1987, at the age of 93, he was found strangled by a piece of electrical flex suspended from a window latch of the prison summer house. The four Allied powers, who had taken turns to guard him, concluded that he had committed suicide. But his family, doubting such an old man had the strength to hang himself, believes he was murdered. One British author, Hugh Thomas, has suggested that the man in Spandau prison was not Hess at all, but a double sent to Scotland in 1941 by SS chief Heinrich Himmler in an attempt to embarrass and discredit Hitler.

As for the prison, it was dismantled brick by brick within weeks of Hess's death to ensure it did not become a neo-Nazi shrine. The site was then turned into a supermarket for British troops stationed in Berlin.

Isherwood Revisited

Christopher Isherwood's sure eye and understated, ironic style were perfectly suited to describing the lives of ordinary Berliners in the tense period leading up to the Nazi seizure of power. Isherwood left the city in 1933 and later wrote two famous books of Berlin stories,

Mr Norris Changes Trains *and* Goodbye to Berlin. *He returned only once, in the 1950s, and found the ruins of the vibrant city he had known profoundly depressing. Isherwood died three years before the Wall crumbled. Perhaps if he had lived he would have come back one final time. A rejuvenated Isherwood might still be teaching English and describing Berliners of all types in his diaries. Nowadays he would not live in Schöneberg, which has become considerably smarter than the district he knew, but in Prenzlauer Berg in the East, the new centre for nightlife and artistic activity. His landlady would probably not be a middle-aged spinster, Fräulein Schröder, but a young, divorced mother of three preferring to go by her first name, Lina. This might be the result:* A Berlin Diary (Summer 1990).

From my window, the cobbled street and line of crumbling tenements, plaster flaking off the neglected, dirty façades. Below, mothers with young children wave to one another as the rusting wheels of their pushchairs slide and scrape over chipped, uneven slabs of pavement. A few weeks ago a balcony on the house opposite crashed to the ground. Nobody was hurt, but now demolition men are busy pulling the entire flat block down. Perhaps the whole street will disappear in a few weeks, by which time everyone will have hard currency in their pockets. The politicians say the people will be rich then and can build brand new houses, or whatever they want. That's not the way most of the people I know see it. Everyone is holding their breath—not because they cannot wait, but because they want the terrible uncertainty, this limbo between decay and renewal, to end.

My landlady is highly amused by a confrontation that took place in our building yesterday. One of the boys from upstairs, Uwe, has got into the spirit of the new market economy and set up his own business, a flat rental agency. A few weeks ago he came round and asked if anyone would mind if he used the common room in the front courtyard for his work until the state property agency allocated him some real office space. Nobody has used the room for years, so he moved in. The poor boy doesn't even have a telephone, but he still has a steady stream of customers. One had trouble finding the right place and knocked on Herr Dubrowski's door by mistake.

'Ah, Christopher, you should have seen old Dubrowski,' Lina said. 'He came running down into the courtyard shouting his head off, so everyone could hear him. "I've worked hard all my life," he fumed, "with my bare hands!"'. (Actually I think he has a desk job at a printing factory in Marzahn; he certainly doesn't look like a real worker, the fat pig.) "What gives you the right to barge into our room, and think you can start taking money off people, just like the Wessis, huh? When do we start seeing some of the action? This is our room, everything belongs to all of us, we should get a share." Naturally everyone rushed to calm him down. He was about to start swinging his fists. Uwe responded magnificently. Go and have a look at the notice he has written in the hallway, Christopher.'

Pinned up on the wall was a sheet of thin, greyish paper with a curt typewritten explanation of Uwe's office space problems. He added at the end: 'I have established my business in accordance with the changing political, economic and social conditions in our country. I thank you for your support. Regrettably, profit-sharing is not possible.'

This dangling carrot, the deutschmark, is driving people slowly crazy. A few weeks ago I saw a television crew in a local bar trying to get some comments from the man in the street about the impending changeover to market economics. The reporter turned to a serious-looking man in the corner who blurted out: 'My name is Doctor Fischer and I want twenty marks for every word.' The reporter choked in surprise. Everyone in the bar started laughing and eventually Doctor Fischer, realizing he was not going to get a penny for his thoughts, slunk out in indignation.

Lina doesn't see any cause to celebrate the arrival of capitalism. 'The future is golden all right,' she says with a smirk. 'Black, red and golden. This is just an excuse for the West to buy up everything on the cheap.' She and her new lover, Axel, had wanted to pool their savings to buy a house on the Baltic Sea coast. 'It's so much healthier for the children. Here they are always restless, always ill. We have to get away. But the prices are incredible. All because the Wessis fancy a cheap holiday home. Good luck to them, but what about us? All you ever hear about this stupid unification is how happy and peaceful we will all be. Well, if this is what it is like, I don't want anyone to reunify me.'

Lina is frightened of losing her job. She works as an architect in the city parks department, but does not get on with her boss. He has joined the Christian Democrat party, the winners of last March's election, and has threatened to get rid of her if she doesn't do likewise. 'It's disgusting, it's just like the Communists, only the names have changed. And the money. The money's changing next. And then what will happen? We don't even know if we're getting paid next month.'

Today is Lina's 'household day' off from work, which all East German women get every month to catch up on shopping and cleaning. She spent half of it waiting in line at the bank to set up a special account for converting her soft-currency savings into deutschmarks. 'After about four hours,' she said, 'someone in front of me commented sarcastically, "Finally a queue that's worth joining". Everybody laughed. You could tell, they were all secretly wondering what exactly they were doing there.'

I went out, too, to give a lesson and go for a long walk on the way back. It is quite extraordinary, after months of nothing but drab grey packaging, to see shelves crammed with Coca-Cola, Marlboro cigarettes and all-natural West German fruit yoghurt. East German goods are being sold off cheap as though the whole country was holding a closing-down sale. Washing machines, bicycles and clothes are all going for a song. But the old etiquette of shopping has not yet vanished. Each store has perhaps twenty plastic baskets. Without a basket, you cannot get into the shop. So there is a queue of people outside each one, waiting for someone to leave so they can go in. It's like a multi-storey carpark with the 'full' sign lit up but only a handful of cars on each level.

The great day, July 1. Out go the tinny old coins and diminutive notes. In comes the solid, shiny small change of the affluent West and those creamy 10- and 20-mark bills. Somehow it already feels more valuable. Last night there was a celebration on Alexanderplatz. At midnight everyone flung their coins into the air, then cursed at how much the sausage sellers in the square were charging. A writer friend of mine, Lutz, took me along while he animatedly made notes. 'Come on,' he finally said. 'Let's go. They're all West Berliners anyway, come to take a look, as though East Berlin were some corner shop holding an inaugural party.' We went off to find a bar in Kreuzberg. By the time we returned at four in the morning, there were already long queues outside the banks. For the first time, in the greyness of the early morning, I noticed how many Western cars there were with East Berlin plates. They had obviously been bought on the never-never before anyone had hard currency to their names. Lutz could not understand my surprise. 'Look,' he said, 'every adult can change four thousand marks one to one. So that's about twelve or fifteen thousand marks for each family. That may not get them very far when the prices shoot up and they lose their jobs, but it's a hell of a lot of down-payments.' I love Lutz's cool, logical explanations for everything. Alone of my friends he seems to think everything will work out fine. God knows why. His girlfriend left him to go to the West.

27

He stands almost no chance of keeping his state writing grant. Moreover, he is as scathing about the Western politicians as anyone. But he says: 'Don't believe those people who moan all the time about how awful it will be. Of course it will be hard, Christopher, but it will be worth it. Nobody wants to go back to what we had before.'

Lutz always makes me feel that perhaps I don't understand how people here feel or think. After all, I'm a foreigner. I can walk out of this city any time I want. I can choose the kind of currency, hard or soft, that I keep in my pockets, even if I can't always determine how much. Many of my friends are frightened by the future, but I have to acknowledge that the electorate voted overwhelmingly for this swift monetary union. The politicians promised them deutschmarks to take on their summer holidays and now they have them. So who's complaining?

Günther is a pupil of mine who works as a trapeze artist in a circus. I met him quite by chance in a café a few weeks ago. He heard me speaking English and came over to ask if I could teach him. He said the circus was being forced to shed its artists because it had lost its subsidies, and he needed a new skill before he too lost his job. I started teaching him and even went to see his show. Announcing Günther's turn, the spangled master of ceremonies beamed and shouted: 'Ladies and gentlemen, I must ask for your special attention for a quite extraordinary and unique act! Our performers will now walk on the ceiling.' Günther began his upside-down walk along a metal beam, then pretended to falter. The children gasped, then started to laugh and clap. The whole show was full of gusto but terribly sad at the same time. As we shuffled out at the end, two of the acrobats came round with collecting caps begging the audience to help save the circus. Günther came round to see me today, almost in tears. He told me he couldn't afford any more English lessons. Not only had he lost his job, so had all the animal tamers. Eight lions and twelve prancing horses had been put down. 'We just couldn't afford to feed them,' he said. 'What kind of a system would let that happen? I thought we were all rich now.'

Axel, my landlady's lover, has lost his job too. Or nearly. He used to work at a publishing house but now he's on short time, which means he only goes to work once a week but still gets paid as much as before. This is a government scheme dreamt up to keep down the unemployment statistics, Axel says. In the new Germany there won't be any redundant people. Just three million workers who are employed but never go to work. Axel, in fact, is very busy. He and a friend get up at three in the morning and drive to the wholesale fruit and vegetable market in West Berlin. They load up their cars with peaches, tomatoes and lettuce and shoot up the motorway to the Baltic Sea coast. Apparently the local state food distribution agencies up there fancy they can get away with charging three times as much for fruit as they do in Berlin. Axel just sells his stuff out of his car boot. Most days he's home in an empty car in time for mid-afternoon tea.

Selling has become a compulsion. Hawkers sell bits of the Wall to tourists at the Reichstag. The other day I saw an East German woman by the side of the road selling maps of Potsdam to day trippers stuck in the traffic going over the Glienicker Bridge. In West Berlin the shops don't know whether to be pleased or appalled by all the new custom. Yesterday I was in a department store where an East German couple were loudly discussing what size of shorts they should get for their son. I overheard one of the shop assistants whispering to her friend: 'All they've done for the last two hours is finger things. They're only going to spend 10 marks, I've seen it all morning. These Ossis are just clogging up the shop.' The two women glared at the couple, who blithely moved on to a bin full of men's underpants and started up their discussion all over again.

West Berliners are beginning to be thoroughly fed up with all the talk of living in harmony in a single Germany. For most of them currency union was yet another party they had to host but could not enjoy. Prices are going up there too. The traffic is getting worse all the time. Everyone is getting steadily more impatient. For 28 years they had their little island paradise where nobody disturbed them and all these changes are getting on top of them, too. Next door to the department store where that East German couple was poking around in the underpants, I saw a clothes shop selling T-shirts which said, emblazoned across the front, 'We want our wall back.'

There's a demonstration nearly every day now. Yesterday it was the civil servants. Today it is the taxi drivers who blocked the main roads and hooted for two hours. The newspapers say that some industrial workers in Dresden and Leipzig have managed to secure modest wage increases. But it seems like a drop in the ocean. Currency union was like an experiment in alchemy. Perhaps it's no surprise that East German base metal did not turn into gold overnight. I am suddenly discovering what a luxury it was to live in a soft currency city. I've had to stop writing and take on some extra translation work. They say that in January heating and rents are going to shoot up. I might just plan to make my exit then.

29

There's not much solace in the present gloom. Nobody can afford to go to theatres or cinemas, half of which look like closing anyway. Lutz keeps dragging me off to political meetings where everyone can feel self-indulgent for a few hours but cannot really change anything.

I feel most sorry for the dissidents who led the revolution last year. Then they were heroes. Now they are forgotten, pushed to one side. At one meeting, four of them sat in a row looking shell-shocked. What are they supposed to think? Their dreams have been rejected. 'My goal is a Germany of solidarity, of renewal, not one that is coerced into unification,' said one of them, the film maker Reiner Schwarz, scarcely believing himself that any such thing was still possible. These people have a tremendous, forceful honesty. But nobody is listening to them.

As I returned home after the meeting, I heard my landlady talking animatedly, but I could not hear any other voices. 'Lina?' I called.

'Wait a minute, Christopher,' she said. She was in the bathroom. A few minutes later she came tearing out with her bathrobe hurriedly wrapped around her. She was sopping wet, holding a large bottle and beaming from ear to ear. I hadn't seen anybody this happy for weeks.

'Want some champagne?' she said excitedly. 'I can't believe it. I finally got my telephone today. After I don't know how many years. Isn't it wonderful news, Christopher? I've just been lying in the bath with a drink and phoning everybody I know.'

History

Perhaps history would have been kinder to leave Berlin as the boggy, disease-ridden, minor provincial trading post of its origins. The city's rise to prominence and power led only to misery, for itself and for the world, and was due almost entirely to the bad influence of outsiders. The Hohenzollern dynasty, which spawned the rulers of Prussia and imperial Germany, first moved to Berlin from Nuremberg in the 15th century; Hitler was Austrian; the architects of the city's postwar division were Russian, British and American; and Erich Honecker, the East German leader who built the Berlin Wall, came from the Saar. Berliners have rarely been masters of their own destiny. Even after forcing open the Wall—with a little help from Soviet leader Mikhail Gorbachev—they found their future being largely determined by a Rhinelander, German Chancellor Helmut Kohl. The city was destined to be the plaything of European and world politics, and has endured tyranny, war and destruction as a result. 'Physically and morally, Berlin is a god-forsaken place,' philosopher Arthur Schopenhauer despaired in 1860. Rarely in its turbulent history has that not been the case.

An Unpromising Start

Ironically Berlin started life as a divided town. The merchants and artisans who settled on opposite sides of a ford (the present-day

31

Mühlendamm) on the Spree river in the early 13th century did not see fit to have formal links with each other for nearly a hundred years. Historical records first mention Coelln, a fishing community on the south bank, in 1237. Berlin, the slightly larger trading town on the north side, appears in documents seven years later. Both had their own ruling council and their own church—Coelln's named after Peter, the patron saint of fishermen, and Berlin's named after Nicholas, guardian of merchants (the Nikolaikirche still exists). The towns' names reflect their provincial modesty. Coelln means sand bank. Berlin is derived from a Slavic word meaning bog, a reference to the unhealthy swamps around the Havel lakes and the Spree. The name has nothing to do with the city's bear emblem, which probably came from Albert the Bear, the Askanian warrior who drove the Slavs out of the area in the 12th century and established the Mark of Brandenburg.

Berlin and Coelln finally formed a single administration in the face of adversity in 1307. After building up a decent trade in rye and timber, the towns had fallen prey to robber barons who abused their noble privileges to pirate wares, demand tributes and keep the populace in a permanent state of fear. But without a standing army, even a combined Berlin-Coelln stood no chance and for the next century it was routed regularly. In 1411 the town appealed to the Holy Roman Emperor, who sent Friedrich von Hohenzollern, Burggraf of Nuremberg, as special protector. The choice was auspicious, if historically fatal: the Hohenzollerns stuck around for 507 years, vastly outstaying their welcome and turning Berlin and the rest of Germany into a stiffer, more pigheaded, aggressive and frightening place in the process.

Within four years Friedrich had dispersed the robber barons and was appointed Kurfürst, or Elector, of Brandenburg. Any hopes the Berliners might have had of returning to their quiet independent life were dashed as Friedrich worked to make their town, with its valuable ford across the Spree, the new capital of the Mark. His successor Friedrich II (known as Iron Tooth) finally reached that goal in 1448, building the city's first castle for his residence, but not before stifling popular opposition by force. Symbolically a metal locket was put around the neck of the city's heraldic bear and remained part of the coat of arms until 1875.

With the Hohenzollerns came the first traces of order and discipline that were to characterize the Prussian state. The Electors wiped away most civil liberties and brought in their own strict administrative structures. By careful redirection of trade routes, Berlin became the focal point for merchandise travelling both north to south and east to west.

The economy boomed thanks to customs tariffs, bringing an influx of bankers, clothiers, milliners, goldsmiths, swordmakers and other new traders. But Berlin was still small and lacked the two vital elements that would later make the rest of the world sit up and take notice: a significant military force and a flourishing artistic culture. During the Thirty Years' War of 1618–48 the city played a largely passive role in the bloody struggle for religious and political control of Germany; it even endured brief occupations by the Swedes and Austrians. The man who changed all that was Friedrich Wilhelm, later known as the Great Elector and the founding father of royal Prussia.

The Rise of Prussia:
Soldiers, Palaces and More Soldiers

> Other states own an army; Prussia is an army that owns a state.
> —Mirabeau

The Berlin that Friedrich Wilhelm found on taking power in 1640 was in deep depression. Ravaged by war and constant plagues, the city's population had halved to just 6000 in 25 years. Thanks to strong ties with Holland (he had been educated there and married Princess Dorothea of Orange), Friedrich Wilhelm secured Prussian territories to the east and Rhineland territories to the west at the 1648 Peace of Westphalia. In an early example of supply-side economics, he eased income tax burdens on merchants and small businesses and introduced a form of VAT instead. The middle classes thrived while the poor were driven off their land and, as often as not, conscripted into the growing army. Friedrich Wilhelm led a series of forays against the Poles and the Austrians to consolidate his territorial gains and turned Berlin into a fortress town with a deep moat (roughly covering the centre of Mitte district). Military strength was the cornerstone of the emerging Prussian state and proved triumphant against the once-mighty Swedes at the Battle of Fehrbellin in 1675. 'A ruler is of no consideration if he does not have adequate means and forces of his own,' Friedrich Wilhelm wrote in his *Political Testament* of 1667. 'That alone has made me, thank God, a force to be reckoned with.'

By the end of the Elector's long reign in 1688, the population had jumped to 20,000 and the city had been transformed. He had eliminated the threat of plague by planting extensive forests on the germ-ridden bogs of the Havel. He had built a new castle, an arsenal (the prototype for the Zeughaus), several fine palaces and the graceful avenue Unter den Linden. And he had eased political and religious freedoms, allowing an influx of persecuted Austrian Jews and French Huguenots who proved crucial in boosting the population, expanding the economy and laying the foundations of a flourishing culture.

Culture was the abiding passion of Friedrich Wilhelm's son and successor, Friedrich III. In fact, so concerned was he to surround himself with riches that he neglected his other duties and virtually bankrupted the state. He crowned himself King Friedrich I of Prussia (including Berlin and the Rhineland territories) in 1701, in a display not so much of political might as unbridled vanity. He began the Prussian mania for art collection by quantity rather than quality and built palace after palace to make up for Berlin's philistine past. He was vain, he was irresponsible, he was hunchbacked, he was unloved. His questionable taste was tempered only by his glitteringly intelligent wife Sophie Charlotte, who brought philosophers to the Prussian court, set up academies for the arts and sciences and oversaw the period's outstanding architectural project, Schloss Charlottenburg. Frederick the Great (in an outrageous case of the pot calling the kettle black) later said of his grandfather: 'The free spending he loved was wasteful indulgence, like that of a vain and extravagant prince. He oppressed the poor to please the rich.'

The kingdom was quickly put back on the straight and narrow by Friedrich's son, Friedrich Wilhelm I, who had only two interests in life: spending money on the army and saving it on everything else. The 'soldier king' halted all cultural projects, conscripted 20,000 Berliners (out of a population that reached 100,000 by his death in 1740), built block-like new housing for his bureaucrats and army staff and obsessively converted Berlin's open spaces into drilling grounds. Commenting in 1764 on the training methods that Friedrich Wilhelm introduced, James Boswell wrote: 'The soldiers seemed quite terrified; for the tiniest trangression they were beaten like dogs. I don't know if these people really make the best soldiers.' The soldiers weren't sure either and deserted in droves. The king, whose own son even tried to run away from the army to England, built a wall around the city in 1735 to hold in deserters and ordered guards to shoot at anyone trying to escape. The Berlin Wall had a precedent.

Ironically the 'soldier king' never fought a war, but his son Friedrich II, better known as Frederick the Great, rapidly made up for lost time.

Weeks after taking the throne he invaded and annexed Silesia. 'Dogs, do you want to live for ever?' he cried at his men on the battlefield. Subsequent wars against Poland, Russia and Austria made Prussia a great European power, but brought misery to most of its people. And the whole enterprise nearly went badly wrong: twice, in 1742 and 1760, enemy troops besieged Berlin and only left in return for large helpings from Prussia's treasury.

Frederick tried to combine the qualities of his three predecessors—judicious diplomacy, military expansion and cultivation of the arts—but ended up compounding all their excesses. As well as a campaigning soldier he was an energetic builder, commissioning the first neo-classical palaces of central Berlin and employing armies of architects, painters and landscape designers for his dream palace at Potsdam. To pay for all these caprices he bled the people dry with taxes. 'They can say what they like as long as they let me do what I like,' he used to say. He also fancied himself as a Renaissance man, a philosopher, a liberal thinker and a wit. He lifted some restrictions on press and religious freedom and cultivated Enlightenment philosophers, notably Voltaire and the Berlin Jewish leader Moses Mendelssohn. But in reality Frederick was a bad philosopher, worse poet and a dire musician; a haughty cynic and misogynist with a withering, unendearing sense of humour; a Jack of all trades but master of only one—tireless self-promotion. 'How can one feel well in Berlin?' fumed contemporary playwright Gotthold Ephraim Lessing. 'Everything one sees there makes one's stomach heave. Don't talk to me about your Berlin freedoms to think and write. It boils down quite simply to making as many tasteless remarks about religion as one likes. Let someone get up in Berlin to defend the rights of the individual and attack exploitation and despotism ... and you'll soon see which country in Europe is today the most abjectly enslaved.'

The Road to Unification, First Time Around

Within 20 years of his death in 1786 as an embittered and lonely old man, Frederick's empire collapsed like a house of cards. His nephew and successor, Friedrich Wilhelm II, was vain, fat and suffered from dropsy (he died after being hit by a flying champagne cork). Friedrich Wilhelm III, who took over in 1797, only woke up to his duties when Napoleon marched triumphantly through the recently completed Brandenburg Gate in 1806. 'The king has lost a battle,' he announced to his people. 'To remain calm is the first duty of the citizen.' In the event Napoleon's two-year occupation was not so bad: he briefly silenced the arrogance of the military and introduced educational reforms that led to the foundation of Berlin's Humboldt University. He also planted the first seeds of yearning for a liberal, united Germany. Despite earlier half-promises Friedrich Wilhelm roundly rejected the idea of a new democratic constitution in 1819, heralding a generation of reactionary conservatism. Karl August Schinkel's ornate neo-classical palaces pandered to Friedrich Wilhelm's delusions of grandeur; the Beidermeier furniture of the period was staid and fussy; and the people, to believe contemporary reports, became unbearable. 'The Berliner is coarse, quarrelsome, unsentimental, vain and cliquish,' the theatre manager Heinrich Laube wrote. 'Not only does he know everything, he knows everything better. Anything a bit different is bad.'

The Industrial Revolution shook the city out of its arrogant torpor. English steam engines, gaslight, water and sewage systems arrived from the 1830s on. Berlin, which had developed as a commercial centre for iron, grain and wool, began building factories for machine tools, dyes, medicines and, later, electrical goods. Fledgling Berlin companies like AEG and Siemens grew into industrial giants. Soon Prussia was the dominant economic force in Germany and, through a system of tariff agreements known as the *Zollverein* (Customs Union), flexed its industrial muscles from the Russian border to the Rhine and from the Baltic to the Alps.

Industrialization brought convulsive change to Berlin, which quadrupled in size in the first half of the 19th century, turning from a provincial capital into a teeming city of 600,000. Cramped high-rise flat blocks known as *Mietskasernen*, or rental barracks, sprang up in suburbs like Kreuzberg and Prenzlauer Berg to house the new working class (see Walks III and V for a catalogue of their miseries at the hands of property speculators and bumbling city administrators). By the 1840s the first murmurings of socialism amplified the calls for democracy that were sweeping the whole of Europe. In Germany there was the first talk of unification and a democratic national assembly. In 1847 Berlin housewives revolted against exorbitant potato prices, overturning and plundering market stalls. When Austria's Prince Metternich was forced to flee Vienna in March 1848, 10,000 people gathered at the King's palace to celebrate, and demanded reform in Prussia too. A nervous Friedrich Wilhelm IV promised to consider the matter and asked everyone to disperse peacefully. Just then one of his soldiers' rifles went off by accident and the crowd, thinking they were about to be attacked, ripped up the streets, built barricades and hurled chimney pots and boiling water. The army fought back and killed 183 people. Revolution had arrived.

Fighting for his political life, Friedrich Wilhelm paraded through Berlin wearing a cockade in the colours of the democratic unity movement—black, red and gold—later turned into the German flag. He promised free elections and restored order with remarkable speed. But the elections never came and Friedrich Wilhelm set up a Bürgerwehr, or armed citizens' militia, to keep revolutionary forces in check. In November General Friedrich von Wrangel dashed any last hopes of reform, dissolving a makeshift popular assembly in the city, disbanding the Bürgerwehr and imposing martial law.

With the democratic path to unity blocked, only one way remained open—force. Although it was clear that Prussia would lead a united Germany, Friedrich Wilhelm always feared the house of Hohenzollern might be made to cede power to a liberal parliament. But the unification issue returned to the agenda with the accession of his brother Wilhelm I in 1857 and the appointment of Otto von Bismarck as Prime Minister of Prussia five years later. Bismarck doggedly pursued his vision of unification through 'blood and iron', ceaselessly negotiating with other German states and fighting no less than three wars—against Denmark in 1864, against Austria in 1866 and against France in 1870. His dream was realized and, in a double celebration of war victory and national unity, Wilhelm was crowned Kaiser (emperor) of all Germany in Versailles' Hall of Mirrors on 18 January 1871.

The effect of unification on Berlin was dramatic. The capital city's population grew at breakneck pace, quintupling to 4 million over the next 50 years. Not only was it the centre of government, it became a magnet for the press, the theatre, literature and the visual arts. As Germany undertook colonial exploits in Africa and Asia, Berlin's museums filled with ever more exotic treasures. As the catastrophe of the First World War loomed, Berlin was aspiring to be the industrial and cultural centre of Europe. 'This city gobbled up talent and human energy with an unparalleled burning hunger,' wrote playwright Carl Zuckmayer, 'digesting, grinding it up and spitting it out again as quickly as possible. Anything on the up in Germany was sucked into the city with tornado force, the false with the true, the failures with the successes.' But the city was still weighed down by the rigid militarism and petty bureaucracy of Wilhelmine Germany. The absurdity of the régime could not have been better illustrated by an incident in October 1906 (later dramatized by

Zuckmayer) that made Berlin the laughing stock of the world. Wilhelm Voigt, an out-of-work cobbler who had spent nearly half his 57 years in prison, conned a detachment of soldiers into believing he was an army captain, took them to his local town hall in Köpenick, arrested the mayor and treasurer and seized 4000 marks of municipal funds. He then requisitioned three horse-drawn cabs and delivered his prisoners to the Neue Wache on Unter den Linden before jumping into a taxi and disappearing. The newspapers hailed the phoney captain a popular hero for exposing Germany's demented respect for uniform. When Voigt was eventually caught and imprisoned, the Kaiser (Wilhelm II) showed a hint of a sense of humour and ordered his four-year sentence to be halved.

War, Revolution and the 'Golden Twenties'

It was the First World War that began to break the stranglehold of Prussia's military mania. The fighting, seen by Germany as a way of furthering its influence in the colonies and in the crumbling Austro-Hungarian empire, was expected to last just a few weeks. But it dragged on for four years and was relentlessly unpopular. Protests began outside the Reichstag, Germany's desperately undemocratic parliament, as early as 1915. Calls for a republic became ever stronger until a wave of strikes and street protests forced the Kaiser to abdicate in November 1918. However, the strongest political force, the Social Democrats (SPD), was bitterly split over the party leadership's support for participation in the war. On 9 November 1918, at the same time as SPD deputy Philipp Scheidemann announced the founding of a democratic republic in the Reichstag, the radical Spartacus League declared communist revolution from a balcony of the Kaiser's palace. SPD leader Friedrich Ebert took control of a provisional government and set about crushing the Spartacist revolt. A clash on 24 December between Ebert's troops and remnants of a navy marine division returning from the front nearly sparked civil war. To dispose of their political enemies Ebert and his tough defence minister Gustav Noske made free use of the *Freikorps*, a loose band of Rambo-like ex-soldiers who could not come to terms with Germany's defeat in the war. 'Anyone found with arms fighting against the government is to be shot instantly,' Noske ordered. Spartacist leaders Karl Liebknecht and Rosa Luxemburg were dragged out of hiding and brutally murdered, and Noske declared martial law.

It was under these inauspicious circumstances that Germany's first democracy, under Ebert's presidency, was founded with the signing of a new constitution in Weimar in 1919. The *Freikorps*, who later formed the backbone of Hitler's stormtroopers, became more disillusioned and violent after the 1919 Treaty of Versailles, which they denounced as a world-wide Jewish plot to besmirch the honour of Germany. On 13 March 1920 a provincial civil servant called Wolfgang Kapp marched into Berlin at the head of a *Freikorps* brigade and declared himself Chancellor, forcing Ebert to flee first to Dresden and then Stuttgart. For five days he held the city in his grip, eccentrically ordering a ban on university exams and confiscating matzo flour from Jewish shopkeepers, before losing his nerve and flying to Sweden. Later that year the head of Germany's delegation to Versailles, Matthias Erzberger, was murdered. In 1922 Walter Rathenau, the brilliant Jewish Foreign Minister who had begun to open diplomatic channels to Germany's wartime foes, was gunned down outside his Berlin home.

The 1920s began badly in Berlin and worse was to come. The hyperinflation of 1923–24, when the price of bread came to be measured first in millions and then in billions of marks, wiped out most people's savings; the Wall Street Crash of 1929 dealt a mortal blow to German industry, sending unemployment sky-high and paving the way for Hitler's rise to power. Despite the hardships, however, the period became known in popular mythology as the 'Golden Twenties'. For a fragile, intense five-year period in the middle of the decade Berlin experienced a dizzy explosion of cabaret, jazz, classical music, theatre, cinema, painting and design. After centuries of stiff conservatism, this was suddenly the most modern city in the world, with glaring street lights, all-night dancing, seedy clubs and backstreet bars. Political instability partly fuelled the frantic free-for-all; you can see it in the garish colours of Expressionist painting, in the apocalyptic overtones of Fritz Lang's film *Metropolis*, in the wry insights of Brecht's plays into human poverty and despair. In retrospect the period seems like a frenzied dance of death, a dark time somehow prescient of even darker times ahead. In the words of historian Klaus Mann:

> Within the city, millions of underfed, corrupt, sex-starved and pleasure-hungry men and women writhe and totter in a jazz-induced delirium. Dance has become an obsession, a mania, a cult. The Stock Exchange hops like a frog, ministers sway on their feet, the Reichstag does a jig. War cripples and profiteers, film stars and prostitutes, former monarchs (with princely pensions) and retired schoolmasters (with no pension at all)—all twist and turn in gruesome euphoria.

Berlin under the Nazis

Berlin never liked the National Socialists and the feeling was mutual. 'Hitler is not one of us,' contemporary historian Friedrich Meinicke said. 'He comes from some race we'd long considered extinct.' Joseph Goebbels, sent to Berlin in 1926 to rouse Nazi support, called the place 'a monster city of stone and asphalt'. His campaign of sending thugs to break up political meetings in working-class neighbourhoods made him few friends. In the flurry of elections in the early 1930s, Berlin bucked the trend of growing Nazi support in Germany and voted resolutely for the Left.

But Hitler made his presence felt in the capital from the moment he became Chancellor on 30 January 1933. Thousands of stormtroopers celebrated that same evening with a torchlit procession through the Brandenburg Gate. Less than a month later the Reichstag was half gutted by a mysterious fire which Hitler used as an excuse to crack down on his left-wing enemies and declare dictatorial powers. On 1 April Goebbels, now propaganda minister, urged a boycott of Jewish businesses at a rally in the Lustgarten and on 10 May he ordered a public burning of books by left-wing and Jewish authors. In a few months the Nazis had stifled the voices at the forefront of Berlin life—its politicians, intellectuals and lively Jewish community. Communists were arrested, imprisoned and shot; professors were summarily removed from their university posts and replaced with Nazi propagandists; theatres, cabarets and bars were shut down as nightlife and sexual freedom were branded as decadent; the lifeblood of the city drained away as the likes of Brecht, Weill and Einstein fled abroad.

In place of the old Berlin came a triumphalist vision of a thousand-year Reich with a rebuilt, marble-decked capital to be called Germania. Hitler broadened the main avenue through the Tiergarten and chopped down the trees on Unter den Linden to make way for military parades. Albert Speer oversaw the construction of new, hulking Fascist buildings, including the Reichsbank (later the East German Communist Central Committee) and the Olympic Stadium which housed the 1936 Games.

But most of the Nazis' giddy architectural plans were shelved in anticipation of war. In 1936 Hitler imposed a command economy geared to weapons production. Two years later he annexed Austria and Czechoslovakia's Sudetenland. Through the Gestapo he set up a network of secret agents and informers to keep the people in check. He also stepped up his persecution of the 'enemy within', the Jewish community

40

which he accused of sullying the earth and conspiring to dominate it. The murder of a German diplomat in Paris by a Jewish activist was used as an excuse for an orgy of looting and destruction of Jewish synagogues, businesses, shops and houses on 9 November 1938, later known as *Reichskristallnacht*, or the night of the broken glass. Thereafter Jews were forbidden to go to theatres or cinemas; their children were thrown out of school; shopowners feared for their livelihoods if they served Jewish customers.

The persecution of the Jews intensified after the outbreak of war. From 1941 they were deported to camps and used as slave labour to help the war effort. The following year the Nazis initiated the 'Final Solution', systematically slaughtering Jews and other minorities in gas chambers. Of Berlin's 160,000-strong pre-war Jewish community, only 8000 remained in 1945. One-third were killed in concentration camps, the rest fled abroad.

The first air raids hit Berlin in 1940 but caused comparatively little damage. Nazi airforce chief Hermann Göring had boasted at the beginning of the war that, as surely as his name was not Meyer, no Allied bomb would hit the capital. He could have been called Meyer hundreds of thousands of times. From 1943 British and American planes carpet-bombed Berlin night and day. The failure of Colonel von Stauffenberg's 1944 plot to overthrow Hitler (see p. 136) signalled the end of Berlin's chances of being spared the worst. By 2 May 1945, when Soviet troops hoisted the Red Flag above the pockmarked Brandenburg Gate, one-third of Berlin's buildings were in ruins and its population reduced from more than 4 million to 2.5 million.

Division and Cold War

Willy Brandt described Berlin in 1945 as 'a no-man's land on the edge of the world with every little garden a graveyard'. This was Year Zero, the end of the nightmare but also the beginning of a hazy and frightening future, a time when the survivors had to come to terms with the barely comprehensible legacy of destruction and death. Most Berliners left the smoking ruins of their city and squeezed into refugee camps in the suburbs. A few stayed in the shells of their former homes. Others were too terrified to emerge from their cellars and makeshift shelters for several weeks. Rationing was limited to two potatoes and half a loaf of bread per day. The black market thrived. Horses were torn apart in the street for meat. The Tiergarten's remaining trees were chopped down for firewood.

Berlin began its painful reconstruction under the supervision of the victorious wartime powers—the Soviet Union, the United States, Britain and France—who had divided Germany between them. Although Berlin fell inside the Soviet occupation zone, the Western allies won control of half the city arguing that it was too big a prize for the Russians alone. The decision to put Berlin under half capitalist, half communist control proved fateful. There had already been no love lost between the two emerging world superpowers, the United States and the Soviet Union, when they discussed the future of Germany towards the end of the war. Now their relationship turned into open animosity as they failed to agree on a constitution or government for the defeated nation. By 1948 it was clear that the two halves of Germany were drifting apart. On 20 June the Western allies revalued the mark in their occupation zones, including West Berlin, and introduced a market economy. Four days later the Soviet Union retaliated with a separate currency for its zone and, in the opening salvo of the Cold War, closed all land routes to West Berlin. Stalin could not tolerate this Western island in a future East Germany and had decided to starve it out.

The Soviet blockade was thwarted by the biggest airlift in history, organized by the British and Americans (see p. 115), which lasted just under a year until Stalin backed down. Two weeks after the blockade ended, the Federal Republic of (West) Germany was founded. Five months later, the communist (East) German Democratic Republic was born. The two states were separated by a fortified border that was eventually closed in 1952. But the future of Berlin remained unresolved. It was still an open city, the only free entry and exit point between the two Germanys. Occupying troops still retained control over their four sectors, nominally sharing responsibility for the whole city but in reality falling firmly into East and West camps.

This precarious situation was unbalanced further in 1953 when Soviet tanks moved into the streets of East Berlin to crush a worker revolt over increased production quotas. The protest, in which 23 people were killed, was a sign of deep disillusion with the ideals of the 'peasants' and workers' state on German soil' and sparked the beginning of a mass exodus of East Germans to the West through the open Berlin border. One and a half million people left over the next eight years, a movement that threatened the very existence of East Germany. In August 1961, with superpower relations deteriorating and the stream of emigrants growing larger by the week, the Communist leadership built the Wall around West Berlin to close the last escape hatch to the West and hold the country together by force.

So began the city's 28-year-long division, with the uncertainties of international politics hovering precariously over it. Every sign of super-power tension was reflected in the nervous claustrophobia of Berlin. The two halves of the city gradually moved far apart. West Berlin, the precious ideological jewel of the capitalist world, became a gilded island subsidized to the hilt by a Bonn government made rich through US aid provided under the Marshall Plan for the reconstruction of Western Europe. New housing grew up on wartime bomb sites, and its streets and shops gleamed. Students and anarchists were attracted by cheap living, raucous nightlife reminiscent of the 1920s and exemption from military service. They were soon to become a powerful voice of radical protest that spawned the German anti-Vietnam peace movement, the Baader-Meinhof terrorist gang and the Greens. East Berlin became the western half's competitor. Although the Prussian palaces of Unter den Linden were restored to their old splendour and Alexanderplatz became a brand new showcase of socialist architecture, the East, with its sluggish economy, could not keep up. Its suburbs were grimy and neglected, its streets drab and still scarred by the war. Above all its people yearned to be able to travel, to see their relatives and friends, to taste the forbidden fruits of the West. The barbed wire and concrete, the armed guards and the periodic reports of deaths at the Wall filled them with stubborn resentment.

Revolution and Reunification

East Germany had always been an artificial political creation, the product of Nazi and Stalinist dictatorship. But as long as the Wall remained, its survival as the communist world's showcase economy seemed assured. When East German leader Erich Honecker visited Bonn in 1987 it seemed the Germanys had ditched all thoughts of unification and were trying to get on with each other as they were. But two crucial outside events changed everything. Soviet leader Mikhail Gorbachev responded to the East bloc's economic and political stagnation with his 'Sinatra doctrine'—letting everyone do it their way. And then on 10 September 1989 Hungary opened its borders with Austria, prompting tens of thousands of East Germans to squeeze through the gap in the Iron Curtain to the West. When East Germany restricted travel to Hungary, its people occupied embassies in Prague and East Berlin instead. Dissident movements such as New Forum organized demonstrations demanding free travel and free elections. At first the protests were small and hesitant, but within a few weeks the streets of every major city were filling with hundreds of thousands of people chanting: 'We are the people!' When Gorbachev came to East Berlin on 7 October to celebrate the 40th anniversary of East Germany, he found a city in turmoil. A few blocks from the official celebration, half a million people were marching in defiance of the swarms of Stasi (state security) agents around them. 'Time punishes those who delay,' Gorbachev told his host prophetically. Honecker refused to contemplate reform but on 18 October, with revolutionary zeal at fever pitch and even his own politburo turning against him, he stepped down.

His successor Egon Krenz failed to stop the rot despite promising change. The demonstrations grew louder and the exodus to the West ever faster. Within three weeks the government had resigned. Then on 9 November, in a last desperate attempt to win back the people, Krenz authorized free travel to the West. Hundreds of thousands of East Berliners swarmed to the Wall and, to their disbelief, were let through. On a night of wild parties, of champagne, dancing, hugs and tears, West Berlin mayor Walter Momper declared: 'We Germans are the happiest people in the world.'

Within weeks Krenz resigned, the party renounced its dominant role and called free elections. The Communist system had evaporated: the question was what should replace it. Continuing street demonstrations began to clamour for 'Germany United Fatherland' but everyone assumed this was a distant prospect. However, one man thought otherwise. Helmut Kohl, West Germany's hitherto bumbling Chancellor, embraced unification as a crusader cause. His Christian Democratic Union (CDU) took over its East German namesake (without worrying too much about the latter's past as a satellite party for the Communists) and threw down the gauntlet to the electorate: vote for us and you will have hard Western currency by the summer holidays. The electorate were won over and the CDU achieved a landslide victory in East Germany's first and last democratic election on 18 March 1990.

The other parties were caught totally off balance. New Forum and other torch-bearers of the revolution accused Kohl of barging in with his money and his slick political machine, making get-rich-quick promises he could not keep. Nowhere was the suspicion of Kohl stronger than in Berlin, whose intellectuals had dreamed of a third way between communism and capitalism, not a wholesale takeover by the West.

But Kohl, virtually controlling the East German government, pressed on, bringing hard currency and a market economy to the East on 1 July against the advice of his own economic experts and central bank. After assuring his neighbours that Germany was not about to return to its aggressive expansionist past, he won the blessing of the wartime Allies and secured Gorbachev's permission for a united Germany to be a member of NATO. Moving at breakneck pace, the Chancellor got his way on everything and managed to see unification through by 3 October, two months before his triumphant re-election in the first parliamentary poll of the new Germany.

It sounds like a fairy tale but it has ended far from happily ever after. Sudden monetary union with the West may have given East Germans hard currency, but it has also destroyed the economy without giving it a chance to adapt to the free market. It has decimated once-booming trade with East European countries who cannot afford to pay in deutschmarks, caused mass unemployment, sent prices soaring without corresponding rises in income and scared off foreign investors who fear the situation is running out of control before basic issues such as property rights have been sorted out.

By simply extending the West German constitution to the East rather than negotiating a new one, Kohl's government has also attacked the very marrow of East German life. Nobody is pretending that a corrupt and inefficient communist state is worth embalming for posterity, but in 40 years the East German people developed a culture, a means of communication, a sense of community which should not just be trashed. The message of the new Germany, however, is that the West is the best. East German books are no longer stocked in shops; East Germany's television news was scrapped just as it was developing a refreshing alternative view of world events; East Germany's widely praised health system has been ditched; even East German eggs, once imported by West Germany, are no longer sold unless they are in Western-produced boxes.

Berlin has inherited its own special problems. The Wall has disappeared except for a few memorial pieces, the borders have vanished and the allied troops have suspended their rights pending full withdrawal. But the city is losing its generous subsidies and does not know if it can survive without them. Although Berlin is nominally the new capital, the government and the revenue it could generate look like staying in Bonn for the time being. The city has also been swamped with East Germans and East Europeans attracted by its affluent western half.

Traffic no longer moves. A severe housing crisis has sparked fierce rioting. Politically the city is becoming polarized, with voters in the West moving to the right and support for the reformed Communists, the Party of Democratic Socialism, remaining strong in the East. Unrest, if it comes, is certain to start in rebellious Berlin.

Kohl hoped that by crushing East German institutions and the economy he would also eradicate the Communist power base behind it, and that new private capital would quickly flood in to rebuild the region in West Germany's image. He won the elections on the understanding that, after a difficult initial period, affluence would quickly spread through the new expanded Fatherland. At the beginning of 1991 it is far from clear whether his gamble will come off.

The Walks

Sculpture,
Mehringplatz

'There's nothing in Berlin that can captivate the foreigner except a few museums, castles and soldiers,' Kaiser Wilhelm II commented disdainfully in 1892. 'After six days, red book in hand, he has seen everything and departs relieved, feeling he has done his duty.' Visiting Berlin nowadays is, fortunately, rather more rewarding than the bilious Kaiser's words suggest. Perhaps one can never feel entirely comfortable in a city so haunted by its past, but there is also much to captivate and surprise. These nine walks mix the grim realities of Prussian militarism, Nazi tyranny and the Wall with the Berlin of landscaped parks, grand palaces and rich museums; they unveil stories of murder, revolution and war but also explore the hedonistic bustle of the city's bars, pavement cafés and spontaneous street art. The blend is not meant to leaven or trivialize the burden of history; rather, it should enhance the ambiguity of the city and leave the visitor not relieved, but exhilarated—if just a little troubled too.

The walks cover longish distances and, in some cases, require some deft use of public transport. At the beginning of each walk are some recommendations on how to tackle the route at hand. The city centre trails (Walks I, II, IV and VII) are easily negotiable on foot, while the rest are a little trickier. One option for the longer walks is to get hold of a bicycle, probably the most rewarding means of transport in Berlin (see Travel section for some addresses of cycle rental agencies).

Walks I–III cover East Berlin; Walks V–IX, West. Walk IV (retracing the Wall) straddles both sides and most vividly brings home the changes since the end of the Cold War. Walk I (Unter den Linden) and Walk VII (the Ku'damm) cover most of the other 'essential' sights immediately associated with Berlin. The rest of the walks are more challenging and perhaps more unexpected. Walk II visits the museum treasures of the Kaisers and the old Jewish quarter. Walks III and V soak up the atmosphere of two quirky and idiosyncratic districts, Prenzlauer Berg and Kreuzberg. Walk VI (the Tiergarten) and Walk IX (the woods and fairy-tale castles of Wannsee) explore the dark undercurrents beneath the tranquil beauty of the city's parkland. Walk VIII juxtaposes the most horrifying of Nazi legacies, Plötzensee jail, and the rococo elegance of Charlottenburg castle.

Some Berlin Leitmotivs

Amid all this variety, some characteristic sights recur in the walks. They include:

Litfasssäulen: 'Everywhere in the city, at regular intervals, there are pretty round pillars, 18 foot high and about as thick as a boar's head,' wrote Mark Twain on a visit in 1891 about Berlin's much loved and frequently copied advertising pillars. Ernst Litfass, the man who invented them, was Friedrich Wilhelm IV's court printer, responsible for publicizing major events around the city. To his horror, the king imposed a ban on public notices in the wake of the 1848 revolution. When Litfass complained, he was told he could continue to stick up his posters, but only on public lavatories and only on condition that he personally took responsibility for keeping them clean, inside and out. In anger and frustration he finally hit upon the ideal solution; the first *Litfasssäule* (Litfass pillar) appeared outside his house in Adlerstrasse on 1 July 1855. It was an instant hit. Soon his pillars were mushrooming all over town. Mark Twain thought they should have been exported to America (they weren't). One joke popular in the 1920s has a drunken man staggering round and round a Litfass pillar shouting: 'Dreadful! I've been walled in!'

Water pumps: Several Berlin districts, notably Charlottenburg, have retained fine *Jugendstil* iron water pumps, worked by a long, ornate handle. They were built at the turn of the century to help clean up after horses on the busy roads. Now they have purely ornamental value. As large warning notices tell you, you can't drink the water.

The Spree: Berlin's river (pronounced *shpray*) was part of the fortified border between the two sides of the city during the Cold War.
Markers show where would-be escapers to the West were shot trying to
swim across. Now the Spree is integrated into the city again, and popular
in the summer for cruises. According to popular legend, it was the Berlin
love of boating that led to the English expression 'to go out on a spree'.
Linguistic experts reserve judgement. A century ago the river was one of
the city's main sources of entertainment. When Lenin studied in Berlin
in 1895 he swam in it every day. Following his example is not recommended nowadays as the waters have grown distinctly murky.

Dogs: When it comes to animals, Berlin is mercifully free from rats
and cockcroaches. But it does have a penchant for pet dogs—some
150,000 of them, or roughly one for every 25 people. Dogs are seen,
heard and talked about everywhere. With typical German thoroughness,
Berliners are conscientious about clearing their pets' business off the
street (they carry little shovels and plastic bags around with them). They
also lavish affection on the creatures, in both life and death. For one of
Berlin's truly bizarre sights, go to the animal cemetery on Dessauer
Strasse in the southern suburb of Lankwitz. Diminutive marble stones
are engraved with tender messages or portraits of the deceased. Most of
the 2,000 animals buried there are dogs, including two police hounds
called Harro and Waldo, both killed in the line of duty.

Berlin's Top Ten

For visitors who do not have time to see everything, here is a list of sights
without which no trip to Berlin is complete:

1. **The Tiergarten** (Walk VI): A vast park of woods and lakes, wide
   avenues and grand monuments, with the Reichstag and Brandenburg Gate looming in the distance.
2. **Checkpoint Charlie Museum** (Walk IV): A detailed and fascinat-
   ing history of the Wall, a record of the cruelty of Berlin's division
   and a celebration of the ingenuity of those who tried to defy it.
3. **Unter den Linden** (Walk I): The grand tree-lined avenue of the
   Prussian monarchs touched up with a little socialist realism.
4. **Platz der Akademie** (Walk I): An unspoiled neo-classical square,
   like an 18th-century print brought to life in the heart of a modern
   city.

5. **Pergamon Museum** (Walk II): Home to some of the most breath-taking ancient Greek and Babylonian booty ever retrieved. Museums don't come any grander than this.
6. **Soviet War Memorial** (Walk V): A dramatic, unsentimental tribute to the soldiers who died in the Battle of Berlin in 1945.
7. **Pfaueninsel** (Walk IX): An isolated pleasure island of follies, peacocks and dreamy views over the Havel lake.
8. **Berlin Museum** (Walk V): A lively, witty and incisive exhibition of the city's history with an authentic-looking Berlin pub inside.
9. **Schloss Charlottenburg** (Walk VIII): Berlin at its most elegant and carefree; a rococo palace set in a richly landscaped riverside park.
10. **Bauhaus Archive** (Walk VI): An insight into the sheer creativity and versatility of one of the 20th century's most influential schools of art, architecture and design.

Five Duds

Some things aren't what they're cracked up to be. The following sights regularly show up in guide books, but don't be deluded:

1. **German History Exhibition at the Reichstag** (Walk IV): Interesting only to see what a watered-down version of history German children are fed when they come here on school trips. Superficial and, for some, offensive.
2. **Multivision Berlin** in the Europa-Center (Walk VII): Does for Berlin what the Reichstag exhibition does for the whole of Germany. A 40-minute bombardment of empty images, remarkable only for what they omit.
3. **Rathaus Schöneberg**: The seat of West Berlin's city government made famous in 1963 when President Kennedy declared from the steps: '*Ich bin ein Berliner*' (I am a Berliner). It's an out-of-the-way, plug-ugly administrative building with little to distract the passer-by. The *Friedensglocke*, the peace bell in the tower, which was donated by the Americans and modelled on Philadelphia's Liberty Bell, is impossible to see from the street and not much of a pleasure to hear when it rings at midday and 6 pm. Kennedy's 1963 speech caused great amusement among local cynics at the time because *ein Berliner* can also mean a jam-filled bun.

50

4. **Funkturm**: West Berlin's radio tower, next to the International Congress Centre in the far west of Charlottenburg. Just about the only thing you can see from the top of this vertiginous metal structure is the knot of motorway junctions below. Come for a congress, but not for fun.

5. **Olympic Stadium**: Built in Fascist triumphalist style for the 1936 Games, the stadium is impressive in its way, but not worth the schlep out to the back of beyond unless you have tickets for a rock concert.

Berlin by Theme

Inevitably each walk presents a big mix of topics and sensations. Here is some guidance for following up individual themes:

Medieval Berlin: Marienkirche and the Nikolaiviertel (Walk I), Berlin Museum (Walk V), Kohlhasenbrück (Walk IX).

The Rise of Prussia: The Brandenburg Gate, Platz der Akademie and Bebelplatz (Walk I), Schloss Bellevue (Tour VI), Schloss Charlottenburg (Walk VIII), Potsdam (Additional Sights).

Biedermeier and Neo-classical Berlin: Unter den Linden and Schinkel Museum (Walk I), Museum Island buildings (Walk II), Kreuzberg monument (Walk V), Schloss Babelsberg, Schloss Glienicke and Pfaueninsel (Walk IX).

Working-class Berlin: Prenzlauer Berg (Walk III), Kreuzberg (Walk V), Moabit (Walk VIII).

Wilhelmine Berlin: Berliner Dom, Rotes Rathaus (Walk I), Reichstag (Walk IV), Siegessäule (Walk VI), Kurfürstendamm and Kaiser Wilhelm Memorial Church (Walk VII).

1920s Berlin: Martin-Gropius-Bau picture gallery (Walk IV), Luxemburg/Liebknecht memorials and Bauhaus Archive (Walk VI), Isherwood's house and Käthe Kollwitz museum (Walk VII), Bröhan Museum (Walk VIII), Brücke Museum (Additional Sights).

Jewish Berlin: New Synagogue, Grosse Hamburger Strasse and Scheunenviertel (Walk II), Jewish cemetery and synagogue (Walk III), Jewish Community Centre and monuments to the victims of the Holocaust (Walk VII), Weissensee cemetery (Additional Sights).

Nazi Berlin: Brandenburg Gate, Unter den Linden, Bebelplatz, former Reichsbank (Walk I), water tower (Walk III), Topography of Terror exhibit, old government quarter and Reichstag (Walk IV), German Resistance Museum (Walk VI), Plötzensee Memorial (Walk VIII), Wannsee Villa (Walk IX).

51

Cold War Berlin: Remnants of the Wall and Checkpoint Charlie Museum (Walk IV), airlift memorial and Elefantengalerie exhibition of Wall art (Walk V), Steinstücken and the Glienicker Bridge (Walk IX), Cecilienhof mansion in Potsdam (Additional Sights).

Communist Berlin: Alexanderplatz and Marx/Engels monument (Walk I), Zionskirche (Walk II), Gethsemanekirche and monuments to communist heroes (Walk III), East Berlin Soviet war memorial (Walk V), former Stasi headquarters (Additional Sights).

Berlin Art Treasures: Museum Island (Walk II), Kulturforum (Walk VI), Charlottenburg museums (Walk VIII), Dahlem Museums (Additional Sights).

Literary Berlin: Brecht's house and Berliner Ensemble (Walk II), Heine statue (Walk II), Isherwood's house (Walk VII), Kleist's grave (Walk IX).

Walk I

From the Brandenburg Gate to Alexanderplatz

Frederick the Great, Unter den Linden

Brandenburg Gate—Unter den Linden—Platz der Akademie—Schinkel Museum—Bebelplatz—Berliner Dom—Nikolaiviertel—Alexanderplatz

> Berlin is a city with two centres—the cluster of expensive hotels, bars, cinemas, shops round the Memorial Church... and the self-conscious civic centre of buildings round Unter den Linden, carefully arranged. In grand international styles, copies of copies, they assert our dignity as a capital city—a parliament, a couple of museums, a State bank, a cathedral, an opera, a dozen embassies, a triumphal arch; nothing has been forgotten. And they are all so pompous, so very correct...
>
> —Christopher Isherwood, *Goodbye to Berlin*

Conjure up an image of old imperial Germany and you might well envisage Unter den Linden, the grand Prussian avenue running through the heart of East Berlin. Its resplendent neo-classical architecture has survived wars and ideological U-turns to bring a peculiarly old-fashioned air to modern Berlin.

Of course, it is one of Berlin's great ironies that Unter den Linden, centrepiece of the Mitte district, should have fallen into the East of the

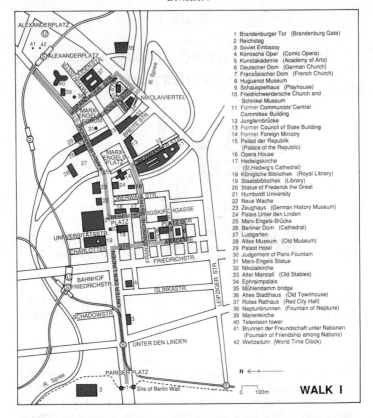

ALEXANDERPLATZ

41 42
ALEXANDERPLATZ

NIKOLAIVIERTEL

MARX
ENGELS
FORUM

MARX
ENGELS
PLATZ

NIKOLAIVIERTEL

OBERWALLSTR.

NEUE WACHE

BEBEL HEDWIGSKIRCHGASSE
PLATZ

PLATZ DER
AKADEMIE

UNIVERSITÄTSTR.

CHARLOTTENSTR.

FRIEDRICHSTR.

R. Spree

BAHNHOF
FRIEDRICHSTR.

GLINKASTR.

LEIPZIGER STR.

UNTER DEN LINDEN

SCHADOWSTR.

UNTER DEN LINDEN

R. Spree

PARISER PLATZ

2   Site of Berlin Wall

N ←

0   100m

WALK I

1 Brandenburger Tor (Brandenburg Gate)
2 Reichstag
3 Soviet Embassy
4 Komische Oper (Comic Opera)
5 Kunstakademie (Academy of Arts)
6 Deutscher Dom (German Church)
7 Französischer Dom (French Church)
8 Huguenot Museum
9 Schauspielhaus (Playhouse)
10 Friedrichwerdersche Church and
   Schinkel Museum
11 Former Communists' Central
   Committee Building
12 Jungfernbrücke
13 Former Council of State Building
14 Former Foreign Ministry
15 Palast der Republik
   (Palace of the Republic)
16 Opera House
17 Hedwigskirche
   (St.Hedwig's Cathedral)
18 Königliche Bibliothek (Royal Library)
19 Staatsbibliothek (Library)
20 Statue of Frederick the Great
21 Humboldt University
22 Neue Wache
23 Zeughaus (German History Museum)
24 Palais Unter den Linden
25 Marx-Engels-Brücke
26 Berliner Dom (Cathedral)
27 Lustgarten
28 Altes Museum (Old Museum)
29 Palast Hotel
30 Judgement of Paris Fountain
31 Marx-Engels Statue
32 Nikolaikirche
33 Alter Marstall (Old Stables)
34 Ephraimpalais
35 Mühlendamm bridge
36 Altes Stadthaus (Old Townhouse)
37 Rotes Rathaus (Red City Hall)
38 Neptunbrunnen (Fountain of Neptune)
39 Marienkirche
40 Television tower
41 Brunnen der Freundschaft unter Nationen
   (Fountain of Friendship among Nations)
42 Weltzeituhr (World Time Clock)

city. The values that imbue every brick of its palaces—class, patronage, imperialism—were the very values rejected by the East German Communists who inherited it after the Second World War. If Isherwood, back in 1932, thought the buildings were sterile and soulless, imagine the Communists' embarrassment. Here, slap in the capital of the 'workers' and peasants' state', was the symbol of imperial Germany, the Brandenburg Gate; a grand statue of Hitler's favourite historical character, Frederick the Great; and the palace of the very same Kaisers whom the Communists had helped to overthrow in 1918.

What to do? The Communists chose not to restore the Kaiser's Palace but blew it up instead. They removed Frederick's statue and dispatched it off to Potsdam. When the Berlin Wall went up in 1961, the Branden-burg Gate conveniently fell within the prohibited border zone and they sealed it off. They replanted the trees that Hitler had chopped down on Unter den Linden and renamed the monument to the heroes of Nazism the monument to the victims of Fascism. At the bomb-ravaged Alexan-derplatz they indulged in a little futuristic socialist realism, including the unmistakable needle-like television tower, and they built a brand new Palace of the Republic on the site of the old Kaiser's residence.

Today the centre of East Berlin (and, now, of Berlin as a whole) is an extraordinary mixture of these opposing traditions. In some ways the old order has returned: the Communists are out and the Brandenburg Gate is open again. Frederick the Great is even back on his pedestal. But the new Germany is very different from the old, and it has a further ironic accident of geography to contend with: in a reunited city where the West dominates everything, its centre is here in the East.

Walking Time: This walk takes about 3 hours and is easily manageable on foot. Most of the sights are open every day, but check the closing times of some minor museums detailed below.

Start: The Brandenburg Gate. The S-Bahn station Unter den Linden is right by the Gate; its end, Alexanderplatz, is a busy junction of both S- and U-Bahns from all directions.

LUNCH/CAFÉS
This is the best gastronomic stretch in East Berlin, which may not be saying much. Picnicking is limited to the park in Marx-Engels-Forum.
Reichstag. A bit of a cheat, as it's in the West. But the food is that much better. There's a quick-bite bar and a restaurant serving sausages, salads, etc. DM 20–25.
Arkade, Französische Str. 25. A former Stasi favourite, it's now a smart tearoom-cum-pub serving light midday snacks and large ice creams. Fine views on to Platz der Akademie.
Café Bauer, Friedrichstr. 158–64. Living off its pre-war reputation as one of Berlin's smart cafés, Bauer is now part of the Grand Hotel and serves coffee and cakes.
Turmstuben, inside the Französischer Dom on Platz der Akademie. A puff up the stairs to get in, but worth it for period furniture and views. The menu is small but not bad. DM 30.
Operncafé, Unter den Linden (next to the state opera house). Great location in the heart of Prussian Berlin. The café downstairs is always

packed. Upstairs is a halfway decent restaurant where you can eat In neo-classical splendour. DM 30.

Quick Tip, Karl-Liebknecht-Str. 5. A cafeteria with reasonable soups and main courses. Part of the Palasthotel, ideal if you haven't hours to waste with slow waiters. DM 15.

Ratskeller, Rathausstr. Atmospheric cellar of the city hall. Above-average food and good beer. DM 20.

☆   ☆   ☆   ☆   ☆

The classical columns of the **Brandenburg Gate** (Brandenburger Tor) are instantly recognizable as the backdrop to rapturous scenes of reunion after the opening of the Berlin Wall on 9 November 1989. This was where friends, lovers and total strangers hugged and kissed, drank and danced, laughed and cried together on an unforgettable night of spontaneous joy. But the Gate also conjures up more disturbing memories, of Prussian officers parading their military glory or of Nazi stormtroopers marching through in torchlit procession. It is now the symbol of the new united Germany, but like much else in Berlin it is riddled with ambiguities.

The Gate, completed in 1791, was originally intended as a symbol of peace, marking a clean break from the warmongering of Frederick the Great who had died five years earlier. Carl Gotthard Langhans' 12-columned design was even based on the Propylea, the entrance to the Acropolis in Athens, suggesting the sanctity of a temple. But the Gate—built across the road out of Berlin to the city of Brandenburg—did not keep the image for long. Two years after it was finished it was crowned with Johann Gottfried Schadow's **Quadriga**, a grand copper sculpture of Nike, the goddess of victory, on her chariot. This curious dual role, as peace gate and triumphal arch, has stayed with the Brandenburg Gate ever since and perhaps helps account for the fascination it exerts as *the* Berlin landmark. The painter Max Liebermann, who lived around the corner in Pariser Platz in the early part of the 20th century, used to tell his visitors: 'To find my house, go to Berlin and take the first left.'

The Gate has acted as a proscenium arch to some of the great exits and entrances of German history. Napoleon marched through to take Berlin in 1806. Kaiser Wilhelm I rode past on a white horse to celebrate German unification in 1871, and Bismarck, the architect of unity, left Berlin in disgrace through its arches after Kaiser Wilhelm II dismissed him as Chancellor in 1890. Wilhelm himself made a similarly ignominious exit in his Daimler after abdicating in 1918. When Hitler came to power on 30 January 1933, his stormtroopers celebrated with a torchlit procession through the Gate. Liebermann, a Jew, watched from his house and commented with a mixture of horror and caustic humour: 'I haven't got room to eat as much as I'd like to throw up.'

In 1945 Soviet troops hoisted the Red Flag atop the war-scarred Brandenburg Gate. Bombs had destroyed the Quadriga, which was later replaced by a West German-made copy. In 1961 the Gate was caught in no man's land behind the Berlin Wall and sealed off with metal barriers guarded by armed border troops. It was only formally reopened to the public on 22 December 1989, six weeks after the Wall was first breached, and shortly afterwards was the centrepiece for the New Year's Eve party of a lifetime, with hundreds of thousands of people popping champagne corks and cheering as fireworks shot into the night sky.

Pariser Platz is now filled with sausage sellers and backpackers, but before the war it was one of the most exclusive addresses in Berlin. Grand neo-classical palaces housed the French and US embassies and the Adlon Hotel, the smartest place to stay in the city. That gilded elegance has lost some of its sheen, but it is still evident along the majestic avenue stretching out ahead, **Unter den Linden***.*

Unter den Linden is named after the trees lining its route (it translates as Under the Limes) which have over the centuries added grace to its grand neo-classical buildings and society cafés much admired by famous visitors from Beethoven to Marx. The Great Elector Friedrich Wilhelm planted the first walnuts and limes at the end of the Thirty Years' War, in 1648, to flank a riding path out towards the hunting grounds of Grunewald and the present-day Tiergarten. He meant the trees to stay, ordering that anyone caught damaging them would have his hand chopped off. Two hundred years later the master architect of neo-classical Berlin, Friedrich Karl Schinkel, made Unter den Linden the centrepiece of his new design for the city, with palaces, museums, embassies and government buildings crowding its 1.5 km extent. Hitler decided to chop down all the trees to make more room for military parades, rendering the avenue sterner and colder. It was replanted as far as Pariser Platz by the Communists; the last stretch of trees up to the Brandenburg Gate was donated after the Wall opened by a West Berlin garden foundation.

The top end of the avenue is flanked by various East European diplomatic missions including the huge former **Soviet Embassy** *to East Germany on the right. Check to see if a bust of Lenin still stands* *in the front garden—in changing times one cannot be sure. The junction with Friedrichstrasse a little further down was once one of the most lively in Berlin.*

The city posted its very first traffic warden here, complete with horse, whistle and trumpet, as early as 1902. It was also the site of three of the city's most famous coffee houses—the Kranzler (now on the Ku'damm), the Café Bauer (now incorporated into the Grand Hotel but originally on the other side of the street where the unappealing Café Lindencorso stands), and the Café Victoria (now the hotel Unter den Linden), which was a favourite with the theatre director Max Reinhardt.

*Take a right onto Charlottenstrasse at the next junction. Don't worry about the sights straight ahead, we're coming back. Walk two blocks until you hit the pedestrian zone incorporating the **Platz der Akademie**.*

The square's easy grace suggests it might have remained intact for two centuries. In fact all three major buildings were badly bombed in the Second World War and the square was little more than a pile of rubble until the late 1970s. This was once Berlin's market square stretching all the way from Unter den Linden to Leipziger Strasse two blocks to the south. In the early 18th century an infantry regiment moved here and it was renamed Gendarmenmarkt. Its modern name stems from 1950 when the Academy of Arts on the left hand side of the square celebrated its 250th anniversary.

In the early 18th century, as now, the square housed a French and a German church with a theatre in between. But it was only after the infantry regiment moved away in 1773 that the present buildings took shape. In the 1780s Frederick the Great had the two churches remodelled very loosely on the twin domes of Santa Maria dei Miracoli and Santa Maria in Montesanto in the Piazza del Popolo in Rome. Built effectively as vanity pieces, they have no religious function today.

*The broad, polished bronze cupola of the **Deutscher Dom** (German church) at the south end of the square is slowly emerging after years of renovation. At the north end, the **Französischer Dom** (French church) houses a **Huguenot Museum** (10–5, closed Mon and Fri, adm) on the ground floor, and a viewing tower and restaurant above.*

The original French church, dating from the early 18th century, was the first for the growing community of Huguenots, or French protestants, who had flooded to the city to escape religious persecution. Elector Friedrich Wilhelm had officially welcomed them with his Edict of Potsdam of 1685, a direct rebuttal of Louis XIV's Revocation of the Edict of Nantes which officially made them *personae non gratae* at home. By the end of the century 6000 of them had flooded in, one-third of Berlin's total population of the time. The museum charts how the Huguenots revived a somewhat depressed, backward Prussia and influenced everything from commerce to the Gallic-flavoured Berlin dialect. An appreciative Frederick the Great once said: 'They helped repopulate our desolate cities and gave us the manufacturing industries we lacked.' The climb to the top of the tall, slim tower (10–6 daily, free) is worth the effort for the view (no lift). There are markers pointing out the sites from the balustrade.

In the centre of the square is the **Schauspielhaus**, or playhouse, currently in its third incarnation. The original by Carl Gotthard Langhans burned down in 1817, just 15 years after it was completed. The present design is by Schinkel, who boasted he had produced a fire-resistant building of great beauty with perfect acoustics and vision, all at a knock-down price. It's too late to know if he was right. The building was wrecked by bombs in 1945 and the renovation, although beautiful, is far from perfect acoustically. It is now a concert hall, memorably used for the late Leonard Bernstein's rousing performance of Beethoven's Ninth Symphony to celebrate the opening of the Wall.

Outside the theatre is the towering marble figure of Friedrich Schiller (1759–1805), one of Germany's greatest writers who wrote the 'Ode to Joy' featured in Beethoven's Ninth. Around him are four muses representing his main areas of work: Euterpe (poetry), Melpomene (drama), Calliope (philosophy) and Clio (history). Erected in 1871, the statue was removed by the Nazis in 1936 because they did not approve of Schiller's liberal philosophy. It languished in a small Charlottenburg park until the renovation of the Schauspielhaus in 1988.

It's worth poking about the warren of building sites beyond the Deutscher Dom to realize how long it has taken to clear up damage from the war. Close inspection reveals bullet holes and scorch marks still on the buildings. Return to the north end of Platz der Akademie and take a right onto Französische Str. Just beyond Oberwallstr. on the left is the **Friedrichwerdersche Kirche** *(10–6 daily, adm), a church containing a museum to the man who designed it, Karl Friedrich Schinkel.*

59

Schinkel is to Berlin what Haussmann is to Paris—the architect of an entire city, a man whose personality and vision is reflected everywhere in central Berlin. The neo-classical stamp he put on Berlin is unmistakable, even in buildings that he personally had nothing to do with. In this part of the city some excellent restoration work has repaired the wartime bomb damage. The Friedrichswerdersche Kirche is one of his least typical works—a neo-Gothic rather than neo-classical design. But his fine sense of proportion shines through, especially in the swooping wooden vaults of the roof. Schinkel built the church at the height of his career in 1830. Downstairs is a collection of sculptures from the period, including one of Schinkel himself (on the right as you go in). Upstairs is an exhibition of his life and work. Born in 1781, he came to Berlin to study architecture under the 18th-century master Friedrich Gilly. Much inspired by trips to Italy, he became a favourite of King Friedrich Wilhelm III and gradually revamped the whole centre of Berlin. He died a rich and famous man in 1841.

Directly opposite the Schinkel Museum is the austere, grey hulk that served both as Hitler's central bank and the **Communists' central committee building**. It was built by the Fascist architect Heinrich Wolff in 1934–8. Either by fluke or a severe lack of aesthetic judgement on the part of the Allies, it survived the war intact and became East Germany's finance ministry before the central committee moved in in 1959. The smudge on the wall to the right was where the party symbol— two hands clasped in solidarity—was displayed until January 1990. The discredited Communists moved out shortly afterwards and the building has since lain idle.

*Walk round the building to get a feel for its outrageous size and to see one of the prettiest bridges in Berlin, which crosses the Spree at Oberwasserstr. The **Jungfernbrücke** (1798) is the only surviving drawbridge in Berlin, but it no longer opens. Standing at the north end, you can see many of the other East German government buildings. The Council of State is to the right. The foreign ministry is just behind the Schinkel Museum. Opposite, across the car park, is the Palace of the Republic which housed the parliamentary chamber, the Volkskammer (see below). For now, retrace your steps down Französische Strasse. Turn right underneath the arch at Hedwigs-kirchgasse. Straight ahead is **Bebelplatz**, back in the heart of Prussian Berlin.*

Frederick the Great and his architect Georg Wenzeslaus von Knobelsdorff dreamed of a square emulating the glories of ancient Rome. It was originally called Forum Fridericianum, later changed to the more mundane Opernplatz. The Communists gave the square its modern name in honour of the 19th-century founder of the German workers' movement, August Bebel. Unfortunately Frederick began to lose interest in the project and the overall result was less than perfect. In fact the square's greatest resemblance to Rome nowadays is that, like many historical sites in the Italian capital, it is blithely used as a car park.

Opernplatz became notorious on 10 May 1933 when the Nazi propaganda chief Joseph Goebbels ordered a ritual burning of 'immoral and destructive documents and books'. Among authors considered too left-wing, too Jewish, or just too un-German to continue in public circulation were Thomas Mann, Albert Einstein, Sigmund Freud and Karl Marx. The burning, deliberately carried out opposite Berlin's traditionally liberal Humboldt University, was one of the Nazis' first major acts of provocation, and the banning, persecution and exile of hundreds of intellectuals soon followed. The Jewish satirical poet Heinrich Heine once commented that if they begin by burning books they end by burning people. The brownshirts flung his works to the flames too.

Knobelsdorff's first building here, the **Staatsoper** (open for occasional tours of the auditorium) to the right, was also his best. Completed in 1743, it was the first public opera house in Prussia. It is based on a Corinthian temple but has some rococo decorative touches. The Latin inscription above the entrance dedicates the building to Frederick, Apollo and the Muses.

Frederick's plan to re-create ancient Rome began to come unstuck with the **Hedwigskirche** (St Hedwig's Cathedral, open 10–5 daily), which was supposed to ape the vast dome of the Roman Pantheon. The story goes that Frederick the Great, asked how he wanted his new church to look, turned over a coffee cup and said: 'Like this.' Begun in 1747, the project quickly ran into technical difficulties, and the church only opened 36 years later with a much simplified design. In fact the troublesome dome was never completely finished until the late 19th century, and had to be rebuilt once again after the cathedral burned to the ground in an air raid in 1943. The clumsy proportions testify to its troubled architectural history. It was the first Roman Catholic church in Berlin and was to remain the only one until 1854. This was not so much a sign of Frederick's religious tolerance as an attempt to appease Catholic Silesia, which he had attempted to overrun twice. St Hedwig is Silesia's patron saint.

The last main building on the square, the **Royal Library** (Königliche Bibliothek) to the left, is modelled on the Hofburg in Vienna and was completed in 1780. Berliners poke fun at its shape and call it the Kommode, or chest of drawers. Lenin worked here briefly in 1895, as a plaque on the outside explains. Now it is part of the Humboldt University.

*The north end of Bebelplatz comes out on Unter den Linden again. The building which replaced the Kommode as the city's main library, the **Staatsbibliothek**, is two minutes' walk to the left, just beyond Universitätsstrasse. Opened in 1910, it has 6.5 million books and manuscripts but sorely lacks material from the Western world written after the war, for obvious reasons. In the courtyard is a 1960s sculpture of a worker indulging in intellectual relaxation with a poem by Bertolt Brecht. Walking back east on Unter den Linden, the next building is the Humboldt University itself. In the centre of the street, is the giant **Statue of Frederick the Great**.*

This equestrian statue is a glorious expression of 19th-century pomposity, fully matching the outsize ego of the man who laid the foundations for imperial Prussia a century earlier through aggressive military campaigns and ambitious cultivation of the arts. It took sculptor Daniel Christian Rauch 15 years to finish and includes pedestal reliefs depicting scenes from Frederick's life, and figures of his eminent contemporaries. It says much about Frederick's often-cited fondness for the artists he patronized that they appear on the rear of the pedestal. Voltaire, the French Enlightenment writer who fell out with Frederick in a monumental slanging match (see pp. 188–9), is conspicuous by his absence. The playwright Gotthold Ephraim Lessing and the philosopher Immanuel Kant, on the other hand, do appear but all historical evidence suggests that Frederick could not abide either of them. Hitler hero-worshipped *der alte Fritz* (old Fritz), but in 1950 the Communists denounced Frederick as an exponent of feudalism and banished the statue to Potsdam. Thirty years later, curiously, Frederick was back in fashion in East Berlin as 'a progressive force in the development of the German spirit' and the statue returned. It's a shame he wasn't given a wash at the same time.

Unlike Frederick, the **Humboldt University** can lay claim to a fine tradition of liberal thinking, with a long list of eminent alumni including the Brothers Grimm, Marx, Engels and Einstein. The Communists paid tribute to Marx by embossing a quotation of his in the marble of the front staircase: 'The philosophers have only interpreted the world in different

ways; the point, however, is to change it.' The site had been an artillery
store and then a minor palace until the writer and diplomat Wilhelm
von Humboldt founded the university in 1806 during the Napoleonic
occupation of Berlin. The pre-war criminal-law professor Eduard Kohl-
rausch used to teach his students about the inaccuracy of eye-witness
evidence by asking them in class how many bronze figures there were
atop the Humboldt building. None of them ever knew (there are 14).
Since unification, the university's 19,000 students have had a miserable
time with cuts and closures, not only in such departments as Marxism-
Leninism, but in medicine and engineering too. They have staged sit-ins
and demonstrations to protest at what they see as a deliberate attempt to
impoverish intellectual life in former East Germany in favour of the
West.

Continue east along Unter den Linden to the **Neue Wache** (new
watch), Schinkel's first major commission. Designed like a Roman
temple, the Neue Wache served as a guardhouse for the Kaiser's Palace
opposite. It was built in 1818 to celebrate victory over Napoleon, but has
reflected a rather more ambivalent attitude to wars since then. It became
Germany's monument to the unknown soldier after the First World
War, then Hitler's monument in praise of militarism, then the Communists' monument to the victims of Fascism. Now there is talk of turning it
into a monument to the victims of Stalinism. In every age soldiers have
performed a ritual changing of the guard every day at 11 am. Goose-
stepping continued here right up until 1990, despite the Communists'
allergy to all things Prussian.

Next door is the old Zeughaus, or arsenal, now housing the
German History Museum.

This was Berlin's first baroque palace, begun by the most unwarlike of
Prussian rulers, Elector Friedrich III (later King Friedrich I), in 1695.
The exterior took 11 years to complete, the interior another 24. Most
distinctive are the **sculptures of dying warriors** by Andreas Schlüter in
the back courtyard, 22 stone heads which display a compassion that is
rare indeed in Prussian military history. In the 19th century the building
became a weapons museum. After the Second World War it turned into
a display on German history from a Communist standpoint. Now it is
used for special exhibitions on historical themes.

Opposite the Zeughaus is the Palais Unter den Linden, a govern-
ment guest house. The bridge across the Spree, called Marx-Engels-

*Brücke but formerly Schlossbrücke and designed by Schinkel, marks the transition from Prussian to modern Berlin. The carpark to the right is **Marx-Engels-Platz**, once the site of the Kaiser's Palace.*

The Communists decided not to restore the palace after the war because of its imperialist connotations and blew it up instead. The site remained bare until 1973, when East German leader Erich Honecker decided to put in his bid for posterity with the best modern building money could buy. The result was a glowing orange glasshouse called the **Palace of the Republic** (Palast der Republik) with conference rooms, restaurants, bars, a bowling alley, picture gallery and chamber for his rubber-stamp parliament. It took three years to finish. But in his extravagant plans for posthumous fame, Honecker made one fatal mistake: he ordered the building to be insulated with asbestos. The building was declared a cancer risk shortly before unification in 1990 and it is now closed, its future uncertain.

*The hapless palace still serves one useful function, reflecting the **Berliner Dom** (cathedral) opposite in its reinforced glass on sunny days.*

Built in the style of the Italian High Renaissance, the cathedral is still being restored. It was designed in the last decade of the 19th century by Julius Raschdorff on the site of an old imperial chapel. Kaiser Wilhelm II, who opened it in 1905, was delighted with its intricate pomp. Inside, a heavy marble staircase gives an idea of how the whole church once was; most of it is still filled with piles of rubble. One sight not to be missed is the **collection of historical photographs** (Mon–Sat 10–5, Sun 12–5, adm). Here, better than anywhere, you can see the Berlin of the 1920s, including Potsdamer Platz and the old Kurfürstendamm. Striking pictures from the Nazi period include stormtroopers marching through the Brandenburg Gate in 1933 and one extraordinary shot of the Französischer Dom on fire in 1943. There is also a small but intriguing section on Nazi propaganda, including a children's game entitled 'Let's Invade England'.

The cobbled forecourt in front of the Dom is the **Lustgarten**, or pleasure garden. In the 16th century it was a patchwork of vegetable beds and fruit trees, but was paved over by Schinkel in the 1820s to fit in with his reworking of the city. Always popular for demonstrations, the Lustgarten was where Nazi propaganda chief Joseph Goebbels called for a boycott of Jewish businesses on 1 April 1933. Now the area is dotted with anti-Fascist memorial stones.

The building at the back is Schinkel's Old Museum (see Walk II).
Go back to the main road and turn left across the second arm of the
Spree onto Karl-Liebknecht-Strasse. Immediately on the left is
another orange horror, the luxury Palast Hotel. In front is an
attractive modern fountain of the Judgement of Paris, showing the
three goddesses, Hera, Athena and Aphrodite, and the Trojan prince
sitting back to back with their toes dipping in the water. Across the
road is the **Marx-Engels-Forum**, *a park crowned by a statue to*
the two founders of communism.

This is a very stiff interpretation, perhaps fitting in a Marxist state which
was itself seizing up when Ludwig Engelhardt sculpted the figures in
1986. Marx is sitting, Engels standing. Berliners call the pair *Sakko und*
Jacketti, a pun on their clothing alluding to an obscure couple of Italian
anarchists called Sacco and Vanzetti.

On the far side of the park, directly opposite the Palast Hotel, you
enter the pedestrianized Poststrasse, leading to a complex of reno-
vated medieval streets.

Few of the medieval-looking houses in this **Nikolaiviertel**, or St Nicholas quarter, are genuine, and the feel is twee rather than picturesque.
Since unification the Nikolaiviertel has turned into the South Molton
Street of Berlin—full of expensive boutiques fancying themselves as
pacemakers of fashion. The period public houses bear such quaint
modern names as Mother Hops and Beneath the Nut Tree. Many of the
monuments were imported from totally different parts of the city.

The most genuine building is the **Nikolaikirche** itself, Berlin's oldest
parish church with roots in the 13th century. This was where the
separate city councils of medieval Berlin and its sister town Coelln
decided to join up in 1307, and where the city's first elected council was
sworn in in 1809. The refreshingly simple interior and twin spires
survived an overhaul in 1878, as well as renovation in the 1980s. The
giant Berlin seal outside the main door was put in place to mark the city's
750th anniversary in 1987.

Down Propststrasse at the riverbank is a good view of the old
imperial riding stables, or **Alter Marstall**, *now used for art*
exhibitions (entrance off Marx-Engels-Platz). There is also a fine
bronze sculpture of St George and the Dragon (1849) by August
Kiss. Turn left and the building on the corner is the **Ephraim-**
palais, *Frederick the Great's present to his court jeweller and*

*chief money minter Nathan Veitel Heine Ephraim. This elegant classical building was dismantled by the Nazis, who had no time for a Jew, not even a dead one, and preferred to use the space to widen the Mühlendamm bridge. The façade was preserved intact and incorporated into a 1980s renovation. On the top floor is a small exhibition on Berlin's origins (9–5 daily, adm), and one storey below is a changing display on Berlin themes. Straight ahead across the main road is the **Altes Stadthaus** (Old Townhouse), an austere building crowned with a grey tower dating from 1911. The East German council of ministers had its offices here; now it is the Berlin branch of the German Chancellor's office. Stay on the Nikolaiviertel side of the road, turning left up Spandauer Strasse back to Marx-Engels-Forum.*

To the right is the **Rotes Rathaus**, or red city hall. 'Red' refers purely to the colour of Hermann Friedrich Waesemann's 1859 building, but it suits the political temperament of the city. Berlin was a left-wing stronghold long before the Communists took power in East Germany, and to a large extent still is. This brick building was the seat of Berlin's ruling council until the administration split in two in 1948. Inside it is a rabbit warren of rather faceless offices. Outside the main entrance are sculptures of a man and woman with digging tools. These 1950s bronze figures are a memorial to the *Trümmermenschen* who cleared away the rubble at the end of the Second World War.

Behind them is the **Neptunbrunnen** (1891), or fountain of Neptune, a late work by Reinhold Begas and one of the most sensual sculptures in town. Crabs, lobsters and other sea creatures scuttle around the god and four naked women representing the four major rivers of Germany: the Rhine (grapes and fishing net), the Elbe (fruit and corn), the Oder (goats and pelts) and the Weichsel (firewood).

Up towards Karl-Liebknecht-Strasse is another historical church, the **Marienkirche**. First mentioned in 1292, the modern building is based on a late 18th-century design by Langhans. But inside is evidence of earlier times, including an organ which Bach played in 1747 and a baroque marble pulpit by the early 18th-century sculptor Andreas Schlüter. The Marienkirche was rebuilt within two years of the end of the Second World War, and remains one of the few old churches in the eastern half of the city.

The last building in this ensemble is also the strangest: the 365-m high **television tower**, known locally as the 'Tele-Spargel'

(TV-asparagus). This is Berlin's most visible landmark, a useful point of orientation from virtually anywhere in the city. Its best attribute is the view from the top (8 am–11 pm daily with slight seasonal differences, adm). The information centre has an interesting scale model of East Berlin.

*Walk under the S-Bahn bridge behind the television tower to come out on **Alexanderplatz**.*

When Alfred Döblin set out to write the definitive novel about the city at the end of the 1920s, he called it *Berlin Alexanderplatz*. The square itself he defined as a 'seething human jumble ... the quivering heart of the city'. Alexanderplatz has since changed dramatically into a showcase of futuristic Communist-era architecture spread over wide-open spaces created by wartime bombing. It's hard to guess this was a cattle and wool market in the 18th century. The square gets its name from Tsar Alexander I of Russia who saw it as a military exercise ground when he visited Berlin in 1805. Later in the 19th century it was the scene of regular housing riots. By Döblin's time it was a teeming traffic junction and a regular meeting point for left-wing activists because the Communist Party headquarters were just around the corner in Kleine Alexanderstrasse. On 4 November 1989 half a million people massed here in the single biggest protest against Communist rule in East Germany. Within five days the government had resigned and the Berlin Wall was open. Nowadays the square fills with junk sellers and foreign tourists. Its most eye-catching landmarks are the **Brunnen der Freundschaft unter Nationen** (Fountain of Friendship Among Nations) and the **Weltzeituhr** (World Time Clock), which tells you who around the globe is having breakfast as you head for dinner, or vice versa. Berliners use it as a convenient meeting point.

Walk II

The Museum Island and the Old Jewish Quarter

Ishtar Gate, Pergamon Museum

Old Museum—Pergamon Museum—New Synagogue—old Jewish cemetery—Weinberg Park—Zionskirche—Brecht's house—Berliner Ensemble

East Berlin is packed with contradictions: bursting with riches, yet desperately run-down; cradle of some the greatest German intellectuals, but also witness to some of the most mindless acts of barbarism in history. This walk explores many of these ambiguities and gives a feel of the psychological and physical jumble of modern East Berlin.

Here is the great treasure-trove of the Kaisers, Museum Island, which started life as a rather pompous showcase for a rising provincial kingdom but grew with the Prussian Empire into one of the most astonishing collections of ancient art ever assembled. Just a few minutes away are the bleak, war-wrecked houses of the Scheunenviertel—once home to thousands of poor Jewish immigrants and now a sobering monument to their persecution and slaughter by the Nazis. Here, too, are traces of Berlin's once-thriving cultural life including two of Germany's towering literary figures, Heine and Brecht. The legacy of their work, bound inextricably to the traumas of German history, continues to haunt the city.

Walking Time: This is a demanding walk, with much to sort out and savour from the plethora of sights and sensations. In the museums, visual delights bombard you from all sides; on the rest of the tour rewards come less easily and need a little excavation. Light relief is not a speciality of the Germans, even less of the Prussians, but the pretty Weinberg Park is strategically placed for a breather about two-thirds of the way through. Art aficionados may want to spend all day in the museums and leave the rest for a separate outing. Otherwise you could absorb just one museum—perhaps the Pergamon—and then take the 2-hour walk around the other sites. The museums, apart from sections of the Pergamon, are closed on Mondays and Tuesdays. Otherwise any day is fine.

Start: The Old Museum, between the Zeughaus and the Berliner Dom (see Walk I) on Unter den Linden. It is a 5-minute walk or a two-stop ride on the 57 bus from Alexanderplatz U- and S-Bahn station. The end

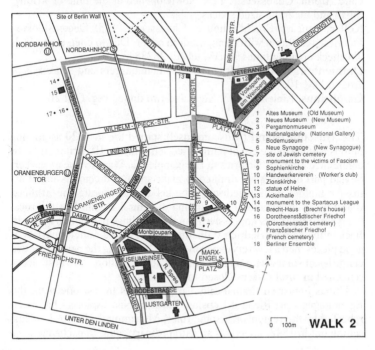

1 Altes Museum (Old Museum)
2 Neues Museum (New Museum)
3 Pergamonmuseum
4 Nationalgalerie (National Gallery)
5 Bodemuseum
6 Neue Synagoge (New Synagogue)
7 site of Jewish cemetery
8 monument to the victims of Fascism
9 Sophienkirche
10 Handwerkerverein (Worker's club)
11 Zionskirche
12 statue of Heine
13 Ackerhalle
14 monument to the Spartacus League
15 Brecht-Haus (Brecht's house)
16 Dorotheenstädtischer Friedhof (Dorotheenstadt cemetery)
17 Französischer Friedhof (French cemetery)
18 Berliner Ensemble

0 100m **WALK 2**

of the walk, Friedrichstrasse station, is a major U- and S-Bahn junction for all directions.

LUNCH/CAFÉS

Food, let alone good food, is hard to come by. There are signs of frantic opening of cafés and restaurants, but for the moment the best recommendation is a picnic. You could buy one in the covered market on Invalidenstrasse (corner of Brunnenstrasse) and then eat it up the road in the Weinberg Park. Treat the following more as a list of last resorts:

Sophieneck, Sophienstr. 38, closed Mon, Tues. Mainly coffee, cakes and ice cream, with a few pizzas and sausages. Pleasant garden in a renovated neo-classical street.

Café Esprit, Invalidenstr. 149, closed Sat, Sun. Coffee and snacks.

Newa, Invalidenstr. 115. The restaurant of this faded, somewhat shabby hotel offers meat, potatoes and cabbage for around DM 25.

Cafe Alpha, Chausseestr. 115. Newly opened at the time of writing. Small and medium-sized snacks.

Keller, beneath Brecht's house, Chausseestr. 125. Decent-looking Viennese restaurant with clean, modern décor. Due to open early 1991. To check opening times/prices, tel (E) 2823843.

Oranienburgertor, Friedrichstr. 115. Hamburgers and schnitzels at around DM 10.

Gambrinus, Linienstr. 133. Meat and two tinned veg. DM 20.

☆   ☆   ☆   ☆   ☆

The **Museum Island** (Museumsinsel) started life in 1820 as an ambitious twinkle in the eye of King Friedrich Wilhelm III. Brimming with confidence after his victories in the Napoleonic Wars five years earlier, he had part of the Spree drained to make space and commissioned his master builder Karl Friedrich Schinkel to incorporate the artificial island in his architectural remoulding of central Berlin. But the royal booty was rather less impressive than the buildings planned to house it. Back in the 1730s Friedrich Wilhelm I said: 'I would rather have lots of good pieces than a few very expensive ones,' so setting the pattern for two centuries of somewhat undiscriminating accumulation. The best pieces remained in royal palaces closed to the public.

Things improved dramatically, largely thanks to just one man, the Egyptologist Carl Richard Lepsius. Previous Nile explorers had been rebuffed by the region's fearsome ruler, Mohammed Ali. But Lepsius, setting out in 1842, pulled off an extraordinary coup. In exchange for a

70

few fine pieces of Prussian porcelain, Ali allowed him to take home all the ancient treasures he could find. Eight years later Lepsius returned home in triumph, giving Berlin the richest Egyptian collection in the world. After such a start, Prussian explorers and archaeologists did not put a foot wrong and brought ever more astonishing prizes not only from Egypt, but Asia Minor, Mesopotamia and the Far East too.

They found a fittingly grand home on Museum Island. Schinkel was responsible for the first of the buildings, the Altes Museum (1830), using the chance to fulfil his dream of constructing an idealized Greek temple. Schinkel's pupil Friedrich August Stüler took over work on the next two buildings, the Neues Museum (opened 1855), and the Nationalgalerie (completed by Heinrich Strack in 1876). By the turn of the century these three buildings were bursting, prompting the construction of the Kaiser-Friedrich Museum (since renamed after its founder Wilhelm von Bode) at the north end of the island. The last of the museums, the Pergamon, was begun in 1909 and completed 21 years later after the interruptions of war and ensuing economic chaos.

The Second World War dispersed the treasures far and wide. Many were stashed down disused mines for safe-keeping, others locked in a cement bunker under Bahnhof Zoo or simply hidden in museum basements. After the division of Berlin, the Western Allies kept what they found in their sectors (including the best of the Egyptian collection) and founded new museums to display them. Some works were looted or destroyed by bombs. But plenty returned to East Berlin. The reunited city authorities now plan to reorganize their museums bringing divided collections back together. At the time of writing it is too soon to tell what will go where.

Nowadays the Museum Island is a bit of a pickle. Rebuilding the bomb damage of 3 February 1945 is still in full swing, making access to the museums something of an obstacle course through cement mixers and scaffolding. The Neues Museum, the worst damaged, is not due to exhibit again until the year 2000. All the rest are functioning and open Wed–Sun 10–5 (adm), with most of the Pergamon open on Mondays and Tuesdays as well. Beware of the fact that sections or even whole floors may shut unpredictably for repairs or special exhibits. The museums are described in the order that a walker encounters them. Of the permanent collections, the Pergamon is the most stunning. The Nationalgalerie gives a flavour of early 20th-century Berlin art. The Bodemuseum, with its huge, diverse but not consistently impressive collection, is more for the specialist.

Schinkel's **Altes Museum** (Old Museum) is neo-classical extravagance on a grand scale: a majestic staircase climbs to an 87-m wide façade propped up by 18 Ionic pillars. The highly polished *granite bowl* (Granit-schale) outside, Schinkel's imitation of similar ancient Roman marble basins, filled contemporaries with awe because the 7-m wide ornament was hewn from a single piece of rock. Less impressionable modern Berliners call it the soup bowl. Inside, a magnificent cupola crowns a spacious entrance hall filled with neo-classical sculptures. The museum originally housed parts of the royal Egyptian collection and a picture gallery; now it just hosts temporary exhibitions.

Behind the Altes Museum and beyond Bodestrasse is a wedding cake of a building, replete with grand colonnades and heavy triumphal stairways, the **Nationalgalerie** (National Gallery). The grand proportions belie a modestly sized painting collection initiated to show off Prussia's mid-19th century artistic talents. The top-floor section is more a testimony to the military severity, and poor taste, of the Kaisers of the period, depicted in a series of stodgy portraits. 'A visit to the National Gallery of Berlin makes me gnash my teeth,' the American critic James Huneker wrote in 1917. 'The sight of so much misspent labor, of the acres of canvas deluged with dirty, bad paint, raises my bile.' But there are soufflés too among the steam puddings: graphic, vivid portrayals of life in factories and foundries by Menzel and Liebermann; and even a sprinkling of French Impressionists and Post-Impressionists, including a Cézanne landscape and a Degas study of two women lying gossiping on a mat. The lower floor gives a rapid overview of early 20th-century German art from the passionately dreamy fantasies of Otto Dix to the stark realism of Otto Nagel's picture of three working men on a bench in the Berlin district of Wedding.

Return to Bodestrasse, turning right towards the Zeughaus. Cross the river and walk right up Kupfergraben. The next bridge up leads directly to the **Pergamon Museum**.

Most museums might be content with a few memorabilia from an ancient archaeological site. Some explorers might think twice about removing treasures from their origin and carrying them thousands of miles away. But not even a whiff of such modesty is evident at the Pergamon Museum, which has reconstructed giant chunks of whole cities. Mythical names from the ancient world—Babylon, Assyria, Mesopotamia—spring to life here. Altars and gates span 20 or 30 m across awe-inspiring exhibition rooms.

In the very first room is the piece that gives the museum its name, the *Pergamon Altar*. A broad staircase sweeps up to a line of stone columns. Around the base, a frieze depicts the furious hand-to-hand battle that Zeus fought against the giants to gain control of Mount Olympus. The figures are incomplete but display a forceful sinewy passion. The altar to Athena, built around 180–160 BC, was built at the height of Pergamon's powers as a city state in the eastern Aegean (now part of Turkey). Its civilization, which once claimed equal status with Athens, was quite unknown until German archaeologist Carl Humann arrived in 1878— the first foreigner in the area for 300 years. Humann spent eight years excavating the altar (and another 20 reconstructing it). He also found a huge library of papyrus scrolls, which explained how the ruler of Pergamon, Eumenes II, built the altar after repelling a Galatean invasion (hence the battle imagery of the frieze). Bergama, the modern Turkish town now occupying the same site as Pergamon, has made repeated requests to have the altar back but has received little sympathetic response.

The other highlight of this section of the museum is the *Market Gate at Miletus*, a giant two-tiered edifice of Corinthian marble columns built by the Romans in Asia Minor in AD 120. The gate collapsed in an earthquake around 1100 but was rescued some 800 years later by Theodor Wiegand and Hubert Knackfuss, who managed to reconstruct it nearly whole.

The next section, the **Vorderasiatisches Museum** (Middle East department), digs further back to the last golden age of Babylon under Nebuchadnezzar II at the beginning of the 6th century BC. The huge crenellated *Ishtar Gate*, made of flaming blue glazed tiles and decorated with horses and mythical creatures, was built at the height of Nebuchadnezzar's career in 580 BC, six years after the Babylonian capture of Jerusalem. The gate leads to a corridor doubling as a Babylonian processional street, also adorned with decorated blue tiles.

The **Islamisches Museum** (Islamic department) contains another wonder, part of the wall of the **Palace of Mshatta**. This desert fortification, built by the Caliphs of the Umayyad dynasty in the 8th century in what is now Jordan, is 45 m long and shows intricate early Islamic patterned reliefs in its weathered rock. The Sultan of Turkey gave it to Germany in 1903. The section also has some remarkable carpets from Iran and Egypt, gaudily decorated walls from a 17th-century Aleppo merchant's house and some remarkable gold and lapis mosque decorations from the 13th century.

Cross back over the river to Kupfergraben, turn right under the S-Bahn bridge and take the next bridge, Monbijoubrücke, to the **Bodemuseum***.*

The Bodemuseum announces the scale of its collections in its grandiose design. Staircases sweep round the cavernous entrance hall, featuring a copy of Andreas Schlüter's statue of the Great Elector and topped by a neo-baroque cupola. Grand marble corridors with arched colonnades lead to the exhibition rooms. This is the storehouse of Berlin's museums, taking you on a diverse and colourful journey from ancient China through Byzantium to medieval Germany and Renaissance Italy. It displays paintings, woodcuts, sculptures, icons, mosaics, ceramics, coins and more—a veritable cornucopia of world civilization. Perhaps the highlight is a 6th-century mosaic fragment from Ravenna in the Early Christian and Byzantine collection (Frühchristlich-byzantinische Sammlung), depicting Christ with saints Cosma and Damian in sharp, clear colours on a deep blue background. Kaiser Friedrich Wilhelm IV bought it from a cash-strapped Pope Gregory XVI in 1844. The Egyptian section (Ägyptische Sammlung) is missing its best pieces, which went west to Charlottenburg after the war (see Walk VIII), but has an extensive collection of well-preserved death masks and stone figures. The Far East collection (Fernostsammlung) is a roller-coaster ride through Chinese, Japanese and Korean art from 3000 BC to the present. The sculpture collection (Skulpturensammlung) has a fine display of medieval German Madonna-and-child wooden sculptures. The picture gallery (Gemäldegalerie) is a rather uninspiring exhibition of 14th- to 18th-century European painting, enlivened by a Rubens of Christ giving Peter the keys to Heaven and a fine Vasari of Saints Paul and John blessing the poor.

Outside the Bodemuseum, turn right and cross the river over Monbijou bridge. The rather sorry-looking park to the right, wedged between the overhead S-Bahn line and the University Women's Clinic, once housed King Friedrich I's summer residence, Schloss Monbijou, which was destroyed by wartime bombs. Keep going until the junction with Oranienburger Strasse. One block to the left, near the corner with Tucholskystrasse, is the semi-renovated New Synagogue, once the heart of the Jewish district.

The contrast with the elegance of the restored museum buildings is immediately striking; it is like stepping out of one city into quite a different one. After the classical elegance of the Museum Island, the streets are now unkempt and full of vacant lots, the houses crumbling and forlorn. In one sense this is typical of East German cities. In Dresden, Leipzig and Erfurt, as in Berlin, the main streets are spruced up while the outlying areas still bear all the scars of the Second World War. But the tumbledown feel of this neighbourhood goes back further: this was the poor *Scheunenviertel*, literally barn quarter, where several waves of immigrant Jews settled from the 17th to the 20th century, struggling to establish themselves and become integrated in city life. The Berlin novelist Theodor Fontane lived here briefly in the mid-1830s and described the area in his memoirs: 'Despite being quite new, everything already looked half decayed, ugly and squalid—a description that went, with a few exceptions, for the inhabitants as well as the buildings. Nothing but failed, lost people lived here in cramped cheap accommodation...'

At the turn of the 20th century, the Scheunenviertel, stretching east from Oranienburger Strasse, was one of the most densely populated areas of Berlin. Crime was rampant, largely because of poverty and the profusion of different cultures and languages which discouraged any sense of community. Jews escaping the pogroms of Russia and Poland had little choice but to settle here, in much the same way as poor Turks settled in the crowded working-class neighbourhood of Kreuzberg in the 1960s. Like the present-day Turks, the Jews made up about 5 per cent of Berlin's population. Exploiting the personal insecurities amid economic and political chaos in the 1920s and 1930s, the Nazis pointed the finger at the seedy Scheunenviertel to spread propaganda about dirty, thieving Jews.

Berlin has had a love-hate relationship with its Jews for nearly as long as the city has existed. Documents refer to them as early as 1295, barely 60 years after the first mention of the twin settlements of Berlin and Coelln. In medieval times they enjoyed periods of relative tolerance and were permitted their own religious ceremonies and a cemetery. However, the community never took proper root; all manner of blame for epidemics, religious deviation and even ritual murder was laid at its door.

The first post-medieval wave of Jewish settlers arrived after an apparently generous offer by the Great Elector, Friedrich Wilhelm, in 1671 to allow 50 Jewish families to escape persecution in Vienna and settle in Berlin. The offer was strongly motivated by self-interest, however, giving the Elector the chance of a political strike against Prussia's great rival, Austria. The families were chosen for their wealth and influence;

they had to pay a special 'protection' tax in anticipation of social resentment; furthermore they were allowed to remain only for 20 years in the first instance. As it turned out they stayed for life, and soon Jews started arriving in Berlin from all directions.

Berlin's Jews began to thrive in the 18th century thanks to the friendship between community leader Moses Mendelssohn and Frederick the Great. By the mid-19th century they enjoyed equal legal rights with all Prussians, were active in business and the arts and lived all over the city. By the time of German unification in 1871, the Jews (known then as 'Israelites') were better assimilated here than anywhere in Europe.

The building of the New Synagogue (Neue Synagoge) was evidence of a flourishing Jewish community relatively free of anti-Semitic rumblings. Two of the city's best architects, Eduard Knoblauch and August Stüler (neither Jewish), conceived its grandiose onion domes and intricate decoration, drawing on Byzantine and Moorish influences including the Alhambra palace in Granada. When the Synagogue opened on 5 September 1866, the Kaiser himself, Wilhelm I, was present.

Such an auspicious start in life proved the building's salvation on 9 November 1938, the night of the Nazis' *Reichskristallnacht* pogrom. Hitler's stormtroopers whipped supporters into an anti-Semitic frenzy of looting and destruction, setting fire to most synagogues throughout Germany. But a lone policeman on duty that night decided that the New Synagogue was too precious to destroy. Invoking a law declaring it a protected historical building, he called the fire brigade to put out the flames and commandeered a troop of uniformed men to stand guard all night. Damage was limited and, remarkably, religious services resumed for two more years. But the synagogue's luck soon ran out. The Nazis requisitioned the building as an ammunition store for the army in 1940. Then in November 1943 allied bombs did what the stormtroopers could not quite manage, and left the synagogue a smouldering wreck.

The slide towards the Holocaust was a particular shock for Berlin, a left-wing stronghold that resisted the Nazis longer than anywhere. And the modern Jewish community has not forgiven the city for letting them down. '*Vergesst es nie*' (never forget) reads the plaque on the front of the building. In the new united Germany, the synagogue is active again. It is being restored and will serve as an archive and community centre as well as a place of worship when it reopens in 1995. Jews hope it will again play a pivotal role—this time to encourage the regrowth of their community. There are just a few hundred of them left in Berlin, most well past retiring age. Thousands of Soviet Jews want to come but at the time of writing it is not clear how many will be let in. Community leaders mutter that while the new Germany is happy to pay for the restoration of buildings and cemeteries, it does nothing to re-establish Jewish life. 'Germany will do anything to help a Jew as long as he is dead,' the saying goes.

The main East Berlin Jewish community has its centre at number 28. The bright red terracotta building on the corner of Tuchol-skystrasse, currently disused, was used at the turn of the 20th century as the stables for some 380 post office horses. Walk back eastwards along Oranienburger Strasse, take the left-hand fork after Mon-bijou Park and turn left into Grosse Hamburger Strasse.

This street bears some of the saddest reminders of Berlin's past. A few metres up to the right is a field marking the site of city's first **Jewish cemetery** (Alter Jüdischer Friedhof) which was destroyed by the Nazis in 1942. Established in 1672, just one year after the arrival of the Vienna immigrants, by 1827 the cemetery had filled and burials ceased. Jews believe that the final resting place of the body is sacred and, unlike Christians, preserve old graves indefinitely. The Nazis made a special point of abusing this tradition, not only smashing tombstones but also digging up the bones of the 12,000 people buried there.

To the left of the cemetery is the moving **monument to the victims of Fascism**. The simple figures, sculpted in the early 1950s by Will Lammert, are of concentration camp inmates in all their raw human defiance and vulnerability, with hollow faces and blankly staring eyes. This is the site of a Jewish old people's home transformed in 1942 into a collection point for prisoners destined for Theresienstadt and Ausch-witz. Some 55,000 Berlin Jews—one-third of the city's community and 10 per cent of Germany's Jewry—passed through here on the way to labour camps and gas chambers.

The elegant grey stone house on the right, number 27, used to be a Jewish boys' school. A plaque commemorates the school's founder, the 18th-century philosopher and Berlin Jewish leader Moses Men-delssohn, who was buried in the cemetery next door. The building is now a training college.

*Further still on the right, opposite the austere St Hedwig's Cath-olic hospital, is a passage leading to the **Sophienkirche** (1732), named after Queen Sophie Luise. It is one of the few architectural* *works from the reign of Friedrich Wilhelm I, the notoriously stingy 'soldier king', and the only surviving baroque church in Berlin. A thin, elegant white tower rises behind a wrought-iron gate. The interior is sparsely decorated and rather block-like, but the church is set in an attractive small park and cemetery looking onto the restored* **Sophienstrasse**.

The tenements lining this street bring to life all those 19th-century watercolour prints showing horse-drawn carriages idling past well-proportioned town houses in pastel shades. While demonstrating their restoration abilities, the East German Communists took a somewhat rose-tinted view of manual workers and dotted the street with twee jewellers' shops, goldsmiths and instrument makers—trades which barely existed here 100 years ago. As well as housing lower middle-class Jewish families, Sophienstrasse was a centre for the burgeoning labour movement. The red brick house at number 18—the **Handwerker-verein** (tradesman's community house) was abuzz with activists, pamphleteers and unionists in the latter half of the 19th century as they campaigned for radical improvements for the industrial working class. A Jewish boys' school existed briefly in the 1920s on the first floor of the backyard. A local museum (Heimatmuseum) at number 23 is due to open in 1991 and is building a collection of period maps, photographs and documents.

> *Go to the end of Sophienstrasse (with the church on the left) and take a right back onto Grosse Hamburger Strasse. This opens onto Koppenplatz, which has an untidy children's playground flanked by a grim school on the left and an equally grim-looking old people's home on the right. Just beyond the top of the square, turn right into Wilhelm-Pieck-Strasse. At the next junction, Rosenthaler Platz, are two turnings to the left. Take the smaller, steeper of the two, Weinbergsweg, to the* **Volkspark am Weinberg**. *This well-landscaped, tranquil park is one of the most attractive in East Berlin and a good picnic spot. Grapes once grew here, hence the name which means vineyard. A pavilion has a café (closed Mon and Tues) and, in the evenings, a disco. Continuing on Weinbergsweg, the second turning on the left leads to the* **Zionskirche**.

Despite the name, this has nothing to do with the Jewish community. It is a Protestant church commissioned to celebrate Wilhelm I's accession to the Prussian throne in 1861; a rather modest brick building completed in

1873 by architect Gustav Möller. The Zionskirche played a key role in the East German revolution, inspiring the first stirrings of dissent against Communist rule. Underground rock bands, many of them banned from conventional venues, used to play in the secluded churchyard. News of the concerts would be kept secret until the last moment, when it would spread by word of mouth around the area. This tradition came to a bizarre and brutal end in October 1987 when a group of skinheads swinging bicycle chains and improvised clubs burst in and beat up the audience. Skinheads were themselves such an unusual phenomenon in East Germany that many suspected the affair to have been staged by the Stasi security police.

The Stasi were back at the Zionskirche just a few weeks later when they raided the cellar beneath the pastor's house. This, at Griebenow-strasse 16 at the north end of the church, was a centre for environmentalists to collect data and print newssheets drawing attention to East Germany's officially hushed-up ecological disasters. Known as the **Umweltbibliothek** (environmental library), it had been considered untouchable because it was on church property. But the Stasi claimed the church had been involved in illegal political activity and briefly detained several people. Outraged locals responded with a week of candle-lit vigils and protest marches—the first open dissent in East Germany for years and an early prelude to the mass demonstrations of 1989.

Go down the hill on Veteranenstrasse, back past the Volkspark. Just before the junction with Brunnenstrasse is a **monument to Heinrich Heine**, *the 19th-century poet and Germany's most outspoken Jew.*

Scourge of Germany's stuffy establishment, iconoclast, polemicist and sparkling wit, Heine blazed a trail of controversy through his restless life. Born in a ghetto in Düsseldorf in 1797, he spent many of his formative years in Berlin before rushing to Paris in the wake of the (failed) 1830 liberal uprising there. Heine broke with the classical discipline of his literary forebears, Goethe and Schiller, and brought modern subjects, including politics, into his verse. The East German Communists revered him, and erected this rather philosophical bronze monument because of his revolutionary credentials and because his analysis of the artist's alienation in society reminded them of Marx's cultural writings. 'I have never placed great value on being a famous poet ... but one thing you should remember is that I was a good soldier in the war for the freedom of mankind,' he wrote in 1835.

In fact, Heine scarcely lived the life of a proto-socialist, depending financially for most of his life on the goodwill of his rich lawyer uncle. But his work is exhilarating and challenging, not least for its exploration of his German Jewish character. At times he was a wild idealist, dreaming of creating a new Jerusalem in Germany that would be a 'citadel of pure spirituality'. At other times he rejected the stiff conservatism of his homeland. *'Denk ich an Deutschland in der Nacht, dann bin ich um den Schlaf gebracht,'* he once wrote (If I think of Germany at night, I cannot get to sleep.) Above all, Heine's Jewishness made him an outsider, a role he occasionally resented but mostly relished until his death in Paris in 1856. The inscription on the 1968 statue by Waldemar Grzimek captures some of his passions and contradictions (but none of his biting wit): 'We don't grasp ideas, ideas grasp us and rule over us and whip us into the arena so that we are forced to fight for them like gladiators.'

*Cross Brunnenstrasse onto Invalidenstrasse, named after a home for invalided soldiers built by Frederick the Great in 1748 at the other end of the street from here. To the left is the **Ackerhalle**, the only covered market in Berlin to survive the war. You might want to take a tram (11, 18, 22 or 46) three stops to the junction with Chausseestrasse. Otherwise the same route is a 20-minute walk past a dilapidated cemetery on Bergstrasse to the right and the wasteland remains of the war-bombed railway station, the Nordbahnhof, on the same side. Turn left into Chausseestrasse. With its extension Friedrichstrasse, this is a fast-changing street where crumbling old buildings and vacant lots are interspersed with skyscrapers and some historical sites, notably traces of the life and work of Germany's greatest 20th-century playwright, Bertolt Brecht.*

Tucked behind a supermarket on the right-hand side is a monument to the Spartacus League, the radical SPD cell which later turned into the German Communist Party. This marks the spot where Spartacus leader Karl Liebknecht founded the breakaway anti-militarist group on 1 January 1916 to protest at the SPD's support of German involvement in the First World War. The building was destroyed in the Second World War and the monument was erected in 1977. It reads: 'Spartacus—that means fire in spirit, that means heart and soul, that means will and action for the proletarian revolution.'

Chausseestrasse 125, also on the right, is where Brecht lived and worked from 1953 until his death three years later. The

Brecht-Haus *exhibition has flexible opening hours; tel (E)*
2829916 for details.

An image of Brecht, with his short-cropped dark hair, heavy round glasses and ever-present cigar, looms large over this part of the city. This was where, as a new arrival in Berlin from Augsburg, he discovered theatre, music and politics in the early 1920s. It was where, after the Second World War, he made his home and founded the company still devoted predominantly to his work, the Berliner Ensemble. And despite recent attempts to tar him with the same brush as the East German Communist system he at first supported, Brecht's theatrical and poetic legacy still retains its bite.

Mixed with his social and political awareness was a hedonistic love of spectacle and song which marks all his best plays from his first success, the 1928 musical *The Threepenny Opera* (written with Kurt Weill) to mature classics like *Mother Courage and Her Children* (1941), *The Life of Galileo* (1946) and *The Caucasian Chalk Circle* (1955). Brecht broke with theatrical realism, using actors not only to portray characters but to discuss them on stage, distancing the audience emotionally from the action and involving them in paradoxical political and moral questions. He saw as his task the transformation of theatre into an effective pedagogical discipline. But he never lost his sense of entertainment and his plays are compelling parables, full of verve and irony.

Brecht and his actress wife Helene Weigel came to East Berlin from exile in the United States in 1948, moving into this modest three-room flat in Chausseestrasse in 1953. 'It is really a good idea to live in houses with furniture that is at least 120 years old; an early capitalist environment until we can have a socialist one,' Brecht enthused to his friend Peter Suhrkamp in characteristically earnest fashion about his new abode. Here are documents, pictures and furniture, including the narrow bed on which Brecht, an inveterate workaholic and chain smoker, died in 1956 at the age of 58. Towards the end, Brecht was torn between his fiercely independent artistic temperament and his allegiance to a communist state that quickly set a strict cultural agenda. Some right-wing critics have tried to hold this against him in the anti-communist backlash following the 1989 revolution. Like his character Galileo who recanted his theories under pressure, the critics argue, Brecht knew what was right but pretended otherwise for his own comfort. But Brecht is too subtle to dismiss that easily. 'Unhappy the land that needs heroes,' says Galileo. Brecht was no hero and never pretended otherwise.

Brecht and Weigel are buried next door in the **Dorotheenstadt Cemetery** (Dorotheenstädtischer Friedhof, open daily dawn to dusk). They are in distinguished company alongside architects Schadow and Schinkel, philosopher Hegel and author Heinrich Mann (ask the caretaker to show you who is where). Adjoining this is a smaller French cemetery, final resting place of Berlin's Huguenot community.

From here it's a 10-minute walk to Friedrichstrasse station. You can also take a tram (22, 46, 70, 71), a bus (57 or 59) or U-Bahn from Oranienburger Tor. This was the old theatre and cabaret district where Brecht first worked in the 1920s. A few of the old theatres, such as the Metropol and the Distel, still exist. Mostly though, skyscrapers and office blocks are springing up to fill the bomb sites.

Just off Friedrichstrasse, to the right on the north bank of the Spree, is the Theater am Schiffbauerdamm, home to Brecht's **Berliner Ensemble**. The theatre itself is a simple, squat building. But it is packed with memories of Helene Weigel's performances as Mother Courage or Shen Te in *The Good Person of Szechuan* and the raucous singing of *The Threepenny Opera*. The Berliner Ensemble went downhill after Weigel's death in 1971, turning in unadventurous, wooden performances mirroring the static cultural environment of late communist East Germany. But it is now back on form. The bookshop is worth plundering for its cheap production posters. Outside is a life-size statue of Brecht by Fritz Cremer, erected to mark the 90th anniversary of the playwright's birth in 1988. Around the seated Brecht are three columns with quotations from his poems.

Friedrichstrasse station has lost the spooky Cold War feel it had when its long corridors were filled with suspicious armed border guards. This was the only rail entry into East Berlin for foreigners and was as heavily watched as the Wall itself. Trains would slow to a snail's pace as they crossed the border, passing between high brick walls before drawing up at the station platform. West Berlin also paid a hard currency tribute to use Friedrichstrasse as a junction for its city rail network. Its lines were away from the other tracks, guarded with hawk-like vigilance. Now the guards, control points and even a platform duty-free shop are all gone—leaving just another normal, busy railway station.

Walk III

Prenzlauer Berg

Lenin Statue

Schönhauser Allee—Jewish cemetery and synagogue—Kollwitzplatz—
Husemannstrasse—Gethsemanekirche—monuments to communist heroes

No district gives a better feel of the energy and sparky wit of East Berlin
than Prenzlauer Berg. Built as a working-class residential neighbourhood in the 19th century, it has retained a Dickensian whiff of vibrancy
tinged with industrial-era misery. Its cobbled streets and rows of stuc-
coed tenements were once crammed with the families of industrial
labourers who lived, worked and died under the thumb of the city's
emerging tycoons and property speculators. The eminent theologian and
anti-Nazi activist Dietrich Bonhoeffer, who worked here in the early
1930s, called Prenzlauer Berg 'the most inspiring neighbourhood in
Berlin despite its considerable political and social problems'. During the
Communist era dissidents escaped the watchful eyes and ears of the
Stasi security police in the area's warren-like alleys and darkened backyards, where they would hold secret political meetings and avant-garde
cultural events.

Today Prenzlauer Berg is physically forlorn. Its houses, largely
neglected since the Second World War, are crumbling away; whole
streets have been abandoned. But it has lost none of its old spontaneity. It
has become a mini-Bohemia for artists, anti-establishment activists and
intellectuals attracted to the buzz of its blocks of flats, working men's

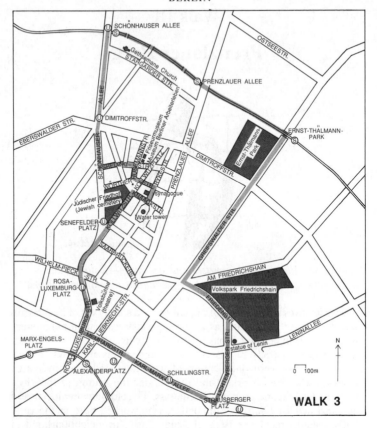

clubs, bars and street theatres. Always a district apart, Prenzlauer Berg has sought to resist the pervasive influence of the West following unification, creating a unique atmosphere of its own. Plays, concerts, political meetings and children's parties take place at a moment's notice in derelict courtyards or crowded squares. Heavy 1950s-style signs still hang outside shops and bars. Bicycles, trams and chugging Trabant cars compete for space with Volkswagens and Audis in the bustling streets.

This walk is intended to reveal the infectious atmosphere of Prenzlauer Berg. It covers few traditional tourist attractions such as museums or churches; its pleasures are less conventional but just as rewarding.

84

Walking Time: Allow 2–3 hours.

Start: The walk starts and finishes at Alexanderplatz (a major U- and S-Bahn junction). It is a good 8 km long and requires a fair amount of tram- and train-hopping. The most versatile way to get around is by bicycle (see Travel section for hiring details).

LUNCH/CAFÉS

The usual caveats about East Berlin apply, although at least the atmosphere, if not the food, is more appetising in this area. Improvised cafés in backyards are often excellent. The best picnic spot is Volkspark Friedrichshain (you could buy the ingredients at the top end of Schönhauser Allee). Otherwise try:

Altberliner Bierstuben, Saarbrücker Str. 17 (at Senefelderplatz). Busy bar-restaurant serving quite imaginative meat dishes and draught beer. DM 20–25.
Wiener Café, Schönhauser Allee 68. Popular Viennese bar.
Bistro 1900, Husemannstr. 1. The best restaurant in Prenzlauer Berg with a small menu but a stylish *art nouveau* interior. DM 20–35.
Krusta-Stube, Stargarder Str. 3. Small sit-down or take-away restaurant specializing in a house variety of pizza. DM 15–20.
Moskau, Karl-Marx-Allee 34. Smart, improving Russian restaurant popular with business people and indulgent midday diners. DM 35–40.

☆ ☆ ☆ ☆ ☆

From Alexanderplatz, cross Karl-Liebknecht-Strasse into Memhardstrasse, then take the first right into Rosa-Luxemburg-Strasse. Straight ahead is the austere concrete façade of the **Volksbühne**, *East Berlin's most important experimental theatre, built in 1913 and a lively venue for occasionally risqué anti-establishment pieces ever since. It is now badly in debt and may be forced to close. Veer left towards the traffic lights and cross straight over Wilhelm-Pieck-Strasse on to Schönhauser Allee. Five minutes' walk up the hill is Senefelderplatz (you can also take a U-Bahn direct from Alexanderplatz).*

This stretch of the road is unusual for Berlin: it is on a slope, albeit a very gentle one. The city is virtually flat apart from Prenzlauer Berg (literally, 'hill on the way to Prenzlau') and Kreuzberg in the West (see Walk V). The two districts have much in common: both were once backwaters outside the city walls, both became teeming residential areas for the industrial working class, both are home to Berlin's modern-day rebels.

Until the 18th century Prenzlauer Berg was a forest popular with the Prussian aristocracy as a hunting ground. As the city expanded under Frederick the Great, farmers cleared the terrain, taking advantage of the area's relative height and wind exposure to build windmills to grind the city's bread. By the 19th century there were 24 mills here, more than half Berlin's total. However, with the advent of the Industrial Revolution, pressure quickly grew to use the space for new housing. The mills kept burning down because their masters, worried about the future, turned to drink and forgot to unclog their machinery regularly, causing sparks to fly from the grating metal wheels.

Among the first people to populate Prenzlauer Berg were the Jews. By 1821 their cemetery in Grosse Hamburger Strasse (see Walk II) was full and they had to find a new site. They eventually settled for a vacant lot at Schönhauser Allee 23–25, just north of Senefelderplatz, and built brand new houses nearby. The **cemetery** (Jüdischer Friedhof, open Mon–Thurs 9–4 and until dark on Fridays, free) became the most fashionable Jewish burial ground in Berlin, in contrast to the more modest, much larger one in Weissensee (see Additional Sights). Admission to one of the plots in this tranquil park of closely planted birches near the city centre was a matter of some pride for the surviving family. Among the names inscribed on the grey marble tombs are those of operatic composer Giacomo Meyerbeer (1791–1864), Bismarck's banker Gerson von Bleichröder (1822–93) and the artist Max Liebermann (1847–1935). The cemetery was forced to close in 1942, partly because space was running out, partly because of Nazi intimidation. Several stones were damaged or ripped out by anti-Semitic vandals and remained unrepaired during the Communist era. The Bonn government has now promised money for renovations. A memorial to the Holocaust, an engraved stone at the cemetery entrance, reads: 'You stand here silent, but when you turn away do not remain silent.'

The statue in the grassy central reserve of Senefelderplatz is of Alois Senefelder (1771–1834), the Berlin-born inventor of lithography, the technique of printing from engraved stone. On the south side of the square is a large tenement brightly decorated with flags and anarchist slogans. This was the first squat in East Berlin after the fall of Communism. The residents are friendly and will readily hand out leaflets, chat and offer coffee. (For the politics of Berlin squatting, see below.) First you should explore the dense tenements which characterize the area. Turn right into Kollwitzstrasse. The third street on the right is Knaackstrasse, leading to a famous **water tower**.

The early inhabitants of Prenzlauer Berg had to collect their water from wells in the centre of the city. Open sewers ran through the streets down the hill to the Spree. In 1843, after several outbreaks of cholera, a Prussian government commission recommended the building of a water system. The water tower, held up by endless bureaucratic dithering, was finally built 13 years later at Prenzlauer Berg's highest point. The original structure, built by an English company with wide experience of water and sewage systems, was the thin tower at the south end of the square. Within 20 years, however, the population had grown so fast that another tower was needed—the broad polygonal building now dominating the square. With so many users, the high-pressure cast-iron pipes frequently burst, squirting out water in impromptu fountains. The Nazis used the tower as a secret concentration camp, murdering 28 local Social Democrats and Communists in its cellars in 1933. There is now a memorial plaque on the side of the building. The water tower fell into disuse after 1952 and is now an eccentric apartment block whose flats have enviable views over the city.

Turn left into Rykestrasse. On the left at no. 53 is the only functioning synagogue left in East Berlin.

Brownshirts were never welcome in this staunchly left-wing part of town, which may explain why the **Rykestrasse synagogue** (services every Saturday) survived the Nazis' *Reichskristallnacht* pogrom of 1938 virtually intact. Since the war it has been the religious centre of East Berlin's Jewish community. Its few score members cannot begin to fill the plainly decorated 500-seat interior. The red-brick building, of classically simple design, was completed in 1904. It was the place of worship for Berlin's liberal Jews until the rise of the Nazis, who confiscated it in 1940 and used it as a munitions store. In the forecourt was a **religious school**, founded in 1926, where boys learned Hebrew, studied the Talmud and picked up Jewish songs. When Hitler came to power in 1933, the Jewish community decided its young people would be less conspicuous in regular German schools and closed down its own. After the schools ejected all Jews in November 1938, about 100 pupils returned to Rykestrasse until it was finally forced to stop functioning in 1942.

Continue down Rykestrasse and take the first left, Wörther Strasse, into Kollwitzplatz.

By now the streets have got narrower, the grey and brown stone houses more tumbledown. Each courtyard is a cluster of flats that barely let in the sunlight over the high roofs. This is the legacy of the 19th-century building boom which determined the flavour of the whole area and, at one stage, made it the most populous city district in the world.

The man who hit upon the idea of high-rise council housing in Berlin was not some industrial-era capitalist; he was none other than Frederick the Great. The philosopher-king believed that his housing law of 1748, giving the go-ahead for new building to accommodate his growing population, would provide plentiful and affordable property for all. He was wrong. His ruling gave property speculators free rein to charge what rent they pleased, no matter how cramped the living conditions. Berlin's first blocks of flats, three- to four-storey buildings around Leipziger Strasse, were despised and earned the nickname *Mietskasernen*, or rental barracks. The visiting Emperor of China commented wrily: 'Europe must be a very small continent if people have so little room on the ground that they have to live in the air.' A more bitter comment came nearly two centuries later when Werner Hegemann reviewed the city's architectural development in his monumental 1930 study *Das steinerne Berlin* (Berlin in stone). He wrote: 'Frederick the so-called Great was too busy composing French poems with his friend Voltaire to realize he had, with haughty indifference, determined the well-being and suffering of hundreds of millions of people.'

Building in Prenzlauer Berg began in earnest in the 1830s. Hundreds of people were crammed into each of the six-storey buildings typical of this area, often with little more than two small rooms for 8 or 10 people, including tenants who slept lined up on the kitchen floor. The back buildings, or *Hinterhöfe*, received almost no daylight. Poorer families lived in dark, damp cellars, or else became *Trockenwohner*—literally, 'drying residents'—wandering tenants who would stay in newly-built flats for as long as the plaster was still wet. The most desperate were forced to sleep in the courtyards. Disease and alcoholism in these damp, overcrowded *Mietskasernen* were rife. Discontent always bubbled near the surface.

Despite a number of official reports and surveys throughout the 19th century, nothing improved. The city encouraged new building to create yet more space, especially in the economic boom of the 1870s. The property speculators obliged, raking in even higher profits and forcing families into ever smaller quarters. Perhaps nothing shows up the parsimonious intransigence of the authorities better than a police report of 1887, prompted by complaints that Prenzlauer Berg had an average of one toilet for every 10 households. No politician could ask for a better primer on how to justify the indefensible:

> Most men are away from the house at their workplace from 5.00–5.30 am to 6.30–7.00 pm. Since stools are mostly passed in the course of the day, they probably don't use the closet at home except in the rarest cases. Small children usually use a pot for doing their business, so that just leaves women and there is only one of them per flat on average. So only 10 or 11 people use each closet. Let us double that figure to 20 to be on the safe side. One sitting takes an average of 3–4 minutes, or five including time to adjust one's clothing even though this is not necessary for women [sic]. Even allowing 10 minutes per sitting, there should still be time in 12 daytime hours for 72 people to use the closet...

By the turn of the century Berlin was the most densely populated city in the world with 76 people per building compared to 51 in Vienna and 38 in Paris. In Prenzlauer Berg the average was a staggering 110 people per building. But the vitality of the district always got the better of the misery. Right from the beginning of the building boom there was a profusion of theatres, bars and shops. Some of the first cinemas in Germany were in Prenzlauer Berg. Many people without a bath at home could swim at one of the district's many sports clubs. To make up for the lack of gardens, families planted shrubs and flowers on their rooftops.

Kollwitzplatz is the centre of Prenzlauer Berg's cultural life, displaying the sense of community in East Berlin at its best. At its centre is a children's playground which holds regular political rallies, funfairs and puppet theatre shows. The bars around the edge are packed all afternoon and evening, spilling out on to the pavements even in cold weather. The square, formerly Wörtherplatz, was renamed after the socialist artist Käthe Kollwitz (1861–1945), whose works have unfortunately landed up on the other side of town (see Walk VII for details of her life and the museum dedicated to her). She lived for over 50 years at Weissenburger Strasse 25 (now Kollwitzstrasse 59, off the south end of the square). The house was destroyed during the war but there is still a copy of her 1935 sculpture *The Mother* at the grassed-over site. The somewhat pretentious tribute on the pedestal reads: 'Käthe Kollwitz created this work in the dark days before the Second World War. The mother wants to save her child, protect it. Where? What from? The darkness threatens fire and murder.' In the centre of Kollwitzplatz itself is another copy of one of her sculptures, a typically sad but unsentimental self-portrait from 1938.

The two cafés on the eastern side of the square are squats, favourite hangouts for the neighbourhood's radicals. The trendy of Prenzlauer Berg are categorized into three stereotypes: the *Hippi* (young; into communal living), the *Muesli* (older; a relic of the spirit of '68) and the *Inti* (more into talking animatedly about politics than actually doing anything).

Squatting has been a contentious issue in the city ever since a series of rent riots in the 19th century. In West Berlin a squeeze on housing in the late 1970s led to a rash of house occupations in Kreuzberg and several fierce clashes with police (see p. 120). In the East, housing under the Communists was cheap but not always plentiful. The authorities completely neglected the old war-damaged buildings near the centre of town, opting instead to build new high-rise blocks on the outskirts. By 1989 there were 25,000 derelict houses in East Berlin, 8000 in Prenzlauer Berg alone. Balconies had crashed to the ground; plaster was flaking off the façades. After the opening of the Wall and the accompanying relaxation of law enforcement, it was easy to move into abandoned houses without official resistance and squats grew up everywhere. The new government even encouraged the practice and promised renovation grants.

The squatters' honeymoon was short-lived, however. The West Berlin authorities, who took effective control of the city in the summer of 1990, a few months before formal unification, were far tougher. They banned the establishment of new squats and worked to regularize some 130 existing ones. To the more militant squatters, it looked as though the West Berlin government was putting on an unwarranted show of strength. Tension grew until November 1990, when the first evictions led to open street battles with police in Friedrichshain (next to Prenzlauer Berg). Squatters built barricades from burned-out cars, furniture and barbed wire, dug deep trenches in the streets and hurled rocks and petrol bombs. The police responded with water cannon, baton charges and volleys of tear gas.

The violence has opened a hornet's nest of post-unification tensions, with 'decent' citizens angrily standing up to radical rebels whom they see threatening the hard-won new freedoms. The squatters, aside from wanting somewhere to live, view themselves in the vanguard of 'resistance' to the Western takeover of East Germany. In Prenzlauer Berg, at least, they have some sympathy. To confuse unfamiliar Western police patrols they have daubed street signs in black or white paint, making them illegible.

At the north end of Kollwitzplatz is **Husemannstrasse**, *a graceful tree-lined street which the Communists chose to restore in period detail in time for Berlin's 750th anniversary celebrations in 1987.*

Next to the crumbling streets all around, it looks like a prize-winning pooch in a pack of unwashed mongrels. Its façades are scrubbed, intact and brightly painted in pastel shades. Its shops, looking more twee than authentic, include a poodle salon and even a horse-and-cart rental agency. The street also boasts two offbeat museums that reflect life in 19th- and early 20th-century Prenzlauer Berg. The **Friseurmuseum** (Hairdressing Museum, opening hours erratic, adm) at no. 8 displays some fashionable period hair-dos on old wooden mannequins and hulking cast-iron driers with perilous-looking wiring. At no. 12 is the **Museum Berliner Arbeiterleben um 1900** (Museum of Berlin working-class life around 1900, open Tues–Sat 11–6, Wed until 8, adm), which shows the interior of a typical working-class house. The main room where a whole family would sleep is crammed with furniture, books, toys, sewing things, pictures and ornaments. The kitchen, dominated by a coal-fired cooking stove, includes old mangles and scrubbing boards for clothes-washing. The stove is still a feature of many households in the neighbourhood, who keep warm by burning bagfuls of brown coal each winter. Not, one suspects, for much longer.

The top half of Husemannstrasse is as derelict as any of the surrounding streets. Turn left on Sredzkistrasse, which leads back to Schönhauser Allee. The large 1891 Jugendstil brick building on the corner was once Berlin's biggest brewery. Now it is a furniture shop and youth club with a disco at weekends. The stretch of Schönhauser Allee to the right, a cobbled avenue with stark iron U-Bahn girders running overhead, is the main shopping street in Prenzlauer Berg. Among the Western advertising placards, neon signs and brand-name café umbrellas are modest, shabby buildings with old, rusty shop signs. Opticians have heavy outsize spectacle frames hanging outside the front door. At Eberswalder Strasse 20 (left at Dimitroffstrasse U-Bahn station) is the only kosher butcher in eastern Germany, served by a specialist wholesaler who flies up from Budapest

once a week. Three more streets up Schönhauser Allee on the right is
Stargarder Strasse, leading to the **Gethsemane Church**.

Were it just for the architecture, nobody would give the Gethsemanekirche a second look. Built in 1893, it has an attractive tall spire but is an
otherwise unremarkable red-brick Protestant building. Nevertheless it
was at the centre of the 1989 East German revolution. Since 1978 the
Church had been granted immunity from state interference on condition
that it did not directly intervene in politics. Protestant pastors, only half
heeding the rules, brought more and more anti-establishment intellectuals under their wing. By the late 1980s their blatant political activism
led to a raid on the environmental library at the Zionskirche (see Walk
II). While thousands of East Germans left for the West through growing
gaps in the Iron Curtain in the summer of 1989, the democracy movement grew ever stronger. The biggest group, New Forum, was founded
in the Gethsemane Church in September and organized debates and
meetings there. Activists held candle-lit vigils and handed out crudely
printed leaflets on the state of the revolution. On 7 October, hundreds of
thousands of Berliners demonstrated in Prenzlauer Berg on the 40th
anniversary of the founding of East Germany. When the Stasi and police
moved in and began beating up protesters, the Gethsemane Church
opened its doors to offer protection.

Occasionally the church relives the spirit of 1989 with commemo-
rative services or speaker meetings. However it, like much of the revolutionary movement, has been almost forgotten in the transition to a
market economy in the new united Germany. But signs of Western
affluence have been slow to reach this part of town. Locals made
redundant or forced to retire early in the economic shake-up like to sit in
nearby bars, passing the time of day playing cards, cracking jokes and
downing their *Molle mit Korn*, beer with a schnaps chaser.

Return to Schönhauser Allee, where the U- and S-Bahn are just to
the right. Having seen how the Communists let the district's old
houses crumble, it's worth looking at the brand new blocks they built
instead. Take the S-Bahn two stops to **Ernst-Thälmann-Park**,
and walk south down Greifswalder Strasse. The park itself is on the
right.

It is scarcely believable that this estate was the pride and joy of the
Communist Party's city planners. Given the choice of a romantic crumbling 19th-century tenement off Schönhauser Allee or one of these

high-rise wonders within screaming distance of a four-lane trunk road, where would you prefer to live? About 4000 party functionaries and their families wound up willy-nilly with the latter. Imagine a victorious candidate for president or prime minister thanking party workers by letting them live in a concrete jungle next to a motorway. There are, however, a few compensations: parkland, shops, restaurants and not least the imposing **statue of Ernst Thälmann** himself, the first of many communist heroes exalted in this part of town.

The 13-m figure, made of black marble from the Ukraine, shows the labour leader and pre-war German Communist Party chief wearing a worker's shirt, his fist raised in defiance. The mood fits the subject. Born in 1886, Thälmann struggled to build up his party during the turbulent years of the Weimar Republic. As soon as the Nazis took power in 1933 he was imprisoned and spent a decade in concentration camps before being killed in Buchenwald in 1944. Unlike many comrades who compromised their ideals and survived (and later joined the corrupt East German élite), Thälmann fought to his death for what he believed. Languishing in prison in 1935, the year of the Nazi propaganda film 'Triumph of the Will', he said: 'I still believe in the triumph of the truth.'

The respect that Thälmann commands across much of the political spectrum might just ensure the survival of his monument in post-communist Germany. Already, however, a plaque with some of his dictums has been removed from the park.

The rest of this walk is intended to be a tour of monuments to communist heroes; you might want to check with the tourist office (tel (W) 2626031) that they are still there. Our next stop is several blocks further down Greifswalder Strasse, so hop onto tram 24, 28, or 58 on the corner of Dimitroffstrasse for two stops (ask for Volkspark Friedrichshain). Turn left into Friedenstrasse, walking with the park to your left (don't confuse it with Am Friedrichshain which is a sharper left turn and hugs the other side of the park).

The **Volkspark Friedrichshain** is a rambling, undulating expanse of trees and open fields ideal for walks or picnics. Its south side has been turned into an honorary cemetery (Friedhof der Märzgefallenen) commemorating those who died in the abortive Berlin revolutions of 1848 and 1918. The simple stone slabs were objects of great veneration by the old Communist leaders. At the entrance is a hulking bronze figure entitled the **Roter Matrose** (red sailor), a reference to a navy revolt in the dying days of the First World War that came within an inch of sparking a Soviet-style communist revolution in Germany. The plaque is not likely to please the masters of the new Germany. It reads: 'Establish the dominance of the working class. Act firmly against anyone who resists.'

The most disputed communist monument of all is a few minutes' walk down down Lichtenberger Strasse in Leninplatz.

The 19-m **statue of Lenin** is a dramatic full-length relief figure against a background of red granite blocks. The founder of the Soviet Union is smiling. East Germany hired a tried and tested professional to build this tribute to Lenin on the 100th anniversary of his birth: Nikolai Tomski was then president of the Soviet Academy of Arts, a position he reached largely on the strength of his previous Lenin memorials everywhere from Riga to Vladivostok. Unveiling the statue on 19 April 1970, East German leader Walter Ulbricht declared: 'The monument to Vladimir Ilyich Lenin on this square will testify to the triumph of Marxism-Leninism in the socialist state of the German nation.' Those words may yet condemn the statue to an early demise. Conservative German politicians, conducting something of a witch-hunt, have vented much of their fury about communist art on this one figure. Less polemical locals quite like it.

Continue on Lichtenberger Strasse to Strausberger Platz, a round-about on one of the most unlovely of East Berlin streets, Karl-Marx-Allee.

Only a sadist of a guide-writer would make you spend more than a few instants at this knot of dual carriageways and depressing oblong blocks. (Incidentally the Communist leaders of the early 1950s prided themselves on having constructed pinnacles of proletarian architecture here). This was where the famous uprising of June 1953 began, when workers protesting against increased production quotas took to the streets and confronted Soviet and East German tanks. In a notorious piece of dictatorial arrogance, the authorities later dropped leaflets along this boulevard saying the government had lost its confidence in the people and only redoubled efforts in the factories would win it back. (In 1953 the street was called Stalinallee, becoming Karl-Marx-Allee eight years later in a general purge of public references to Uncle Joe.)

In 1988 unrest broke out here again during an annual official parade marking the death of communist revolutionaries Rosa Luxemburg and Karl Liebknecht. About 40 demonstrators unfurled a banner with a quotation from Luxemburg that went down like a ton of bricks with the politburo bigwigs: 'Freedom is always the freedom to think differently.' The demonstrators were arrested and imprisoned at the start of a major crackdown on dissent.

Strausberger Platz underground station is just off the square. From here it's two stops to Alexanderplatz. Otherwise it's a high octane 15-minute walk—not recommended except during a U-Bahn strike.

Walk IV

Retracing the Berlin Wall

Wall art—Checkpoint Charlie Museum—Martin-Gropius-Bau—
Potsdamer Platz—Reichstag—Bernauer Strasse

The ghost of the Wall continues to haunt Berlin even though its concrete, barbed wire, watchtowers and sour-faced armed guards are long
gone. For 28 years, 2 months and 27 days it split the city. It tore apart a
people joined by blood, language, culture and much bitterly endured
common experience. It was always far more than a physical divide. Now
that it is gone, Berliners East and West still have to dismantle the walls in
their heads and hearts.

The scar that the Wall has left running through the old heart of the city
is still full of clues to the schizophrenic Cold War period and its
aftermath. The very sensation of walking or cycling through the 'death
strip', the once prohibited patrol zone running through no man's land
between East and West, is surreal; an uncanny marriage of past and
present. But the layers go yet deeper: beneath the death strip lie the
buried remains of Hitler's command centre—his Chancellery, the bunker where he committed suicide with Eva Braun, the headquarters of the
Gestapo. At the centre of this desolation are the Reichstag—the less
than honourable old German parliament—and Potsdamer Platz, once
Europe's busiest traffic junction and now a barren expanse of open
ground slowly being rebuilt for the new Berlin of the 1990s.

96

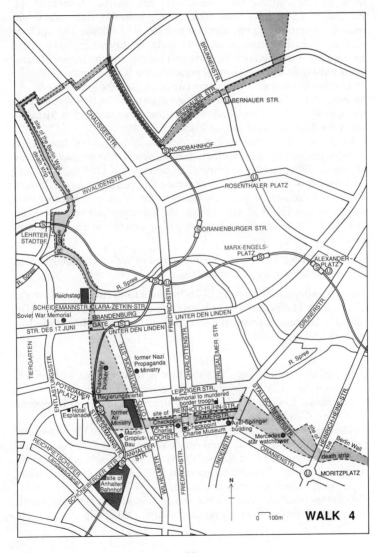

The centrepiece of this tour is the former *Regierungsviertel*, or government quarter, running from the Checkpoint Charlie Museum to the Reichstag, a half-hour walk which, with museum visits added on, provides a stimulating introduction to Cold War Berlin. The opening section, from Moritzplatz, and the coda, to Bernauer Strasse, are atmospheric evocations of life in the divided city and the scenes of some of the most poignant escape attempts across the Wall. Together they take up another hour or so. Don't come late in the day: the area is not lit and becomes even gloomier (and more hazardous underfoot) than usual with the approach of evening shadows. The only day to avoid is Monday, when the Martin-Gropius-Bau is shut.

Of all the walks in this book, this one is likely to go out of date fastest. Some sights may disappear; others may become harder to reach because of new building or road construction. So expect a little upheaval and bring sturdy waterproof boots to negotiate the mud and lumps of broken concrete. Commercial maps are hopeless for orientation because they merely denote the Wall with a thick line superimposed on a pre-Cold War grid. The map on p. 97 shows paths, streets and the death strip much more precisely.

Walking Time: Two hours. Real devotees of Wall memorabilia could keep on walking more or less indefinitely.

Start: Moritzplatz. This is on U-Bahn line 8 from Alexanderplatz; the 41 bus from Hallesches Tor to Kreuzberg also stops there. The end of the walk, Bernauer Strasse, is a short walk to the Nordbahnhof which is on S-Bahn lines 1 and 2.

LUNCH/CAFÉS
Slim pickings around here, but the tour is short enough to complete between meals. The nearby Tiergarten is ideal for picnics.
Schultheiss, Kochstr. 16. Very basic pizza and chicken grill opposite the Checkpoint Charlie Museum. DM 15–20.
Lekkebek, Friedrichstr. 212. A healthier alternative to the above, and just around the corner, with home-made sandwiches and biscuits, salads and freshly squeezed fruit juices. High stools are the only seats. DM 10.
Martin-Gropius-Bau, Stresemannstr. 110. Café with sandwiches and other snacks inside the museum building. DM 10.
Reichstag. Similarly snackish bar and restaurant with sausages, salads etc. Expect crowds of visiting schoolchildren. DM 20–25.

☆   ☆   ☆   ☆   ☆

*From Moritzplatz, head north along Heinrich-Heine-Strasse.
Almost immediately, on both left and right, is a wide band of mud,
grass and broken footpaths winding away between back-to-back
concrete tenements. This is the death strip, the area where border
guards used to shoot trespassers and would-be escapers on sight. Now
families come here to play frisbee and walk the dog. A path runs all
the way along. Turn left and follow it.*

Already city life is beginning to encroach on this once most isolated of
spots. Peeping behind the trees on the left (West) side is a shopping mall
and modest housing estate. A little further on there are even advertising
hoardings along the death strip. Up ahead (marked as Stallschreiberstrasse on maps but in fact just a path) appears to be a watchtower from
the old days, except that it is crowned with a blue neon three-pointed
Mercedes star. It is in fact a piece of art by Hans Haacke, a striking
commentary on the rush towards Western market capitalism that has
followed the demise of the Wall. Erected shortly after the borders
disappeared in July 1990, it is called: *Freedom is being sponsored out of petty
cash*. Its implication that West German big business has seized on the
revolutionary changes in the East to make a fast buck is not perhaps as
far-fetched as it might seem. After all, Volkswagen chairman Carl
Hahn's first reaction to the opening of the Wall was to dream of future
sales prospects in the East, describing the moment as 'an unimaginable
gift of fate'. Mercedes–Benz has not done so badly itself, as can be seen
later on this walk.

*Haacke's watchtower may be a cynical response to the recent changes
in Berlin, but, curiously, it displays the same hard anger that
characterized attitudes to the Wall from the moment it intruded on
the city's life in 1961. Walking westwards through this wilderness, it
is worth turning the clock back and asking just why the Wall was
built in the first place.*

This is how an official East German guidebook (translated into rather
stodgy English) explained it the year after the Wall went up:

[West Berlin] became the rallying point of West German
and other imperialist secret services and organizations of
agents who more and more utilized the open border to
democratic [i.e. East] Berlin to organize comprehensive
diversionist activity against democratic Berlin and the
GDR...

> In order to end the hostile activities of the revengeful and militaristic forces of West Germany and West Berlin, the cabinet council of the GDR in August 1961 decreed the creation of an anti-fascist protective wall and the introduction of a control on the borders of the GDR including the border with West Berlin such as is customary on the borders of every sovereign state.

Needless to say the 'West German and other imperialist secret services' saw things rather differently. Because of its special status, Berlin had stayed open as an East–West crossing point even after other borders between the two Germanys closed in 1952. Over the following nine years 1.5 million East Germans, many of them young and skilled, took advantage of the Berlin loophole and flooded westwards. Some were lured by West Germany's 'economic miracle', which had transformed the rubble of the Second World War into a gleaming new world. Others were disillusioned with the utopian promises of a socialist state already showing signs of high-level corruption and mismanagement. Unable to vote at the ballot box, they decided to vote with their feet.

The crisis heightened in June 1961 when a Krushchev–Kennedy superpower summit in Vienna, called to discuss the exodus, ended in shambles. About 30,000 East Germans were now streaming to the West each month; the lifeblood of the country was simply seeping away. Speculation about counter-measures was rife. East German Communist leader Walter Ulbricht pledged: 'Nobody intends to erect a wall.' But erecting a wall was exactly what Erich Honecker, Ulbricht's security chief and later his successor, was busy planning.

The East Berlin politburo came to the conclusion, with some nudging from Moscow, that blocking the border was the only way to ensure the survival of East Germany as an independent state. So when armed guards began sealing the Berlin border with barbed wire in the early hours of Saturday 13 August 1961, they were not merely establishing a frontier 'such as is customary on the borders of every sovereign state'. They were gambling the future of their country on penning in the people.

The people could scarcely believe it. In the first few hours some managed to jump over barbed-wire barricades or sprint through sewers and underground train tunnels. But it did not last long. Over the next few weeks, border guards drafted ordinary citizens to help build two 4-m high concrete walls separated by a patrol area, the death strip where potential escapers could be shot on sight. The barrier stretched 161 km around West Berlin, about two-thirds of it wall, and the rest—mostly on the outer border with East Germany—iron fencing. Along it were 252 watchtowers and 136 bunkers. At night the guards took Alsatian sniffer dogs on patrol beneath the glaring border lights. For the first two years ordinary citizens were not allowed to cross in either direction. Families, friends and lovers were prised apart.

The West's response was remarkably tame. This was an era of furious nuclear armament by the superpowers—the Cuban missile crisis was just around the corner—and the politicians perhaps felt too scared to take drastic action. Instead there was a flurry of symbolic gestures and a flood of rhetoric, culminating in President Kennedy's 1963 speech on the steps of West Berlin city hall in which he proclaimed: '*Ich bin ein Berliner*'. Axel Springer's press empire, a bastion of West German middle-class conservatism, decided to build its headquarters right up against the Wall as a glaringly visible statement of Western-style freedom. The glass and concrete skyscraper is still there on the corner of Kochstrasse and Lindenstrasse (about 5 minutes' walk west of Stallschreiberstrasse on the left-hand side). Until it was laid to waste by wartime bombs, this area was the hub of Berlin's newspaper district. On the side of the Springer building, huge plastic lettering spells the names of its titles: the sleazy best-selling tabloid *Bild*, the more serious national daily *Die Welt* and the local *Berliner Morgenpost*.

> *Opposite the Axel Springer building on the right-hand (East) side of the death strip rise the blue and white concrete tower blocks of Leipziger Strasse. The East Germans built these monstrosities, used to house diplomats and other foreign residents, in the 1950s and 1960s as evidence of their building abilities. They were high enough to be 'admired' from both sides of the Wall. A detour is not recommended. Continue along the death strip. At one end of a carpark, on the corner of Jerusalemer Strasse and Reinhold-Huhn-Strasse, are four unprepossessing concrete blocks piled on top of each other. Despite its banal appearance, this is one of Berlin's stranger monuments, the* **memorial to murdered border troops** *(Denkmal für ermordete Grenzsoldaten).*

The Berlin Wall claimed its first victims within weeks of being built. Some were shot trying to clamber across, but the majority were intercepted in underground tunnels. For the first few years there was a frenzy of digging beneath street level. Tunnel builders, many of them highly-paid professionals with intelligence contacts as well as engineering experience, would play a high-risk game of cat and mouse with border guards, hoping to ferry out as many East Germans as possible before being discovered. Things did not always go according to plan. On one occasion a digging team lost its way and, instead of surfacing in the West, emerged on a major road in East Berlin where a posse of border guards stood with guns at the ready. Escape became progressively more difficult as security grew ever tighter and more sophisticated. Deep-laid mines effectively deterred the tunnellers from the early 1970s, while searchlights, trip wires and scatter guns made the death strip virtually unassailable. Most escape attempts, and most deaths, occurred in the first five years. In all, 80 people are known to have been killed.

What the Western history books rarely mention is that 25 of them were border guards. The East Berlin authorities on the other hand made maximum political capital of this, hailing the guards as martyrs. The inscription on this memorial reads: 'Their death gives us an obligation.' But the exact circumstances in which many guards met their end were highly controversial. Were they killed in the line of duty, or had some attempted to escape themselves? The most famous case was that of the guard Reinhold Huhn, killed in a tunnel almost exactly at this spot in June 1962. The official East German news agency reported at the time that Huhn was shot by West Berlin 'agents'. The independent West Berlin daily *Tagesspiegel* said he was shot by a colleague who mistook him for an escaper. The truth has never been established.

One of the most poignant civilian deaths is remembered two blocks further west, on the corner of Zimmerstrasse (in the death strip) and Charlottenstrasse.

The wooden cross and wreath here are for Peter Fechter, an 18-year-old East Berliner shot in the lung as he clambered over the Wall in 1962. What made his case particularly cruel and absurd was that he fell wounded in full view of US military police on the Western side of the border. Technically, however, he was still a few feet inside East German territory and nobody came to his rescue. 'Sorry, but this is not our problem,' said one American military guard, who like his colleagues feared the possible international consequences of interfering. A crowd gathered and looked on in horror. Fechter writhed in agony for 50 minutes before dying of his wounds.

Seen with a long, cool historical eye, 80 deaths in 28 years seems a surprisingly low figure given the notoriety of the Berlin Wall. That number might easily be the death toll of a single train crash or bad fire. It is far lower than the annual total of Palestinians killed by Israeli soldiers in the occupied West Bank and Gaza Strip, far lower than the number of Soviet citizens killed by the army in ethnic unrest since the advent of *glasnost*. But Berlin was always more than just a city divided by barbed wire and concrete. Since the end of the Second World War it had been the crucible of East–West tensions, the fuse that could have set the whole world alight. Every death made that fuse a little shorter. If the Cold War ever turned hot, the chances were it would do so in Berlin.

> *One block further west is Friedrichstrasse, once the main crossing point for foreigners and the former site of* **Checkpoint Charlie**. *The death strip at this point has turned into an open-air gallery of Wall memorabilia, including the top of a watchtower, a slab of concrete and the four-language sign that once acted as a warning to anyone about to travel to the East at this point: 'You are leaving the American sector.' All that is left of the border crossing, once a 10-lane control point, is a concrete shell arching across the street. It is hard to imagine that this was the scene of the tensest East–West stand-off in the Cold War.*

Almost immediately after the Wall was built, a row broke out between the East Germans and the Western Allies over the right of occupying forces to move freely through all sectors of the city. US troops complained they were being held up at the border in contravention of the 1945 Berlin Agreement. The East Germans claimed the US presence in Berlin was illegal.

In October 1961 US tanks moved up to the Friedrichstrasse crossing point to reinforce its claims. The Western Allies also built a monitoring post, a prefabricated hut called Checkpoint Charlie that stood in the middle of the road. East German and Soviet tanks quickly moved in to confront the US forces. For three nerve-wracking weeks the world stood on the brink of war as the two sides glared at each other in a deadly game of chicken. In the end it was the East Bloc that backed down first. It never challenged Allied rights in Berlin again.

As for the prefabricated monitoring post, it stayed rather longer than intended. Checkpoint Charlie—so called according to the military alphabet; checkpoints Alpha and Bravo were on the outer Berlin border—entered the mythology of the city, became a favourite location for spy movies and turned into a mini-tourist attraction with Checkpoint Charlie bars selling Checkpoint Charlie cocktails and Checkpoint Charlie pens. Finally on 22 June 1990, during a foreign ministers' meeting to discuss the military and security status of a united Germany, the hut was hoisted away by a giant crane. As British Foreign Secretary Douglas Hurd said at the official ceremony, Charlie had finally come in from the cold.

You should not miss the **Checkpoint Charlie Museum** *(Museumhaus am Checkpoint Charlie) at Friedrichstrasse 44 (open 9 am–10 pm daily, adm), a compelling archive of the history of the Berlin Wall set up and run by a group of civil rights activists.*

Through photographs, text in three languages, paintings, sculptures, newspaper cuttings, videos and other media, it gives a vivid impression of living in a divided city. Its theme is the triumph of non-violent struggle, and one floor of the museum is devoted to material on Gandhi, the US civil rights movement and the rise of Solidarity in Poland. But the museum's greatest attraction is its chronicle of ingenious escapes across the Berlin Wall and exhibition of the contraptions sometimes used. 'Escape is the mother of invention,' reads one slogan. That could be the motto of the whole museum. Here is the balloon in which one East German family flew to the West, and the dummy motorcycle fuel tank where a West German hid his girlfriend. The museum shows how to adapt a pair of suitcases to fit a small adult inside and explains in detail how to hide under the back seat of a car without making the vehicle sag visibly.

Some escapes relied on little more than human cunning. In 1967 a young East German marched boldly up to the Friedrichstrasse crossing, passing several controls until he was stopped. He told a guard he was an Austrian going to see his dying mother in the West. Asked for his passport, he said he had already given it in for checks. The guard called two colleagues to look after him and went looking for the missing passport.

'What's your problem then?' one of the pair asked.

The young man promptly changed his story. 'I am an Austrian and I've just heard my mother is dying in East Berlin. The problem is I've not got my passport on me.'

'Oh no, they'll never let you in,' the guard replied. 'Why don't you just pop back over to the West to fetch it?'

Between Checkpoint Charlie and Potsdamer Platz to the west there is finally a chance to see a real piece of **Wall**.

The city authorities have slapped a preservation order on this stretch of concrete, and not before time. It is pockmarked and crumbling, the result of tireless handiwork by visitors who bashed away at the Wall with hammers in the first few weeks after its opening. In their enthusiasm they destroyed the one good thing the Wall ever had—the wild paintings and graffiti sprayed on its Western side. Over the years artists of varying talent had turned a formidable barrier into a bright carnival of popular art, an ever-changing tapestry of colour, wit and political comment. 'The first person to come through here wins one mark,' one slogan near here used to say. Or another (in English): 'Fuck politics. Fuck religion. Love rules the world. I know, I'm from Ireland.' Sadly the only remnants of that creative energy are a few chipped smudges of paint.

Keep walking westwards. Just after crossing Wilhelmstrasse, an ugly, hulking grey building looms to the right: this was Hermann Göring's **Air Ministry** *which survived more or less unscathed to serve as the East German Communist régime's cabinet offices, the Haus der Ministerien. Now it is the headquarters of the Treuhandanstalt, the state trustee agency responsible for privatizing East German industry. Turn away and head left down Wilhelmstrasse and then swing right at the traffic light onto Anhalter Strasse. At the end are the ruins of the elegant 19th-century* **Anhalter Bahnhof***.*

Just a small section of the façade remains at what was once the third-largest railway station in Europe. This was Berlin's gateway to the south and under Kaiser Wilhelm II became a popular place to welcome foreign dignitaries such as Italian King Umberto I and Tsar Nicholas II. Hitler used the station to stage his triumphal returns to Berlin after the 1938 *Anschluss* of Austria and the German conquest of France two years later. These memories dissuaded the post-war authorities from repairing the limited wartime bomb damage. With the onset of the Cold War the station became useless anyway because the lines hit a dead end as soon as they encountered East German territory. So in 1961, despite widespread public protest, the whole edifice was blown up leaving just one memorial piece.

At the traffic light at the end of Anhalter Strasse, turn right onto Stresemannstrasse. About 200 m on the right is the entrance to the **Martin-Gropius-Bau***.*

The name Gropius may be familiar from Bauhaus founder Walter Gropius (see Walk VI). Martin was his uncle and designed this building in 1877 as the original Berlin handicrafts museum (now in the Kultur-forum, see p. 134). Its magnificent vaulted glass cupola and gilded exhibition rooms are an exhilarating surprise after the rectangular simplicity of the exterior. Its space and airiness make it a popular choice for major exhibitions. But the Martin-Gropius-Bau also houses an outstanding permanent collection of Berlin painting on the first floor, the **Berlinische Galerie** (Tues–Sun 10–6, adm).

This is the best place to chart the history of painting in the city starting from the late 19th century, when artists including Max Liebermann, Lovis Corinth and Lesser Ury experimented with their own brand of Impressionism in a group called the *Berliner Sezession*. They brought to the canvas a new realism which did not shy away from murky or unpleasant subjects and they introduced new techniques of mood and colour similar to those of the French Impressionists. The emblematic picture of this period is Ury's *Leipziger Strasse* of 1898, depicting Berlin's brand new street lights shimmering on the rainswept tarmac. In the first 20 years of the 20th century, the *Sezession* painters were joined by members of the highly influential *Brücke* school from Dresden including Emil Nolde and Ernst Ludwig Kirchner, who experimented with sharper, more abstract lines, and the *Blauer Reiter* movement from Munich, which included Vassily Kandinsky and Paul Klee. Together they formed the basis of German Expressionism, which continued to flourish in Berlin until the rise of the Nazis in 1933. Its combination of gaudy colours, grotesque portraiture and political satire was the perfect artistic commentary on the upheavals of the 1920s. The most original work here is by George Grosz, best known as a cartoonist, and Otto Dix, whose lanky, off-balance portraits reflect the skewed frenzy of the times.

The museum also has an extensive collection of post-war art, beginning with Johannes Niemeyer's crayon drawings of bomb-damaged Potsdam. Wolf Vostell analyzes the new generation's reaction to the Nazi period in a bleak series of montages and collages of the concentration camps. The exhibition comes bang up to date with the first art to emerge since the opening of the Wall. Rolf Händler's *Aufbruch* (Awakening, 1990) depicts apprehensive faces emerging from the new border crossings, suggesting anxiety and upheaval at the momentous changes.

Behind the Martin-Gropius-Bau is a series of building foundations laid bare in the ground and surrounded by bumpy hillocks. This is all that remains of the headquarters of the SS, the Nazis' black-uniformed militia, and their secret police, the Gestapo.

The hillocks are grassed-over piles of rubble from the once grandiose neo-classical buildings. Just a block from Hitler's Chancellery, this was the nucleus of the Nazis' police state. Suspected enemies of the Reich, whether Communists, Social Democrats, freemasons, Jews, gypsies or homosexuals, were registered here in endless secret files, and regularly brought in for interrogation and torture. This was where mail was intercepted, telephones were tapped and reluctant informers black-mailed and threatened. A prefabricated exhibition centre entitled the **Topographie des Terrors** (10–6 daily, free) shows a rather bland series of photographs charting the history of the buildings and some of the horrors perpetrated there. Most atmospheric are the former Gestapo cellars beneath, which form part of the exhibition. But the overall effect is oddly perfunctory, as though Nazi repression was too disturbing a topic to approach with the necessary passion.

*Excavation is a word usually associated with ancient Greek, Roman or Egyptian sites but in Berlin, where time seems to have moved at a terrifying pace in the last century, it refers to painfully recent history. The biggest archaeological site of all is at **Potsdamer Platz**, which you can reach by returning to Stresemannstrasse and following it westwards to a lonely traffic junction in the centre of the death strip.*

At the turn of the 20th century Potsdamer Platz was the very symbol of Berlin's modernity. It was packed with ritzy hotels, cafés and department stores. It boasted Europe's very first electric street lights and had a staggering 600 trams passing through every hour. Mark Twain, who visited in 1891, declared Berlin 'the newest city I have ever come across. Even Chicago seems old and gray by comparison.' In 1920 a surge in automobile traffic brought the world's first traffic light, a rather unwieldy contraption that sat in the middle of the square, but remarkably similar in concept to the modern version with red, amber and green lights.

The war changed everything. Only one building survived the obliter-ation of Allied bombs—the Hotel Esplanade, whose sorry façade you can still see on the south side of the square. Government buildings such as the Gestapo headquarters and Hitler's Chancellery, just to the north, were prime targets. With the building of the Wall, Potsdamer Platz grew yet sadder, a seemingly eternal wasteland trapped in the no man's land between East and West.

When the Wall reopened it at last had the chance to return to normality. The road between the Tiergarten in the West and Leipziger Strasse in the East was reconnected almost immediately and the square

107

became a popular venue for circuses and open-air concerts, including an extravagant multi-million dollar production of Pink Floyd's *The Wall*.

But any chance of returning Potsdamer Platz to its former glory seems to have been dashed. In 1990 Germany's biggest company, Daimler–Benz, snatched up half the site, for a fraction of the market price, to build its new customer services division. Many Berliners were outraged. They felt that big business had muscled in before any serious debate on the future shape of the city could take place. The politicians were unmoved, seeing Daimler's interest as a vital investment for the future.

The remains of the Regierungsviertel, *or government quarter, are scattered in the long, wide stretch of death strip up to the Branden-burg Gate.*

The bump on the right-hand side is the only visible remnant of the **Chancellery bunker** where Hitler spent the last months of the Second World War as the Soviet and US armies closed in on Berlin. On 30 April 1945 he and Eva Braun, the female companion he had married just one day before, committed suicide. The bodies were carried into a courtyard and incinerated, then wrapped in a sheet and stamped into a shell crater. The Chancellery itself was ripped apart brick by brick by the Red Army. The bunker was sealed after the war to prevent it becoming a neo-Nazi shrine.

Further to the right, on the other side of Otto-Grotewohl-Strasse, is the sprawling **former Nazi Propaganda Ministry** *which is still intact. Astonishingly, the building was used at the end of 1990 as a reception centre for Soviet Jewish immigrants hoping to find asylum in the new united Germany. From the Brandenburg Gate (see Walk I), turn left onto Strasse des 17. Juni. A hundred metres on the right is West Berlin's* **Soviet War Memorial** *(Sowjetisches Ehrenmal).*

Unlike the Soviet War Memorial in East Berlin (see Walk V), this is a rather pompous affair. A Soviet tank (a real one) sits atop a fussy marble pedestal (made with material excavated at Hitler's Chancellery). During the Cold War this monument was, however, something of a curiosity. It was an anomalous island of Soviet-controlled territory within the British sector of West Berlin established in the Berlin Agreement of 1945. Steely, sour-faced Soviet troops stood guard at the monument, and British soldiers in turn stood guard over them. Unification has brought this perverse charade to an end and the monument is now in the care of the civilian government.

Turn the corner behind the memorial onto Entlastungsstrasse, then take another right almost immediately to approach the **Reichstag**.

The Reichstag, the former German parliament, is an ignominious building that has rarely lived up to the dedication on its façade—*Dem Deutschen Volke*: To the German People. Built in grand neo-classical style and opened for business in 1894, it has rarely had much to do with democracy and had little success when it did. For the first 20 years of its existence it housed a parliament so beholden to the Prussian aristocracy running Germany that it was little more than a rubber-stamp assembly. Resentment over the First World War gave a stronger voice to the Social Democrats, the largest elected body in the Reichstag, who proclaimed and finally achieved a democratic republic following the abdication of Kaiser Wilhelm II in 1918. However, the republic, constituted not here but in Weimar, proved bitterly disappointing as one weak government followed another in alarmingly rapid succession. The last meeting of the Reichstag before the Nazis came to power in 1933 degenerated into a punch-up in which a chandelier and several windows were destroyed after Nazis interrupted a backroom meeting of Communist deputies. Any claim the Reichstag might have had to being a bastion of democracy ended on the night of 27 February 1933 when a mysterious fire raged through the building. The Nazis, by then in power for a month, blamed a dimwitted Dutch left-winger called Martinus van der Lubbe and hanged him. The chances are, however, that they started it themselves. Hitler used the occasion to ban the Communists from national elections the following week and shortly afterwards declared dictatorial powers.

Gutted by wartime bombs, the Reichstag has now taken on a humbler role. The German parliament, the Bundestag, meets there occasionally but its main function since being restored in 1972 has been as a conference centre. It also houses an exhibition called **Fragen an die deutsche Geschichte** (Questions on German History, Tues–Sun 10–5, free), a government-sponsored display of photographs, text and video. Unfortunately it is as inadequate a treatment of German history as the Reichstag's track record as a successful democratic forum. The photographs, films and text do not have the courage to address any historical questions properly. Explanations of such events as the 1848 revolution, the Nazi annexation of Czechoslovakia and the extermination of the Jews are couched in disturbingly comfortable terms. Hitler is vaguely alluded to as an excessively aggressive man, but few of his misdeeds are properly catalogued. Despite being a compulsory stop for German children on school trips to Berlin, this is a pop-up view of their country's history that teaches little and seems shockingly matter-of-fact.

*The Wall sliced right between the Reichstag and the Brandenburg Gate. Now tat merchants blithely hawk their wares here. For an altogether more desolate stretch of no man's land, hop onto S-Bahn line 2 at Unter den Linden, just behind the Brandenburg Gate. Three stops north at Nordbahnhof, follow the signs out to **Bernauer Strasse**.*

The death strip arches up a long hill, a bleak stretch lined with wooden crosses and wreaths in memory of many of the Wall's victims who died here. Bernauer Strasse suffered perhaps the cruellest division of all since the Wall ran down the middle of the street. Residents on the East side suddenly saw armed men laying barbed wire outside their house and bricking up their downstairs windows. As period film footage has disturbingly portrayed, several of them, including pensioners, tried jumping into the West from the tops of their houses. West Berlin firemen rushed to the scene with nets whenever they heard of an escape attempt. Some 20 people died, either falling to their deaths or shot by border guards.

Perhaps fittingly it was at Bernauer Strasse that the first East Germans were allowed through the Wall on 9 November 1989—although as it turns out the whole event could have been a bureaucratic bungle. The East German Communist leadership was in turmoil. The government had resigned and re-formed two days earlier, a mass exodus to the West via Hungary showed no signs of letting up and pro-democracy demonstrations were growing ever stronger. In a panic the politburo drew up new rules allowing limited travel to the West and hastily passed them on to the party's Central Committee for approval. Somewhere along the line it became unclear if those allowed to leave would be let back into the country. When party spokesman Günter Schabowski read out the regulations at a news conference on the evening of 9 November, he did not know himself. He did not even realize that the rules only came into force the next day. He told the public they applied immediately, a mistake that made history. Border guards were caught unawares as thousands of people thronged to frontier posts around East Berlin. At first they tried to tell everyone to return home, but that quickly turned out to be futile. Finally, at 9.15 pm, at a crossing point on the junction of Bernauer Strasse and Brunnenstrasse (four blocks east of the Nordbahnhof), the first East Germans were let through. It is still hotly contested whether the guards acted alone or if an emergency order came from above. At the time nobody dared admit that anything had gone wrong. Now, with the Berlin Wall firmly in the past, all kinds of people are eager to claim credit and secure a place in the history books.

Walk V

Kreuzberg

Punk Statue

Airlift Memorial—Viktoria Park—Berlin Museum—Oranienstrasse—
Turkish market—Oberbaumbrücke—Soviet War Memorial

'Berlin is a fine city,' wrote Mikhail Bakunin, the Russian revolutionary, on a visit in 1841, 'excellent music, cheap living, very passable theatre, plenty of newspapers in the cafés. In a word, splendid, quite splendid—if only the Germans weren't so frightfully bourgeois...' Had Bakunin come to Kreuzberg 150 or so years later, he would have found the music, the theatre, the cheap living, yes even the newspapers in the cafés—but this time in one of the most resolutely anti-bourgeois city districts in Europe. Kreuzberg is West Berlin's rebellious heart, a bubbling mixture of punks, artists, left-wing intellectuals, Turkish immigrants and drop-outs. The area has spawned every radical movement in West Germany from 1960s anti-Vietnam protesters to the Baader–Meinhof terrorist gang to the Greens. The very mention of Kreuzberg fills every order-loving middle-class German with fear and loathing. But to the visitor the area offers a colourful mixture of street art and street life: free-wheeling Berlin at its most exuberant. Beneath an intimidating surface, Kreuzberg is a friendly if restless place, wanting nothing more than to be left alone to its alternative lifestyle.

This walk starts at the tamer, western end of Kreuzberg with the hill that gives the district its name. It traces many past upheavals (the

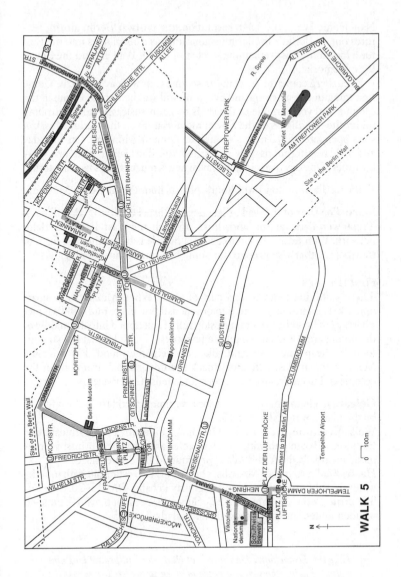

WALK 5

0   100m

113

Napoleonic Wars, the 1848 revolution, the postwar Berlin airlift), features one of Berlin's livelier museums and, as a coda, slips into the East for a look at the last remaining stretch of Berlin Wall art and the Soviet War Memorial.

Kreuzberg comes to life at night, so time your walk accordingly. Come first thing in the morning and everyone will still be in bed. Come in the evening and you can idle in the cafés of Oranienstrasse before strolling under the floodlights of the Soviet memorial. Even the Berlin Museum stays open late (till 10 pm), although it is shut on Mondays. On Tuesday and Friday afternoons you can catch the Turkish market on Maybachufer. One day to avoid is 1 May, when Kreuzberg has its annual riot.

Walking Time: Allow three hours, plus an hour for the Berlin Museum.

Start: The start of the walk, Platz der Luftbrücke, is on U-Bahn line 6. Treptower Park, at the end, links up with the East Berlin S-Bahn network. With nearly 10 km to cover, a bicycle is by far the best form of transport. Otherwise prepare for some bus- and train-hopping.

LUNCH/CAFÉS
There's nothing fancy in this part of town. When Maxwell's, a smart upmarket restaurant, moved into Oranienstrasse in the mid-1980s it met a barrage of hostility (including a skip full of shit tipped into the middle of the dining area) and closed after a few weeks. Don't let that put you off: food is cheap and tasty and, like the neighbourhood, has a strong Mediterranean bias. The ideal snack is a doner kebab from one of the countless Turkish take-away shops and stalls. Otherwise try:

Golgatha, Viktoriapark. Perfect for a summer breakfast in the open air by the park's waterfall. DM 15.
Weissbierstube, in the Berlin Museum, Lindenstr. 14. An atmospheric traditional Berlin pub with wooden tables and historical prints. Home-made meatballs, beer and salad for around DM 20 per head.
Hasir, Adalbertstr. 12. No-frills, cheap Turkish restaurant with mouth-watering aubergine starters and yoghurty kebabs. DM 15–20.
Taverna Pella, Zeughofstr. 22. Simple Greek pub with candle-lit wooden tables and great souvlaki and salads. DM 15.

☆   ☆   ☆   ☆   ☆

Take the Tempelhofer Damm exit at Platz der Luftbrücke U-Bahn station. Facing you across a patch of green to the left is a sprawling

Nazi-era building, the headquarters of the Berlin police. Just in front is the **Monument to the Berlin Airlift**.

Not the most beautiful of monuments, this curved slab of reinforced concrete nevertheless recalls one of postwar Berlin's hairiest moments—Stalin's attempt to starve out the western half of the city at the beginning of the Cold War. On 23 June 1948, with tensions near fever-pitch between Moscow and the Western Allies and the division of Germany looking increasingly inevitable, the Soviet command announced that road and rail links to and from West Berlin were 'temporarily closed to traffic on account of repairs'. An innocent-sounding order perhaps, but it signalled the start of an 11-month blockade intended to eradicate the West's last outpost behind the Iron Curtain. The commander of the US Allied Forces in Berlin, General Lucius Clay, quickly realized Moscow's intentions and set up what was to become the biggest airlift in history. US and British planes brought 1.8 million tonnes of food, fuel and medical supplies on nearly 300,000 flights to Tempelhof airport, which stretches away to the south of here. At the height of the airlift, planes were landing every 90 seconds, day and night, with a turnaround time of just six minutes. Five years earlier, during the wartime air raids, the din of US and British military planes filled West Berliners with terror. Now they fondly dubbed them *Rosinenbomber*, or raisin bombers.

The three prongs of the monument, erected in 1951, symbolize the three Western Allies—the United States, Britain and France—and the three air corridors through the Soviet occupation zone where their planes were allowed to fly. The overall effect, however, is unfortunately fork-like. The Berliners call it the *Hungerharke*, or hunger rake. A memorial slab lists the 70 British and US airmen who died in accidents during the airlift. 'They gave their lives for the freedom of Berlin,' it reads.

> *Like most open spaces in Berlin,* **Tempelhof Airport** *was once a military drilling ground, established by King Friedrich Wilhelm I in the 1730s. After the Wright brothers used it to demonstrate their pioneer planes in 1908, it developed into Berlin's main airport despite being so close to the centre of town. The Americans took it over as their airforce base in 1945 and have kept it open for just a few civilian (mostly charter) flights. Moving on, cross Tempelhofer Damm onto Dudenstrasse and take the first right, Methfesselstrasse, to the top of the* **Kreuzberg hill**.

Kreuzberg literally means 'mountain of the cross', a grand name for an irreligious bump standing no more than 66 m above sea level. But it is the highest point in flat Berlin and offers a panoramic view of the modern city as well as an insight into the origins of the district. At first known as Tempelhofer Berg, the hill was a famous wine-growing spot at the centre of a tranquil farming area until the 17th century. But with the growth of Prussia as a military power it gained strategic importance. The Great Elector Friedrich Wilhelm, never one to agonize over human considerations, burned down every house and vineyard here in 1641 to clear a firing line to the advancing Swedes in the Thirty Years' War. So began Kreuzberg's resentment of the power of the state which has continued more or less unbroken to the present day.

Now the hill is dominated by Karl Friedrich Schinkel's **National Monument** (Nationaldenkmal) to the Wars of Liberation against Napoleon. There is a crusader flavour to this neo-Gothic cast-iron ornament, its religious overtones more to do with dispatching Frenchmen to the next world than making one's peace with God. Taking the form of a cathedral spire topped by a cross, it celebrates Prussia's victories from Leipzig in 1813 to Belle Alliance (better known as Waterloo) in 1815 in a series of plaques beneath life-size figures of war heroes.

The real pleasure of this site is the **Viktoriapark**, a series of terraces and gardens leading down from the monument with Hermann Mächtig's 1894 gushing artificial waterfall as their centrepiece. Ahead is the long, straight Grossbeerenstrasse leading up to the ruins of the Anhalter Bahnhof. To the right, among the tenements of modern Kreuzberg, is the prominent outline of the 19th-century Apostelkirche on Urbanstrasse. 'There lies the city, heavy, grey and white,' was how Ernst Blass, a late 19th-century poet, described the view. Behind the Schinkel monument is the bright brick **Schultheiss Brewery**, home to the city's biggest beer-maker for 100 years. Ever conscious of tradition, the brewery used horse-drawn carts to carry out its kegs right up to 1981.

Mehringplatz is a 10-minute walk down the hill (go to the end of Methfesselstrasse and walk four blocks down Mehringdamm) or else a two-stop U-Bahn ride from Platz der Luftbrücke to Hallesches Tor.

The battle of Waterloo was not just won on the playing fields of Eton, but on the drilling grounds of Prussia too: **Mehringplatz** was one of the more famous and was even called Belle-Alliance Platz for most of the 19th century. But Kreuzbergers took their military duties, like every other State imposition, with a certain reluctance. Conscripts would dress up as women to fool the guards at the fortified Hallesches Tor gate (now gone and remembered only as the name of the U-Bahn station) and seek refuge with families outside the city walls. Mehringplatz is now a rather soulless circular housing development with just a gaudy 19th-century statue of winged Victory in the centre (by Daniel Christian Rauch) as a reminder of the glorious past. At the north end is an altogether more striking aluminium statue of two disembodied legs, both with left feet, called *Where do we come from where are we going* by Rainer Kriester (1975).

> *We are now entering the 'boring' part of Kreuzberg, a series of long straight roads first built by Kaiser Friedrich Wilhelm I to house civil servants in the 18th century and described by Goethe as a 'monstrous piece of clockwork'. The area proved less than boring during the 1848 revolution when the local people built barricades around Mehringplatz and Lindenstrasse and held out against the army for three days—longer than anywhere else. The centre of bureaucratic activity was the Kammergericht (appeal court) at Lindenstrasse 14, now the Berlin Museum. At the top of Mehringplatz, turn right onto Franz-Klühs-Strasse and then left onto Lindenstrasse. Otherwise take the 41 bus from the south end of the square (beneath the overhead U-Bahn line), which will drop you three stops later outside the front door.*

The **Berlin Museum** (Tues–Sun 10–10, adm) is a mishmash of pictures, furniture, maps, models, clothes and toys which bring the city's history vividly to life. The exhibition makes a virtue of simplicity—for example, explaining the opening of the Wall by contrasting two newspaper front pages. West Berlin's *Tagesspiegel* has a huge picture of the revelry and the headline: 'The night of open borders'. The East German Communist Party daily *Neues Deutschland* buries a dry account of the new travel rules beneath details of a forthcoming party congress.

The first delight of the museum is the building itself: a restored yellow classical façade by Philipp Gerlach (1735). Above the portal is the Prussian coat of arms supported by allegorical bronze figures of Justice and Truth. (In fact neither of these virtues was much in evidence during the appeal court's first hundred years or so since the King took all important judicial decisions himself.)

Don't expect too much order in the museum—the first thing to greet you is a painted slab of the Berlin Wall, followed by the small Jewish collection displaying mainly religious art, followed by some 18th-century landscapes of the Berlin area. But there are some real gems. Susette Henry's witty 1790 painting of a *Berliner Familie* is a hilarious portrait of Prussian pomp and complacency. The stern father is wearing a flashy blue frock coat which fails to hide his bulging belly; the mother, plump and prematurely aged, is trying desperately to entertain her seven children with a faded old print. Behind them is a ludicrous marble *Venus pudica* perched on a tile oven.

A series of drawing rooms charts the evolution of middle-class Berlin's often questionable taste in furniture, from the plain, heavy Biedermeier style of the post-1815 restoration to the lighter, playful curves of 1920s *Jugendstil*. There is a mock-up of a working-class kitchen, and paintings of the seamier side of 1920s Berlin by Zille, Kirchner and Baluschek.

The museum also gives an insight into Hitler's giddy architectural plans for Berlin, showing a scale model of his intended 300-m high white-domed congress centre, the *Grosse Halle*. Set next to copies of the city's most famous landmarks on the same scale, the Grosse Halle looks like it could eat a hundred Brandenburg Gates for breakfast. Otto Risch's photographs of views of the city before and immediately after the Second World War show Hitler's true architectural legacy.

Kreuzberg, like much in Berlin, is split into two parts. So far this tour has explored staid 'Kreuzberg 61'; now it's time to discover the wilder 'Kreuzberg 36' (the numbers refer to the post code). Get back on the 41 bus outside the museum and take it four stops east to Oranienplatz.

While '61' attracted civil servants and other middle-class families in the 19th century, '36' was filling with the same cramped *Mietskasernen*, or rental barracks, which were springing up in Prenzlauer Berg (see Walk III). If anything the authorities made more mistakes in Kreuzberg, provoking a series of housing riots. In 1872, for example, the fire brigade simply tore down a series of wooden huts near Kottbusser Tor to make room for middle-class homes. In 1893 the *Vossische Zeitung* reported that many of Kreuzberg's cellar flats (about 10 per cent of the total) were so small that the average person could not stand upright in them. Prisoners in Plötzensee jail had more living space than the average Kreuzberger. The cartoonist and satirist Heinrich Zille commented: 'You can fell a man with an apartment like you can with an axe.'

Perhaps the most disastrous episode in relations between workers and the state occurred around Oranienplatz. The strip of grass running roughly north to south through the square was once the **Luisenstadt Canal**. In 1848 the city authorities, terrified of discontent among unemployed workers after the March revolution that year, decided to join the Spree and the Landwehr canal through a special scheme for the jobless. They hired more than 5000 people to dig the canal trench, but decided to use a steam-powered pump to drain the ground water. The workers, who had not been told about the pump and feared they were about to be fired, smashed and burned the machine and took to the streets to protest. Thirteen of them were killed in ensuing fighting with the *Bürgerwehr* (armed citizens' militia), and the rest were sacked. The 2-km canal took another four years to complete. Partly because of anxieties about the unrest, boats shunned the new canal and it gradually silted up. In 1926 it was refilled, ironically in another work scheme for the unemployed.

> *Oranienstrasse is the main street in Kreuzberg, packed with bars, kebab stalls, dingy clubs and shops, many on the upper floors and back courtyards of converted 19th-century factories. It is also covered in graffiti and wild wall paintings. Within minutes of getting off the bus you will be bombarded with Turkish power slogans, women power slogans, freedom for El Salvador slogans. Welcome to Kreuzberg.*

Is this really Germany? Whatever happened to that orderly, slightly smug and above all *clean* country? And why is there a wafting smell of garlic and rosemary in this north European metropolis?

Salman Rushdie once speculated what might happen to London's cool reserve and petty snobberies if the city acquired Bombay's climate overnight. Well, maybe the result would be a bit like Kreuzberg. What unites the district's residents is a desire to melt away the stifling conformity of middle-class Germany, to be able to visit shops that don't open and close exactly within the hours prescribed by law, to lie on grass regardless of 'keep off' signs, to be able to live in multi-cultural communes rather than isolated three-room family flats. Above all, many Kreuzbergers want to be able to forget that they are in Germany, forget the legacy of discipline, order and bourgeois complacency that has lingered even though the excesses of Prussian militarism and Nazism are long gone.

Despite Kreuzberg's attempt to escape from history, there's no doubt the district was very much fashioned by it. The Cold War turned West Berlin into a haven for non-conformist young people as the German government offered cheap living, extended nightlife and exemption from military service to keep the city alive. When the Wall went up in 1961, Kreuzberg became a perfect vacuum for them to fill. With concrete and barbed wire on two sides, many factories and businesses in the area moved out or closed down altogether. In flooded the first waves of Turkish immigrants, who could not afford to live anywhere else and had to put up with dilapidated housing. In, too, flooded black-clad students, anarchists, underground musicians, artists and left-wing activists who made the district their own with all-night bars and clubs, the first wholefood and vegetarian shops, backstreet cult cinemas, theatre work-shops, gay and lesbian centres and women's support groups.

The colourful home-made shop signs and shabby window displays make Oranienstrasse a provocative counterweight to the bright neon and flashing lights of the Ku'damm. Follow the road down to Adalbertstrasse, then take a right down towards **Kottbusser Tor***, the Piccadilly Circus or Times Square of Kreuzberg.*

Known locally as the 'Kotti', this square has long been a crucible for the district's passions as well as the junction for its main U-Bahn and road links. Its graffiti-strewn concrete building developments, street stalls and all-night Turkish bars around the iron girders of the railway have again and again been the scene of evictions, housing rallies, anti-estab-lishment demonstrations and riots. The worst of the violence came in the late 1970s and early 1980s, when landlords systematically emptied houses and kept them vacant in the hope that a tighter market would push up property values. Housing was scarce in any case and outraged young people began occupying the buildings and daubing them with defiant slogans. *'Legal, illegal, scheissegal'* was their battle cry ('Legit or illegit, who gives a shit'). In December 1980 an attempt to clear one of the houses led to pitched battles between riot police and the squatters, who set up barricades around the Kotti. However, the Social Democrat city government, sensing a degree of public sympathy for the protests, stopped short of ordering a general eviction. By the time the Christian Democrats won control of the ruling Senate the following year, there were more than 150 squats in Kreuzberg. The crackdown came, but slowly. Landlords stopped relocating tenants to new high-rise blocks on the outskirts of the city and the squatters were eased out of their strongholds. By the end of the 1980s just two or three squats remained.

The spirit of rebellion continued long after the last militant squat was cleared. When President Reagan visited Berlin in 1987, the city authorities stopped all public transport to and from Kreuzberg for fear of disruptions. (In retaliation, a conceptual art group called the 'office for unusual measures' set up a cardboard mock-Berlin Wall at Kottbusser Tor, questioning anyone who passed and issuing special 'visas'.) A year later, during an IMF/World Bank meeting in Berlin, a phalanx of police blocked off the centre of town to thousands of demonstrators accusing the visiting officials of 'murdering' the poor of the Third World.

There is something strangely ritualized, even decadent, about all this rebellious activity. For all the anti-capitalist talk, the anarchists of Kreuzberg only exist because of the indulgences that capitalist West Berlin offers them. The loudest generally have no pressing material or political worries. And for all the non-conformism, Kreuzberg trendies are suspicious of anyone who does not behave and think exactly like them. They are remarkably uniform in their appearance, lifestyle and political views—as uniform in their own way, in fact, as the middle-class Germans they so despise. Black drainpipe trousers, mottled T-shirts, black and white cotton neckscarves and pebble glasses make them instantly recognizable. They streak their hair red and keep it straggly. They roll their own cigarettes and worry about Third World hunger and global warming. On local issues such as racism against the Turks or unemployment in East Berlin, they generally have nothing to say. They talk about their holidays spent with the Berbers of Morocco or the tribes of thè Amazon, which may have been more 'ideologically correct' than the average bourgeois family's jaunt to the beach in Greece or Turkey but certainly cost no less. Above all, they wish they weren't German and repeat how badly they want to move away.

The ritual of rebellion reaches its annual climax every May Day, when for no reason (except perhaps habit) bands of masked anarchists group around the Kotti spoiling for a fight. Invariably the police arrive and beer cans and stones begin to fly. For some, rioting is a form of recreation, an alarmingly gratuitous gesture of defiance. But the iconoclasm is in the end harmless just because it is such a ritual—the city carries on regardless.

Two Kreuzberg punks are immortalized in bronze on Admiralstrasse (off the Kotti directly opposite Adalbertstrasse), in a 1985 monument by Ludmila Seefried-Matejkova. At the base of a composite sculpture in the middle of the road sit a man with a harmonica and a woman listening to a Walkman, both—of course—with straggly hair and drainpipe trousers. Above them is a 3-m high sandstone hourglass which is also a platform for two bronze admirals standing back-to-back with telescopes—a playful juxtaposition of past and present, of authority and rebellion. Kids from the local school use the monument as a giant climbing frame.

It would be wholly out of step with the spirit of Kreuzberg to tell you exactly where to go. So spread out, using Kottbusser Tor as base. At Oranienstrasse 25, the **Elefanten Press Galerie** *has the city's only extensive exhibition showing photographs of the mural art and graffiti that used to be displayed on the Berlin Wall (now all gone, along with the concrete barrier itself). The best pieces, featuring colourful political allegories, distorted and abstract figures, always were in Kreuzberg. You might meet a nostalgic artist still mourning the day the bulldozers uprooted his or her masterpiece. Naunyn-strasse and Waldemarstrasse have some of the Kreuzberg's best house murals—explosions of colour giving the flat walls perspective, depth and a touch of surreal madness. (The tableaux change regularly as landlords love to restore the walls back to boring old white.) In Mariannenplatz is the* **Künstlerhaus Bethanien**, *a magnificent 19th-century brick hospital, with two imposing neo-Gothic towers, now used as a cultural centre. At the south end of the square is a humorous monument to the city's fire brigade, showing clumsy Prussian fire fighters with outsize bulbous noses tripping over each other's water pipes. Wrangelstrasse is lined with the best local food shops including a mouthwateringly cosmopolitan covered market on the corner of Eisenbahnstrasse. On Maybachufer by the canal is the enticing* **Turkish market** *(Tues and Fri 12–6 pm).*

Kreuzberg's punks and anarchists might make the most noise, but the group that has struggled hardest and made the deepest imprint on the neighbourhood is the Turkish community. Since the first *Gastarbeiter* (guest workers) came over in the early 1960s, Berlin has acquired the second-biggest Turkish city population in the world after Istanbul, with 140,000 people. About a third of them live in Kreuzberg. The market shows them at their most flourishing and exuberant. Veiled women offer aubergines, sweet peppers, spices, pulses, beans, fresh figs and dates on sumptuous stalls. Bearded men haggle with customers over cloth, jewellery and ornaments. The scent of freshly prepared kebabs fills the air. Newsstands have locally-produced Turkish newspapers with details of local Turkish television and radio stations. The Middle East has come to Prussia. But not without a struggle.

When the first immigrants, largely from Anatolia in central Turkey, arrived to make up a labour shortfall in West Germany's economic miracle, they were put on factory assembly lines or given menial work like street cleaning or rubbish collecting—jobs that Berliners were no longer willing to do themselves. Their flats were usually small and without bath or toilet. In the early days they were temporarily housed in buildings due for demolition to help landlords raise cash to buy new property. When Turks tried to go to bars or nightclubs, they were regularly shown the door. Small ads would specify 'no foreigners'. As a result their social life was discreetly introspective. Women would rarely appear out of doors. Their mosques were little more than the backrooms of flats.

Things have improved as many Germans have come to appreciate Turkish culture, starting with food and drink. A middle class of shop-keepers and restaurant owners has established itself and indeed thrived with the increased custom since the opening of the borders. But racism has also become more virulent. The far-right Republicans campaigned for the 1990 Berlin city elections with a poster of a young Turk being arrested by riot police under the slogan 'Keep Berlin German'. Young Turks, suffering more than their share of unemployment and depri-vation, have set up street gangs for the first time to fight skinheads and loot and steal from the white middle classes. Authors and community leaders who promote a multicultural society have earned the respect of German intellectuals, but are given little chance to air their views through the mainstream media.

*The overhead U-1 U-Bahn running through Kottbusser Tor is popularly known as the Orient Express, and the area between here and Schlesisches Tor is dubbed Little Istanbul. It's two stops by U-Bahn or a 10-minute walk to Schlesisches Tor (if you have wandered over to Wrangelstrasse then you will be close by). Next to the station is a small park leading to the river and the **Ober-baumbrücke**. This rickety iron footbridge marks the border be-tween Kreuzberg and Friedrichshain, between West and East Berlin.*

In the days of the Wall, the Spree served as the 'death strip', sandwiched on each bank by concrete and barbed wire, so divorcing the river from the city. 'Beware deadly danger!' the signs said. 'The water belongs to the Eastern sector.' There are crosses and a memorial stone to East Germans shot trying to swim across. The Oberbaumbrücke was the city's customs entry checkpoint in the Middle Ages. Excise officials blocked the river with tree trunks at the end of their working day to stop merchant ships stealing through in the dark. The current bridge dates from 1896.

It's easy to forget in Kreuzberg just how close the Wall used to be. Life there was so insulated that for many people the East virtually did not exist. When the revolution came in 1989, many Kreuzbergers at first did their best to ignore it. 'Why should I go to East Berlin?' one artist said. 'I see it on television and can imagine what it's like.' His house is five minutes' walk away from the Oberbaumbrücke. But there are signs that the end of the Cold War may alter Kreuzberg beyond recognition. Instead of being an isolated oddity, the district is now in the centre of the city and ripe for development. Already prices have jumped; property speculators are beginning to move in. West Berlin is about to forgo its special subsidies and has lost its exemption from military service. Some of the anarchists and artists (and kebab stalls) have moved to cheaper areas like Friedrichshain and Prenzlauer Berg in the East. Kreuzberg may yet become as 'frightfully bourgeois' as the Berlin that Mikhail Bakunin found in 1841.

> *Take a look to the left of the Oberbaumbrücke on the eastern side for signs of an open-air picture gallery. In early 1990 the East Berlin authorities decided to keep a piece of Wall here and invite artists to use one segment each to reproduce the kind of art that long predominated on the western side. The result included some striking images, such as a black-red-gold German flag with a star of David in the centre, or a picture of Brezhnev and Honecker kissing each other on the mouth with the caption: 'Will nobody save me from this deadly love?' However, at the time of writing, the gallery's future is uncertain. There is talk of taking it to a museum, or on tour to London and New York, or simply to the scrapyard.*
>
> *This is the end of the Kreuzberg walk, but one outstanding sight is tantalizingly close. The Soviet War Memorial (Sowjetisches Ehrenmal) in Treptow is such a powerful monument to the Second World War that it is a must, whether now or on a separate trip. From the Oberbaumbrücke walk straight ahead to Warschauer Strasse station and take the S-Bahn two stops to Treptower Park. Walk alongside the park on Puschkinallee until you reach a marble entrance arch adorned with laurel leaves bearing the words (in German and Russian): 'Eternal fame to the heroes who fell for freedom and the liberation of their socialist homeland.'*

After four decades of Cold War rhetoric it is sometimes forgotten in the West just how much the Soviet Union sacrificed to defeat the Nazis. Twenty million of its people died during the Second World War—more than 10 per cent of its total population. In the final battle for Berlin alone, 15,000 Soviet soldiers were killed. Here, in the peace of a suburban English-style park, they are celebrated in imposing style.

A grieving woman in marble, representing Mother Russia, stands before two high stone slabs bearing reliefs of the Soviet flag. Two soldiers kneel on either side, their guns resting on their helmets. The two slabs form a theatrical opening on to the main cemetery, a series of white stone tombs stretching away to the centrepiece of the memorial, an 11-m high bronze figure of a soldier clutching a child to his breast with one hand while spearing a swastika with a mighty sword in the other. The tombs bear relief sculptures showing soldiers leaving their families, training for battle, and defending cities such as Odessa and Stalingrad. Each relief is accompanied by a quotation from Stalin praising the bravery of his people. A small mausoleum inside the pedestal of the giant soldier is filled with flowers and an inscribed gold mosaic on the wall: 'Today everyone recognizes that the Soviet people through its sacrificial struggle saved European civilization from the protagonists of the Fascist pogroms.'

Despite the somewhat heavy-handed Stalinist overtones, this monument is moving by any standards. It was erected by a Soviet military committee of commanders and artists in 1946–49, using marble from Hitler's wrecked chancellery and granite stored for the planned rebuilding of Berlin in triumphant Fascist style. Despite its overt atheistic purpose, there are Christian overtones in the Madonna-like figure of the grieving mother, or the Christ-like theme of sacrifice for the benefit of all humanity. The giant soldier clutching the child could be an image of St Christopher, who, according to legend, carried the baby Christ across a river. The figure also recalls a legendary Soviet sergeant-major, Trifon Lukyanovich, who died while protecting a child from the SS in the last few days of the war.

125

Walk VI

The Tiergarten

Bahnhof Zoo—Siegessäule—Schloss Bellevue—Kongresshalle—
Kulturforum—German Resistance Memorial—Bauhaus Archive

'The Tiergarten is the only place where the Berliner can convince himself that the world contains nature, green trees and the darkness of woods at night,' the poet Josef Victor von Scheffel declared in 1846. But even this idyllic haven of parkland, woods, lakes and fine houses did not escape the barbarisms of the 20th century. Beneath the tranquil surface lurk tales of revolution, dictatorship, war and murder. Revolutionaries Rosa Luxemburg and Karl Liebknecht met their violent end here in 1919. The 1944 bomb plot against Hitler was hatched and then foiled a block away from the park. For 28 years one end of the Tiergarten ran into the dead end of the Wall.

The Tiergarten is also a symbol of Berlin's renewal. Bauhaus and later experimental buildings have sprung up in place of bomb sites. The Berlin Philharmonic orchestra and the West Berlin National Gallery have their home here. The park was also the setting for many of the scenes in Wim Wenders' haunting 1986 film about his home city, *Wings of Desire*.

This is a highly pleasurable walk, but be warned that it is some 8 km long. You might want to consider renting a bicycle (see Travel section for details) or, possibly, attack it in two goes. Many of the attractions are out

126

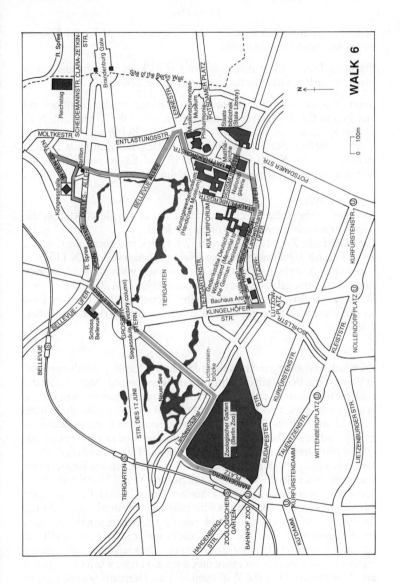

WALK 6

N

0   100m

R. Spree

SCHEIDEMANNSTR. CLARA-ZETKIN- STR.

Brandenburg Gate

Site of the Berlin Wall

Reichstag

MOLTKESTR.

ENTLASTUNGSSTR.

Pavillon

Kongresshalle

JOHN- FOSTER- DULLES- ALLEE

BELLEVUE ALLEE

R. Spree

ENNESTR.

Musikinstrumenten-
Museum

PHILHARMONIE

Philharmonie

POTSDAMER PLATZ

MATTHÄIKIRCHSTR.

Staats-
bibliothek
(State Library)

Matthäi-
kirche

Kunstgewerbemuseum
(Handicrafts Museum)

KULTURFORUM

Neue National-
galerie

Kunstbibliothek

STAUFFENBERGSTR.

SIGISMUNDSTR.

Gedenkstätte Deutscher
Widerstand (Memorial to
the German Resistance)

Reichpietsch
UFER

Landwehrkanal

UFER

Bauhaus Archiv

TIERGARTENSTR.

KLINGELHÖFER
STR.

LÜTZOW-
PLATZ

SCHILLSTR.

LÜTZOW UFER

KURFÜRSTENSTR.

POTSDAMER STR.

NOLLENDORFPLATZ ⓤ

KLEISTSTR.

BELLEVUE ⓢ

BELLEVUE- UFER

SPREEWEG

Schloss
Bellevue

GROSSER
STERN

Siegessäule (victory column)

TIERGARTEN

Neuer See

Landwehrkanal

Lichtenstein-
brücke

STR.

KURFÜRSTENSTR.

BUDAPESTER
STR.

TAUENTZIENSTR.

WITTENBERGPLATZ ⓤ

LIETZENBURGER STR.

TIERGARTEN ⓢ

STR. DES 17. JUNI

Zoologischer Garten
(Berlin Zoo)

HARDENBERG-
PLATZ

ZOOLOGISCHER
GARTEN ⓢ

BAHNHOF ZOO ⓤ

HARDENBERG-
STR.

KURFÜRSTENDAMM

KUDAMM

127

of doors, so aim for fair weather. The museums clumped in the Kulturforum are closed on Mondays.

Walking Time: Allow at least 2 hours of walking, plus the amount of
time you wish to linger in the museums and galleries.

Start: The tour begins at Bahnhof Zoo, the biggest junction of rail and
bus lines in the city. It ends at Lützowplatz, where the 29 bus leads back
to the Ku'damm or on towards central East Berlin and Kreuzberg.
Weary travellers can take the 69 back to Bahnhof Zoo from Schloss
Bellevue or the Kongresshalle. The 48 and 83 go south from the
Kulturforum to Kurfürstenstrasse U-Bahn station.

LUNCH/CAFÉS

Extremely thin pickings, with no restaurant of any description in the
Tiergarten itself. Picnicking is of course ideal.
City Grill am Zoo, Hardenbergstr. 29. Quick and convenient, with a
good Turkish kebab and salad bar. Next to Bahnhof Zoo. DM 15.
Reichstag. A slight deviation, but the only place midway round the walk
route. Sausages, salads, sandwiches and snacks. DM 20–25.
Bauhaus Archiv Restaurant, Klingelhöferstrasse 14. The best food
on the tour, with fresh pastas and simple meat-and-vegetable dishes.
DM 20.

☆   ☆   ☆   ☆   ☆

Every self-respecting metropolis should have a teeming, seedy core and
in West Berlin that place is **Bahnhof Zoo** (Zoo station). Named after the
zoological gardens next door, it is something of a human zoo too. Pimps,
beggars, con men, street vendors and drug dealers all peddle their living
here. Many of them are poor East Europeans who came in search of
gold-paved streets but ended up hawking cigarettes or lighters instead.
    The place has been witness to barely-scraped livings and shady deals
for generations. It was a major black market during various 20th-century
economic crises. In the years after the Second World War the currency
became so worthless that black market bosses would light up their
Chesterfields and Lucky Strikes with rolled up 100-mark notes. During
the division of the city you could buy East German marks here at a
heavily discounted rate. The Stasi security police loved to spy on illegal
currency buyers at Bahnhof Zoo, phoning through their car number
plates to border guards to ensure they got a hard time when they crossed
into East Berlin. After the Wall opened, East Germans flocked here to

offload their worthless money for hard Western cash, then as often as not crossed Hardenbergstrasse to peer at the Beate Uhse sex shop opposite.

*Opposite the station, the main rail link to points west, is the entrance to the **Berlin Zoo** (Zoologischer Garten) itself (open 9–sunset daily, adm). Although claiming to be the biggest collection of caged exotic animals in the world, the zoo is a disappointment; by skirting round the outside you can see quite a few of the animals anyway without paying admission. Much of the original stock imported and bred from the 1840s on was wiped out by wartime bombing. The present-day elephants and rhinos look rather sad and unhealthy in this most non-tropical of climates. At the end of Hardenbergplatz, on the western side of the zoo, follow the footpath running between the railway track and the fenced-in animals. In a few minutes, the city seems far away as the traffic and roads give way to trees, lakes and paths. Turn right at the canal, and continue until the next bridge, Lichtensteinbrücke.*

Here, in perhaps the most discreet corner of Berlin, the bodies of Rosa Luxemburg and Karl Liebknecht were dumped after their brutal murder during the abortive communist revolution of January 1919. Both fiery products of turbulent times, Luxemburg and Liebknecht have become heroes of the German Left and respected across the political spectrum as antagonists of the dying Prussian aristocracy. The pair broke away from the Social Democratic Party beacuse of its support for German involvement in the First World War. Liebknecht, the activist, formed the radical Spartacus League in 1916 and spent two years in jail for subversion and incitement to pacifism. Luxemburg, the theorist, distanced herself from Lenin's idea of a vanguard, or revolutionary élite, and developed a concept of democratic socialism. When the Kaiser, facing the consequences of a lost war and a restless workforce, abdicated in November 1918, the Spartacists struggled to establish a communist state. They were thwarted by the Social Democrats who, under Friedrich Ebert, attempted to steer a moderate path through the chaos. In December 1918 and January 1919, bands of revolutionaries fought furious battles with disgruntled companies of right-wing ex-soldiers from the front known as *Freikorps*. Liebknecht called for a general strike, while Luxemburg urged workers to take the Reichstag by storm. On 8 January Ebert and his tough defence minister Gustav Noske declared they were prepared to use force to quell the revolt and Liebknecht and Luxemburg went into hiding. A week later they were caught in a

Wilmersdorf flat and taken for interrogation to the Eden Hotel (on the site of a present-day savings bank on Budapester Strasse on the southern flank of the zoo). There they encountered Captain Waldemar Pabst, later a notorious Nazi, who had his men beat and sexually humiliate them. Liebknecht was hustled out of a side entrance and shot, his body then flung into the Neuer See, the lake just north of the Lichtensteinbrücke. Luxemburg, told she was being taken to Moabit prison, was escorted out of another entrance and clubbed to death. She was dumped in the Landwehrkanal by the bridge. Her body, with weights attached, was not discovered for six months, when it bobbed eerily to the surface. It took several more years of official cover-ups for the truth of the murders to come out. The affair continues to arouse passions today. In 1986, after a bitter debate over their historical merits in the city parliament, the West Berlin authorities agreed to erect memorial plaques to Luxemburg and Liebknecht but put them in virtually hidden places. Luxemburg's plaque is on the underside of the Lichtensteinbrücke. Liebknecht's is on a bank of the Neuer See.

Cross the bridge and keep going straight through the Tiergarten until you reach the main road and the Siegessäule, the Prussian victory column erected to celebrate victory in wars against Denmark, Austria and France in the decade leading up to German unification in 1871.

The **Tiergarten** (literally animal garden) was originally a private hunting estate outside the city walls for the Electors of Prussia and their chosen subjects. Plans to turn it into a public park were hatched as early as 1700 when Friedrich I began building a road through from the city to Schloss Charlottenburg to the west. However, the plans only came to fruition in 1742 under Frederick the Great, who reversed his father Friedrich Wilhelm I's obsessive conversion of large tracts of the Tiergarten into military parade grounds. Its modern paths, artificial lakes and layout of trees were the work of Berlin's prime landscape architect Peter Josef Lenné in the 19th century.

The park was devastated by bombs in the last days of the Second World War. During, the following winter its few remaining trees were chopped down for firewood and the bare terrain parcelled into plots for growing vegetables. The Swiss novelist Max Frisch described it in 1947 as a 'bare steppe . . . filled with splintered pedestals and choking in weeds'. Two years later Berlin's mayor Ernst Reuter ceremonially planted the first new tree, a lime, and today it is hard to tell that the vegetation has not stood undisturbed for centuries. It is a favourite spot for summer sunbathing. Berliners, displaying impeccable German obedience, keep strictly to the patches indicated by signposts as *Liegewiesen*, special fields designated for lying in. But their sense of propriety does not extend to their clothes: people of all ages and shapes romp around naked with no sign of the slightest inhibition.

The golden goddess of Victory who sits atop the **Siegessäule** looks remarkably harmless thanks to her gracious position halfway along the grand Strasse des 17. Juni, which runs through the heart of the Tiergarten to the Brandenburg Gate. The 67-m high sandstone column with a red granite colonnaded base looked rather more forbidding in its original location outside the Reichstag. It was moved in 1938 to form the centrepiece of Hitler's military parades along the main boulevard (then called the Ost–West Axis). You may recognize the column with affection from *Wings of Desire* as the perch for two angels who come to Berlin to seek out human warmth in a despairing world. But on close inspection this is an ugly, puffed-up piece of Prussian pomp. On the northern side of the road intersection are statues of the heroes of the unification wars—Chancellor Bismarck, Field Marshal Moltke and War Minister Roon. For a bird's-eye view of the Tiergarten, climb the Siegessäule (entrance through tunnels on Strasse des 17. Juni, closed Mon morning and December–March, adm).

> *Walk along Spreeweg (directly opposite the path on which you approached the Siegessäule) and on the left is the elegant neo-classical* **Schloss Bellevue**.

Siegessäule

131

Built in 1785 as a summer house for Frederick the Great's brother, Prince August Ferdinand, Schloss Bellevue is a little gem of a building set by the banks of the Spree. The airy, gold-embellished rooms behind the long pastel façade are unfortunately not open to the public as the building is the official Berlin residence of the German President. You can, however, visit the perfectly manicured English garden at the back when the head of state is not in town. In the past the palace was used variously as an art gallery and a discreet venue for political meetings. Hitler turned it into a government guest house, entertaining the likes of Soviet Foreign Minister Molotov (he of the eponymous cocktail) before wartime bombs wrecked the building. The restoration was completed in 1959.

*Turn right onto John-Foster-Dulles Allee, named after President Kennedy's Secretary of State, which winds away from the river and leads to the futuristic **Kongresshalle**.*

This building, with its ambitious cantilevered front, is popularly dubbed the 'pregnant oyster'—a vivid description of its yawning red and yellow concrete façade. The hall, a present from the US Allied Command for an international architecture fair in 1957, apes the stretched awnings of tents which provided entertainment for Berliners in this part of town in the 18th century. However, in 1980 the pregnant oyster had a mishap and the building collapsed. It is now back to its full glory, hopefully in permanence, and used for conferences and the odd exhibition.

At the back of the building is a street called In den Zelten (literally, in the tents), marking the site of the old outdoor funfairs and street theatres. The only trace of that tradition is the part-canvas, part-concrete Tempodrom nightclub, which hosts rock concerts in the summer.

Back on John-Foster-Dulles Allee, just beyond the Kongresshalle, is the **Carillon**, a gleaming concrete and steel bell tower whose 68 bells peal out twice a day at noon and 6.00 pm. This exemplary piece of bad taste was a present from Daimler–Benz on the 750th anniversary of Berlin in 1987. Since the chief executive of Daimler was Edzard Reuter, son of Berlin's famous post-war mayor, nobody was in a position to stop him.

The tour now darts off to the south side of the Tiergarten. The most enjoyable route is along the winding pathways straddling the Strasse des 17. Juni. The best measure of your bearings is Entlastungsstrasse to your left. If in doubt take the road, or the 83 bus one stop. At the

*corner of Tiergartenstrasse are the unmistakable golden-yellow con-
crete gables of the **Philharmonie**, home of the Berlin Philharmonic
orchestra.*

Hans Scharoun's Bauhaus-inspired Philharmonie has become famous
for its revolutionary layout and near-perfect acoustics. The orchestra sits
surrounded by the audience instead of facing them, permitting a much
greater sense of involvement in the performance and ensuring flawless
vision from all 2200 much-coveted seats, which are arranged like vineyard terraces on nine levels. If you want seats, book as many weeks or
even months in advance as possible. There are also guided tours at
Sunday lunchtime; phone ahead on (W) 269251.

The orchestra itself has fully matched the reputation of the home it
moved into on 15 October 1963. Founded in 1882 as a breakaway group
from a chamber orchestra at the court of the Kaisers, the orchestra
blossomed before the Second World War under Wilhelm Furtwängler
and then attained superstar status with its legendary post-war conductor,
Herbert von Karajan. Karajan, who retired in 1989 a few months before
his death at the age of 82, oversaw the drawn-out move to the Philharmonie after the orchestra's original premises, near Anhalter Bahnhof, were destroyed in an air raid in 1944. He also became notorious for
his fits of artistic temperament, which caused delays in concert season
openings and even strikes over details of programmes or points of
interpretation. The constant intrigues and scandals emanating from the
Philharmonie prompted the press to dub the place 'Karajani's Circus'.
Both Karajan and Furtwängler had to live down their association with
the Nazis (both had publicly supported Hitler), and rarely enticed the
world's leading Jewish musicians to play with them. The current conductor, Italian maestro Claudio Abbado, is the first non-German in the
job and has maintained towering professional standards without the
tantrums or whisperings about the past.

*Scharoun masterminded a series of new buildings in this corner of
the Tiergarten called the **Kulturforum**. The space was badly
bombed during the Second World War, but had in fact been largely
cleared already by Hitler as he prepared to build a triumphalist
Nord–Süd Axis (North–South Axis) from the Brandenburg Gate to
a new complex of Fascist buildings. Heated debate over plans for the
Kulturforum have kept the complex in a state of non-completion for
30 years. The demise of the nearby Berlin Wall has reopened the
discussion about what should be built where. For now the Forum*

contains the Philharmonie, the adjoining Musical Instrument Museum to the left, the Handicrafts Museum to the right, the National Gallery behind to the south and the State Library away on the other side of Potsdamer Strasse.

The angular white **Musical Instrument Museum** (Musikinstrumenten-Museum, open Tues–Sun 9 am–5 pm, free) charts the development of the piano, lute, guitar and trombone and related instruments. Highlights are the harpsichords made either of highly polished wood or ornately decorated with animals, plants and abstract symbols. The most intriguing pieces are 17th-century trumpets and trombones, whose long thin tubes look a precarious challenge for any player. Unfortunately visitors are not allowed to touch, let alone play, any of the exhibits and have to content themselves with tinny recordings. Specialists can apply for a guided tour (in German only) at weekend lunchtimes; phone (W) 254810 in advance.

Next door is the newest building in the ensemble, the **Handicrafts Museum** (Kunstgewerbemuseum, open Tues–Sun 10 am–5 pm, free), a hotchpotch of art and artefacts from medieval communion cups to modern teapots. From the old gold and silverware to the 18th-century elephant paperweights and unicorn clockholders, the collection shows the Prussian aristocracy's mania for the fussy and the exotic, and above all a passion to amass and possess. Perhaps the most vivid single piece is a late 15th-century reliquary of St George, resplendent with its silver armour, golden hair tresses and shining sword about to strike at the dragon as the monster bites into the shield. The red-brick museum, started in 1985 by architect Rolf Gutbrod and still being finished at the time of writing, is functional and spacious but no great beauty.

Just outside is Matthäikirchplatz and the **Matthäikirche** (Church of Matthew) itself, the only surviving building here from the 19th century. The mottled red and white brick church, built by August Stüler in 1846, is virtually derelict inside and closed to the public, but in its heyday it was a popular place of high society worship, a 'rendez-vous of the pious, of lieutenants and the daughters of intelligence officers, who prayed and danced together,' according to contemporary poet Franz Hessel.

*The architectural highlight of the Kulturforum is the **National Gallery** (Nationalgalerie, Tues–Sun 10–5, free), the last work of Bauhaus master Ludwig Mies van der Rohe, who returned to Germany at the end of his life after a long exile in the United States.*

Completed in 1969, the year of Mies van der Rohe's death, the building is a simple 65 m by 65 m glass box with a flat black roof. From the outside it looks enticing and challenging with its multi-layered terraces and sculpture garden (including a Henry Moore bronze on the north side called The Archer). *Inside it gives an exhilarating sense of space, light and freedom.*

The collection, part of the heritage of the Nationalgalerie in the East, confronts you with some highly experimental modern works on the ground floor, from Frank Stella's canvases of simple shapes and colours to Joseph Beuys's montage of blackboards flung chaotically around a schoolroom. Downstairs is an exquisite collection of Impressionist and Expressionist painting, taking the visitor from the lazy summer idylls of Renoir and Monet to the harsh, garish world of 1920s Germany. Of particular Berlin interest are Adolph von Menzel's sweatily realistic chronicles of industrialization in the 1840s; Ernst Ludwig Kirchner's skew, uncomfortable images, painted at the beginning of the First World War, of the Brandenburg Gate and other sites tinged with military overtones; and finally George Grosz's chaotic, Bosch-like allegory of the pre-Nazi period, *Stützen der Gesellschaft* (Pillars of the Community)—a montage of grotesques including pompous mustachioed businessmen, uniformed thugs and a red-faced shopkeeper with a tea cup on his head.

Across the busy Potsdamer Strasse is the sprawling **State Library** *(Staatsbibliothek), built by Scharoun in 1978 and a pleasure to visit whether or not you want to consult books.*

Wim Wenders picked up the atmosphere of light and space, of comfort and isolation, of silence and concentration in a scene of *Wings of Desire*. Wenders' lingering views of wasteland and Wall behind the library at Potsdamer Platz have of course been overtaken by history. But, as in his film, the spot is still popular with circuses. For more on this former border area, see Walk IV.

We now return west along the canal. Two blocks (or one stop on the 29 bus) along Reichpietschufer, turn right on to Stauffenbergstrasse. About halfway up on the left (there are signs) is the Bendlerblock, the former Nazi army headquarters housing the **Gedenkstätte Deutscher Widerstand**, *the memorial to the German resistance and the men who tried to overthrow Hitler on 20 July 1944.*

One great scandal of the Allied occupation of Germany at the end of the Second World War was the British and American refusal to acknowledge the existence of an organized resistance to Nazi rule. Up to a million people were active in opposing the Third Reich, and this building tells some of the bravest, and most harrowing, stories about them. By 1944 an influential group of army officers, led by army Chief of Staff Claus Schenk Graf von Stauffenberg and General Ludwig Beck, had become horrified by the war and the régime they were fighting for. From this building they planned the overthrow of the government and on 20 July Stauffenberg, a conservative aristocrat, planted a bomb in a brief-case under Hitler's seat at his East Prussian command centre in Wolf-schanze near Rastenburg. Back in Berlin, Beck was ready to arrest all the Nazi leaders as soon as the assassination was carried out. But bad luck and the pedantic obedience of a German major caused the meticulously planned plot to fall apart. By a fluke the briefcase was moved round behind a heavy wooden table leg just before it exploded, and Hitler escaped virtually unscathed. Beck pressed ahead with the plan regardless, arranging for news of the Führer's death to be read out on the radio. Confusion reigned for hours. But it was a stiff Prussian officer, Major Otto Ernst Remer, who unwittingly scuppered the plot. Beck sent him to arrest Goebbels in the Propaganda Ministry. Goebbels received him calmly, asking him to sit down while he made a phone call. He then dialled through to Hitler in Wolfschanze, who promoted Remer to colonel on the spot and ordered him to go back to the Bendlerblock to round up the conspirators. Used to obeying orders from his superiors without question, Remer did what he was told.

Hitler's revenge was terrible. Stauffenberg, who had returned to Berlin, and four of the other main conspirators, were shot in the court-yard of the Bendlerblock the same night. Beck was granted leave to kill himself. In the following weeks some 200 people, including innocent relatives and acquaintances of the plotters, were rounded up and either shot or hanged slowly with piano wire at Plötzensee jail (see Walk VIII).

The courtyard has been turned into a memorial for the conspirators, considered in modern Germany as martyrs. In the centre is a bronze statue of a defiant, naked young man in chains. The names of Stauffenberg and the others are inscribed on the left-hand wall. A stone on the ground bears the message: 'You could not endure the shame, you resisted, you gave the great eternally vital sign of change, sacrificing your glowing lives for freedom, justice and honour.'

Inside on the second floor is a **museum** *(Mon–Fri 9–6 and Sat–Sun 9–1, adm) with extensive documentation on the German resistance (some in English).*

Room upon room of photographs and period documents testify to the extent and complexity of the German resistance, from workers and left-wing intellectuals to artists, the Church, Jewish leaders and conservatives such as Stauffenberg and the future Chancellor of West Germany, Konrad Adenauer. It punctures the myth later perpetuated by the occupying Allies that all Germans who did not die or flee the Third Reich must have been Nazis. But the museum is not complacent about the past: the resistance, after all, barely dented Hitler's broad support base before the war and failed to topple him after it started. The exhibition gives prominence to the guilt and complicity that many members of the resistance felt. 'We have been dumb witnesses to evil deeds,' runs a quotation from Dietrich Bonhoeffer, an eminent theologian murdered by the Nazis. A banner displays Berlin pastor Martin Niemöller's famous reflection on solidarity and betrayal:

When the Nazis came for the Communists I said nothing, for I was not a Communist. When they locked up the Social Democrats I said nothing, for I was no Social Democrat. When they came for the trade unionists I said nothing, for I was not a trade unionist. When they came for the Jews I said nothing, because I was not a Jew. When they came for me, there was nobody left to protest.

Return to the Reichpietschufer and turn right along the canal, lined with trees and fine houses. After the next bridge is a path running between the canal and the road. It passes the **Villa von der Heydt**, *an elegant neo-classical mansion that once housed the Chinese embassy and is now the administrative headquarters of Berlin's state museums. Just behind are the distinctive curved northlights of the* **Bauhaus Archive**.

No architectural movement this century has proved as influential as Bauhaus, nor deemed so subversive. Working from the principle that art is an extension of industrial production, its exponents sought to master all working materials and techniques of creating shapes to achieve what founder Walter Gropius described as 'a new unity between art and technology'. In other words utilitarian objects like cutlery, furniture or machine tools were to be appreciated for their beauty; conversely, paintings, sculptures and buildings should create their beauty through the use of everyday materials, shapes and techniques. The result was a felicitous combination of artistry and practical application that revolutionized architecture and design. For example, Marcel Breuer's 1928 chair design, exhibited at the Archive, using a curved metal frame instead of legs, is still a standard of modern Habitat and Ikea models.

The movement, begun in Weimar in 1919 and run by a constant rotation of directors, opened up wide vistas of new creativity. Artists like Klee, Kandinsky and Stravinsky flocked first to Weimar, then Dessau and Berlin, to see the new methods and adapt them for their own work. But the movement was also seen as potentially revolutionary for knocking art off its exalted pedestal and declaring workers and artists to be part of the same creative force. Nazis, whose notions of art were more in line with the triumphalist neo-classical style of Unter den Linden, constantly harassed Bauhaus schools in the 1920s. Finally in 1933 stormtroopers raided the movement's last headquarters in Germany, a former telephone factory in the Berlin suburb of Steglitz, and arrested 32 students. Twelve later died in concentration camps. Bauhaus exponents like Gropius, Mies van der Rohe and Oskar Schlemmer fled to the United States where they influenced a whole generation of buildings in New York, Chicago and elsewhere.

The archive itself (Wed–Mon 11–5, adm, free on Mondays), housed in a Gropius-designed building, gives a brief history of Bauhaus and displays the movement's extraordinary artistic diversity. There is much more here than glass-box buildings and sleekly designed silverware. Franz Scala's painting *Birth–Dream–Desire–Death* is a striking blend of Freudian themes and Chagallian fantasy within a strict formal framework. Laszlo Moholy-Nagy's *Light-space modulator* is a mechanical mesh of metal, plexiglass, grotesque kitchen utensils and a wooden ball which rotates and casts shadows on the backing wall at the touch of a button.

Outside the western entrance to the Bauhaus Archive is a busy traffic junction. Turning left into Schillstrasse, you will find a bus-stop for the 29 and 69 back to the Ku'damm.

Walk VII

The Kurfürstendamm

Kaiser Wilhelm Gedächtniskirche

Nollendorfplatz—Isherwood's house—KaDeWe—Europa-Center—Kaiser Wilhelm Memorial Church—Ku'damm—Käthe Kollwitz Museum—Jewish Community Centre—Savignyplatz

The Kurfürstendamm—referred to popularly as the Ku'damm—is quintessential West Berlin. Noisy, glossy and unashamedly materialistic, it is the ultimate showcase of Western capitalism. Leather boots, fully fitted kitchens, designer knick-knacks—they are all here. During the Cold War, while the East Berlin Communists talked about the inevitability of crisis in the capitalist system, here on their doorstep was evidence that crisis was far, far away. The Ku'damm sought to prove that the West really was the best. Of course generous subsidies from the federal government in Bonn had more than a little to do with it. And with the Wall barely a mile off, the apparently easy affluence was all too fragile. When West German singer Udo Lindenberg wrote in 1982 'the Russians will be on the Ku'damm in 15 minutes', he was only half joking.

Nowadays the Ku'damm has taken on a new symbolism as the premier shopping street in the capital of a united Germany. It doesn't need subsidies any more: it can rely on the hundreds of thousands of rich visitors and new residents who have descended on the city since the opening of the Wall. Having a coffee on the Ku'damm is still a byword for self-indulgence for many East Berliners. Like it or loathe it (and there are plenty of people in both camps) it is still a magnet of tremendous force.

The Ku'damm straddles two strongly flavoured districts, Schöneberg and Charlottenburg, both filled with cafés, bookshops, idiosyncratic monuments, street sculptures and quirky shops. Come during the week if you can; the Ku'damm overflows with people and cars at the weekend, and the shops aren't even open after 2 pm most Saturdays because of Germany's draconian opening laws. If the shops and museums aren't as important to you as soaking up the atmosphere, come in the evening when the shimmering lights cast the Ku'damm in its best colours.

Walking Time: About 3 hours.

Start: Nollendorfplatz. This is on U-Bahn lines 1 and 4, and buses 16 and 19 stop there too. The 19 and 29 buses run all the way down the Ku'damm and cost just DM 1 instead of the usual DM 2.70 per trip. The finish, at Ernst-Reuter-Platz, is on U-Bahn line 1.

LUNCH/CAFÉS

There are hundreds of excellent places in this area (see Charlottenburg in Food and Drink section), so it's a shame to hit a dud. Two rules: avoid the Europa-Center, and be wary of the pavement cafés and restaurants on the Ku'damm itself. They may look nice but they are generally bad and overpriced. Two of the better ones, neither of them cheap, are:

Café Möhring, corner of Ku'damm and Uhlandstr. Faded elegance and impeccable service; where rich, middle-aged Berliners have coffee and cake and reminisce.

Café Kranzler, Ku'damm 18–19. Slightly more upbeat and brash, with glass exteriors and neon lights.

Elsewhere you can't go too far wrong. Often a large breakfast is as good an option as lunch:

Nolle, at the Nollendorfplatz market. Closed Tues. More of a watering hole than a restaurant, this looks out on the flea market and oozes charm. Solid home-made cooking and a wide variety of beers. DM 10.

Schlemmer Pylon, Marburgerstr. 9a. For professional shoppers. Wacky building which used to be the base of a footbridge to the Europa-Center. Delicious freshly squeezed juices, soups and sandwiches. Stand up or take away. DM 10.

Café Savigny, Grolmanstr. 53. Great breakfasts and good value French-style lunch. Stylish, young clientèle. DM 20.

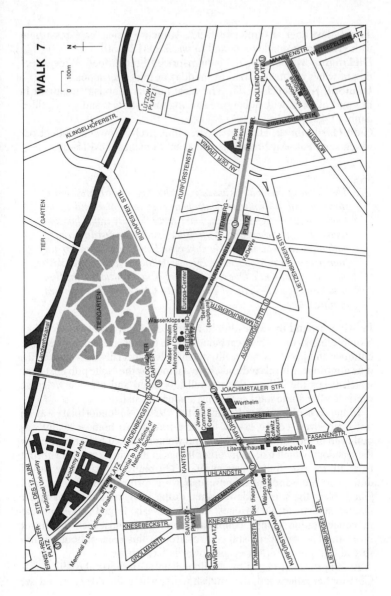

WALK 7

N

0   100m

WINTERFELDTPLATZ

MASSENSTR.

NOLLENDORF-
PLATZ

WINTERFELDTSTR.
Isherwood's

EISENACHER STR.

MOTZSTR.

LÜTZOW-
PLATZ

KLINGELHÖFERSTR.

Post
Museum

KLEISTSTR.

KURFÜRSTENSTR.

AN DER URANIA

BUDAPESTER STR.

TIER-
GARTEN

TAUENTZIENSTR.

WITTENBERG-
PLATZ

KaDeWe

LIETZENBURGER STR.

TIERGARTEN

Europa-Center

MARBURGER STR.

AUGSBURGER STR.

Landwehrkanal

"Berlin"
(sculpture)

Wasserklops

BREITSCHEID-
PLATZ

Kaiser Wilhelm
Memorial Church

ZOOLOGISCHER
GARTEN

JOACHIMSTALER STR.

HARDENBERGSTR.

ZOO

Academy of Arts

Technical University

KURFÜRSTENDAMM

Wertheim

MEINEKESTR.

Jewish
Community
Centre

FASANENSTR.

Käthe
Kollwitz
Museum

Literaturhaus

Grisebach Villa

STR. DES 17. JUNI

STEINPLATZ

KANTSTR.

UHLANDSTR.

Memorial to the Victims of Stalinism
Memorial to the Victims of
National Socialism

CARMERSTR.

GROLMANSTR.

Set theory clock

Maison de
France

ERNST-REUTER-
PLATZ

KNESEBECKSTR.

SAVIGNY-
PLATZ

KNESEBECKSTR.

MOMMSENSTR.

KURFÜRSTENDAMM

LIETZENBURGER STR.

GROLMANSTR.

SAVIGNYPLATZ

141

Tucci, next door at Grolmanstr. 52. Attractive Italian café-restaurant with great home-made pasta and *tiramisú*. DM 20–30.

Diekmann, Meinekestr. 7. Medium-priced French food. Wide selection of wines and teas. Good for midday or mid-afternoon.

Istanbul, Knesebeckstr. 77. The most popular Turkish restaurant in this part of town, with aubergine and yoghurty starters and spicy grilled lamb. DM 25.

Café Hardenberg, Hardenbergstr. 10. A lively, crowded student bar which serves all-day breakfasts and snacky lunches. DM 15–20.

☆　　　☆　　　☆　　　☆　　　☆

*The theme of this walk is modern, flashy, high-tech Berlin, but it starts modestly at Nollendorfplatz, where the iron girders and ageing track of a disused U-Bahn line loom above the busy traffic junction below. This is Schöneberg, a cheerful, residential district teeming with antique shops, tea parlours, bars and nightclubs which stretch from here away to Motzstrasse, Eisenacher Strasse and Winterfeldtplatz just to the south. One of the most unspoilt attractions is the **flea market** (open 11–7, closed Tues), which takes place on the disused overhead line.*

Prowling around the wares in old railway carriages makes you feel like Skimbleshanks the railway cat being busy in the luggage van. Some of the antiques and jewellery are really worthwhile, especially early in the day. The atmosphere is relaxed and chatty, helped by the Nolle pub next door which keeps the sellers' throats well lubricated and offers a welcome reprieve after some hard searching among the stalls.

In the days of 'naughty Berlin' in the 1920s, Nollendorfplatz was an unusually overt centre of gay life at a time when homosexuality was outlawed in most of Europe. Men and women flocked to Berlin to enjoy the freedom, which like many other things in this city came to an abrupt halt with the rise of the Nazis in 1933. The clubs and bars were closed down and thousands of homosexuals were tortured, imprisoned, and killed. Near the south-side entrance to the U-Bahn, a pink triangular plaque similar to the badges that the Nazis forced gays to wear in concentration camps commemorates the homosexual victims of Fascism. The gay scene still centres around this area, although it has spread out quite a bit, especially towards Kreuzberg.

Among those attracted by the liberalism of Berlin in the 1920s was Christopher Isherwood, the English writer who brilliantly captured the sense of foreboding of the pre-Nazi period in wry, understated prose in such novels as *Mr Norris Changes Trains* and *Goodbye to Berlin*. Isherwood came to Berlin with W. H. Auden in 1929 and left four years later, shortly after Hitler replaced Hindenburg as head of state and declared dictatorial powers. Much of Isherwood's writing is based on his experience as an English teacher living in a rundown Schöneberg tenement block with his warmhearted landlady, a middle-aged spinster referred to in the books as Fräulein Schröder. The house was in Nollendorfstrasse, which you can reach by walking south along Maassenstrasse and taking the first right. Isherwood lived about half-way down on the right at number 17—a plaque marks the spot. The 'deep solemn massive street' and the 'houses like shabby monumental safes crammed with tarnished valuables' that he describes in the celebrated opening to *Goodbye to Berlin* have smartened up quite a bit in the intervening years. Much of Nollendorfstrasse was destroyed in the war and replaced with some particularly unpleasant coloured concrete monoliths. But Isherwood's house has remained, redolent of the old coal-fire stoves and living rooms smelling of cabbage.

Most people are familiar with Isherwood only second-hand, through the hit film musical *Cabaret* starring Liza Minelli. Although based loosely on the characters of Isherwood's books, the film conveys a somewhat distorted impression of 1920s Berlin. Minelli's character, Sally Bowles, comes across as an exuberant, confident cabaret singer with all the world at her feet; in *Goodbye to Berlin* she is altogether sadder, letting men take advantage of her in a vague and rather despairing attempt to become a singer. Isherwood's Berlin, even before the Nazi takeover, was darker than the film suggests. His friend Stephen Spender encapsulated it strikingly after a visit in 1930:

> There was a sensation of doom to be felt in the Berlin
> streets. The feeling of unrest went deeper than any crisis.
> Berlin was the tension, the poverty, the anger, the
> prostitution, the hope and despair thrown out on the streets.
> It was the blatant rich at the smart restaurants, the
> prostitutes in army top boots at corners, the grim
> submerged-looking Communists in processions, and the
> violent youths who suddenly emerged from nowhere and
> shouted: '*Deutschland erwache!*'.

Follow Nollendorfstrasse to the end and take a right up Eisenacher Strasse. Cross the road at Kleiststrasse, full of state-of-the-art but soulless office blocks, and turn left. In the central reserve of the junction with An der Urania is the first of several curious pieces of modern art on this walk that were created for Berlin's 750th birthday celebrations in 1987.

It looks like an outsize piece of lead piping—the sort Colonel Mustard might use to murder the Reverend Green in Cluedo—or maybe a giant tick giving a self-satisfied city 10 out of 10. In fact the 18-m high black steel tube is called **Curve of 124.5 degrees**, by Bernard Venet. Foolhardy young Berliners use it as a high-risk skateboard track. If you are lucky you will see some, rapidly pursued by several policemen.

Around the corner at An der Urania 15 is the **Post Museum** (Mon–Thurs 9–5, Sat–Sun 10–5 adm), recommended for an entertaining half-hour looking at impossibly intricate 19th-century pioneer telephones and telex machines.

Go back to Kleiststrasse and along to Wittenbergplatz, the site of a rather junky flea market on weekdays. The elegant Jugendstil U-Bahn station was built in 1913 and renovated in the mid-1980s. On the left of the central island is a modern signpost that looks as if it might be listing bus stops but in fact catalogues the most notorious Nazi concentration camps with a simple 'lest we forget' message. The design seems very matter-of-fact, and a busy shopping square is an odd place for such a reflective monument. Most people barely notice it.

Shopping here begins with a bang. The Kaufhaus des Westens, or **KaDeWe** (pronounced *kah-deh-veh*), is unmissable on your left. Emblazoned with flags, this giant department store is the Berlin equivalent of Harrods or Bloomingdale's. The 'department store of the West' claims to be the largest shop in continental Europe. It is certainly the most striking in Berlin—an object of near-reverence, its name printed on every telephone directory, the pinnacle of consumer culture.

Inside, it is one non-stop fashion show. Drapes, perfumes, designer clothes—everything looks perfect. Almost too perfect. Straight ahead of the entrance is an information booth, where the attendant will provide every last statistic about the shop in just about any language. An area of 63,000 square metres. Six storeys. Some 2400 employees. Home deliveries, credit cards, gift wrapping.

Founded in 1907, the KaDeWe was always a little bit special. Despite being badly bombed, it quickly reopened after the war, a beacon of shameless luxury to help overcome the misery and ruins of 1945. When the Berlin Wall came down in November 1989, thousands of East Germans crowded in to gape at its impeccable opulence. However, its conspicuous consumerism has also made it a target for anti-establishment protest and it was one of two Berlin stores bombed by anarchists on the eve of unification in October 1990. With perfect unruffled *savoir-faire*, the shop ensured that every sign of the damage had disappeared within days.

The highlight is undoubtedly the food hall on the top floor, the *Feinschmeckeretage*, where of an afternoon you can nonchalantly gulp down fresh oysters with champagne. There is even an express lift which goes straight there to cause minimum delay.

The KaDeWe fronts onto Tauentzienstrasse, traditionally a shoe-shopping street. Two great pre-war names, Stiller and Leiser, are still putting leather on feet today. Stiller in German means quieter, and Leiser means softer—giving rise to a famous Berlin joke about an out-of-towner asking where he can buy shoes. 'Stiller,' replies a Berliner. The stranger asks again, this time lowering his voice: 'Excuse me, where can I buy shoes?'. 'Leiser,' comes the response. 'Excuse me,' he whispers, 'where can I buy shoes?'. 'Stiller . . .'

In the middle of Tauentzienstrasse is another 750th birthday sculpture, entitled **Berlin**, *by German artists Brigitte and Martin Denninghoff, its twisted chrome-nickel tubes intending to symbolize the skew vision each side of the city had of the other. On the right-hand side is one of the great monstrosities of Berlin, the* **Europa-Center**.

Full of tacky shops and dud restaurants, the Center is an exercise in Cold War bad taste, a 20-storey skyscraper topped with a glowing Mercedes three-pointed star built high enough to be seen from East Berlin. By the Tauentzienstrasse entrance is a computer-operated waterfall of purple, green, blue and yellow neon lights which locals call the fruit-juice machine. On the ground floor inside is a modern French sculpture entitled the *Lotus Stream*. Metal lotus leaves fill with water, then tip over and gush their load into another leaf. The sign asks you not to disturb the sculpture, described as a celebration of 'the fruitfulness of eternity'. Berliners have great fun ignoring this and trying to throw coins into the cup-like leaves. Upstairs is a special screening room called **Multivision Berlin** which several times a day puts on a 40-minute film that has absolutely nothing interesting to say about the city at all. It is superficial and smug, more like a commercial for life insurance than a documentary,

145

and—more worryingly—fails to mention the Holocaust or offer any substantial account of life in East Berlin. Finally, there is a lift up to the top floor (open 9 am–11 pm daily, adm). Through some Cold War architectural quirk, the view extends in every direction except one—east.

Walk out on to **Breitscheidplatz***, a pedestrian zone buzzing with tourists, shoppers, buskers, junk-stall holders and punks, and crowned by the ruins of the Kaiser Wilhelm Memorial Church. Right outside the Europa-Center is another outdoor artwork, the* **Weltkugel***, or globe. Water rushes over the smooth granite, hurtles down staircases around it and squirts through abstract sculpted figures. This is popularly known as the* Wasserklops*, or water dumpling. As you will have gathered, the Berliners don't have a great deal of respect for their city's modern art.*

Breitscheidplatz has changed character completely, in keeping with Berlin's volatile political and social fashions. Originally called Viktoria-Luise-Platz after the daughter of Kaiser Wilhelm II, it was a monument to Prussia's military might. The Memorial Church (*Gedächtniskirche*) was built to commemorate Kaiser Wilhelm I, the hero of the Franco-Prussian war. A full military parade honoured the church's opening in 1895.

All that changed completely in November 1943 when British bombers wrecked the Ku'damm and left the church a smouldering ruin. In a total *volte-face* after the war, the square was renamed after Rudolph Breit-scheid, a Social Democrat politician murdered by the Nazis. As for the church, it stayed as a memorial, no longer to glorify war but as a semi-destroyed reminder of war's ravages. In the 1960s student groups used Breitscheidplatz to protest against the Vietnam War. Their heirs, especially punks and bikers, still like to hang around the church steps. The church is torn between welcoming their presence and wondering how to pay for the DM 80,000 in damage they do to the buildings each year.

The American historian Gerhard Masur described the **Memorial Church** as 'one of the few buildings to be improved by the fall of bombs and the ravage of fire'. The original was a 19th-century neo-Gothic exercise in self-glorification and kitsch. Now, with just the nave and the crumbled remains of the tower remaining, it is strikingly powerful. Inside (open Tues–Sat 10–6, Sun 11–6, free) you get a good idea of the spirit of the original from the gold-inlaid mosaics on the ceiling celebrating military campaigns from the Crusades on. A photographic exhibition shows how the church was wrecked during the war and includes pictures of the destroyed tombs of the Kaisers.

Around the ruin are new church buildings, all unfortunate combinations of breeze blocks and bright blue stained glass. The bell tower is inaccessible apart from a Third World bookshop at its base; the chapel, with its glowing octagonal interior, looks more like something out of *Doctor Who* than a place of worship. At the back is a Samaritan-style crisis centre where down-and-outs can wash, eat and kip down for the night.

Head now for the Kurfürstendamm U-Bahn and then take a right onto West Berlin's main street.

If the size, scale and slight tackiness of the **Kurfürstendamm** remind you of the Champs Elysées in Paris, that is no accident. The boulevard was the brainchild of none other than Count Otto von Bismarck, the Iron Chancellor who unified Germany with Prussian severity in the 19th century. He fell in love with the Champs Elysées after Prussia beat France in the 1870–71 war and resolved to build a street like it back home.

A road, of sorts, had existed since the 16th century. The city's rulers, or Electors, gave it its name (Kurfürstendamm means Avenue of the Electors) and used it as a riding path to go hunting in the Grunewald forest. Bismarck, however, had grander plans. The new street was to be 3.8 km long and 53 m wide, with a tree-lined riding path down the middle and fine patrician houses along its route. 'The people of Berlin should be able to promenade in the open air in comfort... and the upper classes practise on their horses,' Bismarck's cabinet decreed in 1875. Dream, however, took some time to become reality and by the time the boulevard was finished, Bismarck was long dead.

The Ku'damm, like much of Berlin, had its heyday in the 1920s and 1930s, when American poet Thomas Wolfe described it as the largest coffee house in Europe. Streetcars whizzed along the grassy central reserve. New theatres and cabarets attracted full houses every night. The big, swish city had arrived where windmills once swayed over peaceful fields. Writers such as Robert Musil, Joseph Roth, Thomas Mann and the budding Hollywood film director Billy Wilder gathered in a cluster of cafés concentrated at the Memorial Church end of the street. This was where high society went on display, but not for long. In 1933 the Nazis broke up the artists' liberal haven and arrested, killed or expelled the Jews and left-wingers among them. Then in 1943 British bombs destroyed 80 per cent of the fine houses built only decades earlier.

147

After the war the Ku'damm made a remarkable recovery, mirroring the economic miracle in the rest of West Germany. Within 20 years smart new houses, shops and hotels made of steel and glass had replaced the fine patrician houses. Great shops of the pre-war period, such as Wertheim (previously on Leipziger Strasse) moved here and re-established themselves. Businesses, fashion stores and computer warehouses set up shop on the boulevard alongside cinemas, restaurants and souvenir stalls.

Berliners often complain about the Ku'damm's profusion of fast-food joints, neon signs and peep-shows. This is 'coca-colanization', they complain, 'hamburglary'. But to moan about over-commercialization is to miss the point. The Ku'damm is overtly, unashamedly commercial. That is its *raison d'être*. It is the shop window for Europe's powerhouse economy and looks like staying that way.

On the south side of the street is the **Wertheim department store**, *traditionally the smartest retail chain in Germany. Before the war there used to be jokes about Wertheim and its more down-market rival Hertie, founded by the Berlin Jewish businessman Hermann Tietz. Berliners used to say:* 'Bei Tietz bringt man nichts von Wert heim', *an untranslatable pun which can mean either 'At Tietz you find nothing of Wertheim's' or 'At Tietz you find nothing of any value'. An ironic postscript to the story is that now Hertie and Wertheim belong to the same concern. Take the second left down Meinekestrasse, which has some of the best surviving examples of turn-of-the-century town houses. Go round the block to the right on Lietzenburger Strasse, dotted with casinos and tacky restaurants, and then onto the elegant Fasanenstrasse. No. 25 is* **Villa Grisebach**, *a* Jugendstil *palace used for occasional exhibitions. Next door at no. 24 is the* **Käthe Kollwitz Museum**, *a moving celebration of one of Berlin's most remarkable artists (Wed–Mon, 11–6 adm).*

A socialist and feminist, Kollwitz produced woodcuts, drawings and sculptures reflecting her political commitment and bitter personal experience. Born in Königsberg (now Kaliningrad in the Soviet Union) in 1867, she studied in Berlin and married a doctor there. They had two sons of whom the younger, Peter, died on a battlefield in Flanders in the opening months of the First World War. When the Nazis came to power, she was forced to leave the Academy of Arts and give up teaching. Eventually she was banned from exhibiting. In 1943 she fled the US and

British bombing raids on Berlin and settled in the country near Dresden. She died in 1945, days before the end of the Second World War.

The museum is not Kollwitz's house, which was in Prenzlauer Berg in the East and destroyed during the war, but a privately run venture in a smart villa—slightly incongruous, perhaps, with her modest lifestyle and socialist ideals. The exhibition is spread over four small floors, starting with searing early woodcuts about hunger, disease and death, and following her artistic career towards more personal work, including some intensely sad self-portraits. Her studies of women, either together or with children, are particularly striking. The sculpture *Tower of Mothers* (1939) is an early example of 'women power' feminism.

*The next house, number 23, is a bookworm's paradise, the **Litera-turhaus Berlin**. It has a large bookshop and art gallery, and a peaceful winter garden for browsing, reading the newspapers and drinking coffee. Frequent literary events include visits by English-language authors. Return to the Ku'damm at the top of the street, cross over and continue up Fasanenstrasse towards the **Jewish Community Centre** (Jüdisches Gemeindehaus) at no. 79–80.*

This used to be the most impressive synagogue in town. Built in Byzantine style with three domes, it served a Charlottenburg Jewish community of over 20,000 in the 1920s. When the Nazis came to power it was an obvious target for anti-Semitic attacks. During the looting and destruction of Jewish property by Nazis on *Reichskristallnacht* (night of the broken glass) on 9 November 1938, the Fasanenstrasse synagogue was burned to the ground.

After the war, the site was turned into a community centre (closed Sat, the Jewish sabbath) serving a Berlin community of just over 6000. Surviving pieces of the old synagogue façade have been incorporated into the new building. Outside the centre is a modern bronze sculpture pleading for racial tolerance. The words on the scroll, from the book of Moses, read: 'Let there be one law for the people and for the foreigners among you.' Inside you can pick up information about the Jewish community including synagogue services and meetings. A kosher restaurant offers *gefilte* fish, chopped liver and other Ashkenazim specialities.

*Return to the Ku'damm, cross the road and walk down to the right. On the corner with Uhlandstrasse is a taste of old Berlin at the Möhring Café, and a French cultural centre, the **Maison de France**. It has original-language French films, occasional* *exhibitions and a café. Cross over to the central reserve just west of the Uhlandstrasse junction for one of the more intriguing modern additions to Berlin.*

The strange flashing lights are in fact a clock, called the **Mengenlehre Uhr,** or set theory clock. To tell the time, count the illuminated rectangles. Each light in the first row is equivalent to five hours. In the next row, one hour. A square in the long third row lights up every five minutes, with a red light every 15 minutes. Finally, each light in the bottom row represents one minute. Intrigued? Confused? Blame it all on a certain Dieter Binninger, a Heath Robinson-style inventor who built the clock in 1975. Beneath his invention is an address where you can get hold of your own miniature version to infuriate friends and neighbours at home.

The Ku'damm continues for about 2 km, featuring more shops, restaurants, fine houses and striking modern sculpture. At Rathenauplatz is Wolf Vostell's montage of two Cadillacs (real ones!) buried in concrete. Our walk, however, leaves the Ku'damm at Uhlandstr. Take the left-hand fork, Grolmanstrasse, up to Savignyplatz. There's nothing much around here in the way of sites or museums, but it is a glorious area for sitting in cafés and browsing in bookstores. Some of the most fertile streets include Knesebeckstrasse, Mommsenstrasse and Carmerstrasse. Consult the Shopping section (pp. 223–4) for more details.

Kantstrasse, the broad avenue cutting across Savignyplatz, is traditionally the place for cheap shopping in West Berlin. Packed with discount food and hi-fi stores, it was the first stop for thousands of Poles who flocked into the city after the opening of the Berlin Wall. Despite a tightening of visa restrictions they still come to stock up on consumer goods that they can then sell for hard currency back home. Berliners are less than charitable about the Poles' technique of arriving by the coachload, stripping the shelves bare in discount stores like Aldi and Pennymarkt, then disappearing again. The locals complain they can't get near their own shops any more. The street has acquired the nickname Warsaw Boulevard, and Aldi has been rechristened Poldi. Some shopkeepers have begun selling 'bring back the Berlin Wall' T-shirts. Others have smartly put out signs advertising *Piwo Zimne*, Polish for cool beer. The Germans have never liked the Poles much at the best of times. But these days bitterness is running alarmingly high.

*From Savignyplatz, walk along the peaceful, tree-lined Carmer-
strasse towards Steinplatz, a rather ordinary grassed-over square
which has turned into something of a shrine to the horrors of Berlin's
past.*

In the north-west corner is the **Memorial to the Victims of Stalinism**,
a simple tombstone-like piece which is West Berlin's answer to the
memorial to victims of Fascism on Unter den Linden in the East. The
Memorial to the Victims of National Socialism is on the north-east
side. The stone, embossed with the letters KZ (standing for *Kon-
zentrationslager*, or concentration camp) is a piece of the destroyed
synagogue on Fasanenstrasse (see above). The location of this simple but
effective memorial is extraordinarily unfortunate. Just to the left are the
offices of the German chemical giant Hoechst, which during the war was
part of the I.G. Farben group, producer of the Zyklon-B gas used at
Auschwitz.

*Opposite Steinplatz on Hardenbergstrasse is the elegant Hochschule
der Künste (Academy of Arts). The end of the walk, Ernst-Reuter-
Platz, is five minutes away to the left. Named after the first mayor of
West Berlin and hero of the 1948–49 Soviet blockade (see p. 115),
this busy traffic junction used to be known as the* Knie *(knee) because
of the way it broke the junction between Bismarckstrasse and
Hardenbergstrasse.*

Walk VIII

The Plötzensee Memorial and
Schloss Charlottenburg

Schloss Charlottenburg

*Moabit—Plötzensee Memorial—Schloss Charlottenburg—Egyptian
Museum—Bröhan Museum—Canal walk—Charlottenburg Gate*

This walk could be subtitled Beauty and the Beast. Schloss Charlottenburg is the finest building in West Berlin, a magnificently restored
rococo palace with expansive, much-loved gardens and a cluster of
museums boasting treasures spanning more than four millennia, including the celebrated bust of Nefertiti. Plötzensee, on the other hand, is
one of the most chilling memorials to the brutality of the Third Reich,
the place were hundreds of political prisoners were mercilessly slaugh-
tered between 1933 and 1945. Both are in the district of Charlottenburg,
and between the two you catch a flavour of the area's mixture of smart
town houses and elegant canals set against factories and modest residential streets.

Walking Time: The main sights take about 3 hours to cover, but on a
sunny day you may well be tempted to do as the Berliners frequently
do—spend a whole day idling in the Charlottenburg palace gardens and
museums (closed on Mondays except for the Egyptian Museum which is
closed on Fridays).

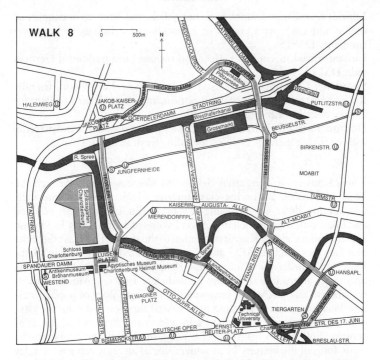

Start: The walk starts and finishes at Tiergarten S-Bahn station, a convenient vantage point for transport. The 23 bus leads from the S-Bahn to Plötzensee. From Charlottenburg you can either follow the canals back to the Tiergarten, or cut the walk short by taking the 9 or 54 bus towards Bahnhof Zoo. There is also a nearby U-Bahn station, Sophie-Charlottenplatz, 5 minutes' walk down Schlossstrasse. This route makes a good bicycle tour (see Travel section for hiring details); car drivers will find thinnish traffic in this part of town and reasonable parking.

LUNCH/CAFÉS

The Schloss gardens are perfect for picnicking—just as well, because cafés and restaurants are rather thin on the ground. There's nothing near Plötzensee, and such a spooky place does not make you feel like eating anyway. These are the best near Charlottenburg:

153

Lenné, Spandauer Damm 3–5. For salads and light main courses or coffee and cake, with copies of Expressionist paintings to keep you company. DM 15.

Luisenbräu, Luisenplatz 1. Beer and sausages in a traditional German pub. DM 15.

Samovar, Luisenplatz 3. Closed for lunch Nov–Feb. Good, friendly Russian restaurant with a seafood extravaganza called Tsar's Delight for parties of eight or more. DM 30–40.

Delfino, Kaiser-Friedrich-Str. 105. Fair Italian restaurant and pizzeria, with changing daily specialities including fresh seafood. DM 35.

☆ ☆ ☆ ☆ ☆

The 23 bus from Tiergarten S-Bahn to Plötzensee runs through the heart of Moabit, a working-class quarter which shows an unusually unassuming, down-to-earth side of West Berlin. Its streets are cobbled and filled with friendly neighbourhood shops of a kind sorely lacking on and around the glossy Kurfürstendamm to the south. This was where the first factories, such as AEG and Borsig, appeared during Berlin's late-flowering industrial revolution in the 1840s; the tenement blocks sprung up shortly afterwards. Berliners immediately associate Moabit with its courthouse and jail, which have entered the mythology of popular culture because so many working men passed through it during the dark days of poverty, unemployment and war in the first half of the 20th century. Folk heroes from Wilhelm Voigt, the out-of-work cobbler who made fools of the military by masquerading as an army captain for a day in 1906, to Franz Biberkopf, the fictional hero of Alfred Döblin's *Berlin Alexanderplatz*, did time in the redbrick prison on Turmstrasse (just off the bus route at Beusselstrasse). Since unification, insiders have tipped Moabit as the up-and-coming neighbourhood of Berlin. Unlike Kreuzberg it has stuck to its working-class origins and remains refreshingly unspoilt. At least for now.

The bus crosses a disused railway line and passes the Grossmarkt, *or wholesale food market, on the left. The Plötzensee stop is on Saatwinkler Damm and comes just after a busy junction above a motorway. Opposite the bus stop is a narrow cobbled road, Hüttigpfad. The memorial, which is signposted, is two minutes' walk on the left.*

Two stark, grey concrete pillars mark the entrance to the **Plötzensee Memorial** (Gedenkstätte Plötzensee, open 8–6 daily, slightly earlier closing in winter). It is flanked on both sides by the high brick walls of a juvenile detention centre that was once part of the prison. The surrounding area is filled with overgrown allotments and shabby houses. This is a cold, isolated part of Berlin, in keeping with the grisly events that took place here. After the concentration camps, perhaps nowhere witnessed greater Nazi brutality than Plötzensee prison. Thousands of political detainees raked up by the Gestapo were held here in constant fear of torture or death, many of them arrested at random or on the flimsiest of unsubstantiated accusations. More than 2000, some as young as 17 or 18, were executed by rope or guillotine. According to eyewitness reports, prisoners who fell ill would be ordered to squat for hours on a cold stone floor. When they begged for help, the guards would merely say: 'What's the difference? You're going to have your head chopped off anyway.' At the height of a Nazi crackdown on dissent in September 1943, 186 people were hanged in a single night. The bodies were taken to the city's Anatomical Institute where they were used for experiments in support of Nazi theories on racial supremacy. As Plötzensee's chaplain later testified at the Nuremberg trials, prison staff were so overwhelmed with corpses they could not transport them to the institute fast enough to keep up with the pace of executions, and left them piled up in an outhouse.

'The measures I take will not be inhibited by any legal considerations... My job is not to administer justice but only to destroy and exterminate, nothing more,' said Hermann Göring, who as Prussian Interior Minister began rounding up political prisoners at Plötzensee in 1933. The horror stories that leaked out from here and other similar jails terrorized the German people into submission during the Nazi period and encouraged many to turn informer rather than risk coming under suspicion themselves. Those who stuck to democratic principles did so at a terrible risk. Resistance figures, Roman Catholic priests, Social Democrats, even politicians who had served under the Nazis were all killed here. One detainee who had distributed transcripts of BBC news broadcasts in Hamburg, Helmuth Hübener, was just 17 when he died. After Stauffenberg's failed plot to overthrow Hitler in July 1944 (see p. 136), nearly 200 people connected with the conspiracy, however vaguely, were arrested and executed. Eighty-nine of them were brought to Plötzensee, where they were strung up with piano wire—a particularly slow form of execution. Hitler had the proceedings filmed so he could watch the deaths over and over again.

The memorial, erected in 1952, contains the squat brick building used for the executions. The forecourt has been paved over and redesigned to give the site the dignity of a cemetery. To one side is an urn filled with soil from several of the Nazi concentration camps. One wall of the execution building has been built up with heavy stones to resemble a mausoleum and bears the words: 'To the victims of Hitler's dictatorship in the years 1933–1945'. There are two exhibition rooms. Inside the execution chamber, usually filled with wreaths and flowers, you can still see the hooks where up to eight people were hanged at a time. Next door is a display of death warrants and legal documents, chilling for their bureaucratic perfunctoriness. There are printed cards inviting Nazi officials to attend an execution as a reward for good service. One reads: 'If you intend to be present, please arrive at Plötzensee Prison *at least* half an hour before the time stated (dark suit). I enclose an admission card. You are required to maintain the strictest *secrecy* concerning the impending execution. Should you not wish to make use of the admission card, kindly destroy it.' Another document details a judicial 'error' when the wrong Czechoslovak national was executed because he shared the same name as an intended victim. The prison official writing the report explains how he 'corrected' his mistake the next day by finding the right person and hanging him too.

The journey from here to Schloss Charlottenburg is, unavoidably, rather tricky. Turn left at the exit to the Memorial and continue along Hüttigpfad to the end of the road. Pick up the 23 bus again (westbound) just to the right of the junction with Friedrich-Olbricht-Damm. Get out five stops later, on Reichweindamm, and continue walking along the street which turns into a motorway slip-road (with a pavement) called Goerdeler Damm. About two minutes away down here to the right is Jakob-Kaiser-Platz, a major bus and U-Bahn as well as road junction. Get on the 9 or 62 bus (southbound), which will drop you four stops later at the junction of Otto-Suhr-Allee and Kaiser-Friedrich-Strasse, in front of the castle.

Schloss Charlottenburg was the first building of any noteworthy artistic merit in Berlin, and the city's architects have rarely bettered its cool symmetry and rococo elegance. The palace and gardens owe their existence to the fortuitous pairing of a man of means and a woman of taste—Elector Friedrich III (later King Friedrich I) and his wife, Queen Sophie Charlotte. Together, at the turn of the 18th century, they set out to give Berlin the cultural credentials it had lacked almost entirely in the first 500 years of its history. By the time Friedrich died in 1713, Berlin had become known as *der Spreeathen*, Athens on the Spree.

The royal pair could not have been more different. Friedrich loved spending money, especially on himself, but possessed almost no qualities as a statesman and based his artistic judgement solely on one criterion: the more, the better. In short, he was vain and rather stupid. A reluctant ruler living in the shadow of the Great Elector Friedrich Wilhelm, his immediate predecessor, he once said: 'I am only doing what my father began and wanted me to complete.' Such meekness did not prevent him risking the wrath of the Holy Roman Emperor and crowning himself King of Prussia in a lavish show of self-aggrandizement in 1701. Nor did it hold him back from spending the hard-won earnings of his father and starving the poorest of his subjects to death to satisfy his vain whims: with every new palace, thousands of peasants came flooding into the city holding up begging bowls.

Sophie Charlotte, on the other hand, was intelligent, cultured and much-loved by the people. The daughter of the Duke of Hannover, she spoke four languages, played the piano with great proficiency and had a passion for philosophy and the natural sciences. She was firm friends with the Enlightenment philosopher Gottfried Wilhelm von Leibniz and brought him to Berlin as president of the newly founded Academy of Sciences in 1700.

It was she who first conceived of Charlottenburg in 1695, as a refined country setting for intellectual discussion. Together with architect Johann Arnold Nering the Queen picked a site on the Spree near the village of Lietzow, 8 km outside the city walls. Friedrich merely consented to the idea and put up the money. The original building, completed in 1699 and known at first as Lietzowburg, comprised just the 11-window central section of the present-day palace with a small formal French garden behind. Sophie Charlotte spent six years holding impassioned debates with Leibniz at the new palace and inspired his most influential work, the *Théodicée* published in 1710. In 1705, at the age of just 36, she caught a throat infection and died. Perhaps nothing sums up her enthusiasm and spirit better than the note she wrote on her deathbed: 'I go now to satisfy my curiosity about the basic cause of things, which Leibniz was never able to explain to me, about space and the infinite, about being and nothingness; and for the King my husband I prepare the drama of a funeral, which will give him a new opportunity to demonstrate his magnificence.'

Sure enough, Friedrich mourned her in style, renaming the palace after her and commissioning a new architect, Eosander von Göthe, to build a west wing, the present Orangerie. But Berlin's cultural renaissance was over. Charlottenburg and other building projects, such as the Zeughaus, an original version of present-day Platz der Akademie and the now-destroyed Schloss Monbijou had bankrupted the kingdom. Leibniz suggested a state lottery to raise funds; Friedrich toyed with the notion of a silkworm farm. Both ideas came to nothing.

Work on Charlottenburg ground to a halt with the accession of Friedrich Wilhelm I, the dour 'soldier king', in 1713. Commissions for frescos and paintings were halted, walls were left semi-plastered and the garden was transformed into a cabbage patch. It was only some 30 years later, under Frederick the Great, that building resumed. Georg Wenzeslaus von Knobelsdorff's east wing was the most impressive architectural achievement of all, completing the palace's present-day long, sleek, cream-coloured façade. However Frederick's interest, too, quickly waned. In a somewhat backhanded compliment he called Charlottenburg 'the rendez-vous of people of taste', then promptly turned his attention to his new palace in Potsdam and never set foot there again.

Scores of artists and architects have worked on Charlottenburg since, including Carl Gotthard Langhans (the designer of the Brandenburg Gate), and the master builder of neo-classical Berlin, Karl Friedrich Schinkel, who respectively built the belvedere and mausoleum in the palace grounds. Two immediately striking features at the entrance are in fact recent additions, made during work to repair the damage of a wartime air raid.

The first, Andreas Schlüter's **Statue of the Great Elector** in the forecourt, used to stand on a bridge opposite the Kaiser's Palace (today's Rathausbrücke in East Berlin). It underwent a remarkable journey to its present site. The bronze statue spent the war years safely tucked away in Potsdam and should by rights have returned to East Berlin. But on its way back in 1945 it sank in the West's Tegeler See and was dredged up only seven years later. By then the Cold War was well under way and the West Berlin authorities decided to keep the statue for themselves. Sculpted over 10 years (1699–1709), it depicts a rather portly Friedrich Wilhelm on his horse. The allegorical reliefs and figures of four slaves in chains around the base are not by Schlüter but were added later. The second 'new' feature is the gold figure of the goddess of Fortune crowning the central tower. The original by Eosander did not survive the war; this version, based loosely on the original, dates from 1957. It turns in the wind like a weather vane.

The only way to see the central apartments is by guided tour in German beginning inside the main entrance (on the hour, Tues–Sun 9–5, adm). A separate entrance to the right leads to the Knobelsdorff Wing (adm) and the Galerie der Romantik (free) where visitors can roam alone. The garden can be reached by walking around the palace in either direction.

If the exterior design of Schloss Charlottenburg demonstrates Queen Sophie Charlotte's sure architectural eye, the **royal apartments** inside show only the wayward artistic sense of her husband. Full of family portraits, tapestry and furniture from the 17th century, they lack nothing for splendour but contain little outstanding work. The highlight, for its unashamed sumptuousness, is the porcelain cabinet which Friedrich had built after the death of his wife. It is crammed with painted vases and ornaments displayed against gold-inlaid walls. Mirrors make the room shimmer with opulent colours. The glass and porcelain dates from the last 40 years; the original pieces were smashed by Allied bombs in 1943.

More impressive is Knobelsdorff's **New Wing** (Neuer Flügel), including the architect's masterpiece, the Golden Gallery (Goldene Galerie). Unlike the porcelain cabinet, this broad, airy room is delightfully understated. It has no furniture, just a highly polished wooden floor and gold-embossed walls and ceiling which sparkle as the daylight streams in from both sides. The White Hall (Weisser Saal) is devoted to the rather precious 18th-century paintings of Antoine Watteau and his school for which Frederick the Great had a great fondness. One picture is a great work by any standard—Watteau's dreamy *Voyage à Cythère* (1720).

The best paintings of the collection, however, are downstairs in the **Galerie der Romantik**, which includes a stunning room devoted to the work of the master of German Romantic painting, Caspar David Friedrich (1774–1840). Friedrich's moody landscapes, making dramatic use of light and warm colours that seem to melt off the canvas, present an idealized view of nature which outraged his contemporaries. One critic called him 'irreligious' for presuming to improve on God's creation; another said he 'robbed landscapes of their real features'. Nowadays Friedrich's canvases, whether of mountains in the mist or sunrise over a field of grazing sheep, exude a mesmerizing, ethereal quality. The gallery also shows master architect Schinkel turning his hand to painting, with a series of idealized buildings depicted in perfect harmony with

159

Nefertiti

their natural surroundings; one might see these as an architecturally rigorous reworking of Claude Lorrain's 18th-century fantasy castles. Eduard Gärtner's faithful cityscapes of mid-19th century Berlin display a rather more down-to-earth approach to painting buildings, at the risk of seeming a little pedestrian. They show a scrubbed, symmetrical city with no hint of the seedy, run-down subculture that dominates the work of succeeding generations. Finally, one surprise to look out for in the corner of the Gärtner room is Jacques Louis David's impassioned portrait of Napoleon crossing the Alps (1800).

Immediately behind the Schloss is the formal French garden originally laid out for Queen Sophie Charlotte. However, the grounds extend way beyond into a carefully landscaped English park of curved lawns, large beds of flowers and shrubs, and a central artificial lake. If the sun is shining, the gardens are sure to be crowded—this is one of the city's most enchanting spots. On the other side of the Schloss, just across Spandauer Damm from the main entrance, is Charlottenburg's complex of four museums. The twin-domed neo-classical buildings on either side of the junction with Schlossstrasse, designed by Schinkel's pupil August Stüler, were originally the mess for officers in the garde du corps, the royal body guard. Now the one on the left is the Egyptian Museum, the one on the right the Museum of Antiquity. Between them in the middle of the street is a statue of Prince Albrecht, a hero of the 1870–71 Franco-Prussian War. The Bröhan Museum, an exhibition of Berlin Jugendstil and Art Deco, is tucked behind the Museum of Antiquity. Finally, just behind the Egyptian Museum on Wulf-heinstrasse is the Charlottenburg district museum.

The star of the **Egyptian Museum** (Ägyptisches Museum, open 9–5 except Fri, free) is a one-eyed beauty on the first floor called *Nefertiti*. Her bust has fascinated Berlin museum-goers ever since its discovery at Tell al-Amarna on the upper Nile in December 1912. The long neck, strong cheekbones and warm gaze are unparalleled in any other surviving work from ancient Egypt. Nefertiti was the wife of Akhenaton, who ruled Egypt from Amarna in the 14th century BC. The bust was used as a model by a contemporary sculptor called Tithmosis, who never painted in the left eye. When Ludwig Borchardt, a Berlin Egyptologist, came across Nefertiti on his third expedition to the area in 1912, she had been preserved deep in the sandy soil for 3000 years, intact apart from a slightly chipped ear. If he was excited by his good fortune, he certainly did not let on—possibly as a ploy to ensure he could take the bust back home with him. His report on the find, aside from one reference to 'the most lifelike of Egyptian artefacts', is remarkably dry and perfunctory.

The splendour of Nefertiti should not detract from the rest of the museum which boasts some exceptionally well-preserved and brightly painted busts, mummies and death masks going back to 5000 BC. Each work is dramatically exhibited by spotlight against a background of almost total darkness. A stern bald head in green stone dating from the early Ptolemaic period of 300 BC, known as the *Berlin Green Man*, is particularly powerful. On an altogether larger scale is the *Kalabsha Gate*, built for the Roman Emperor Augustus around 20 BC and depicting him in relief sculptures as a Pharaoh attending a sacrifice to the goddess Isis. Mysteriously, the gate was dismantled shortly after it was built and, but for the persistence of a few German archaeologists, it might never have been seen again. When Egypt decided to build the Aswan Dam in 1960, UNESCO managed to organize an international mission to dig up any valuable remains in the area first, on the understanding that each partici-pating country was entitled to anything it found. The Germans, who were responsible for Kalabsha, suffered a severe setback when the Nile rose and flooded the area in 1963. Four years later they were about to claim the excavated Gate when Cairo broke off diplomatic relations with

Bonn for its condemnation of the Six Day War against Israel. It was only grassroots contact between various scientists and archaeologists that kept the German claim alive. In 1973 President Sadat finally agreed to hand the Kalabsha Gate over. It took another five years to reassemble; some 80 per cent of the original had survived.

Berlin's Egyptian collection dates from the time of Friedrich I, but only got going in 1827 when Friedrich Wilhelm III bought several hundred pieces for his new Museum Island from a shady Triestine art dealer named Giuseppe Passalacqua. The booty retrieved by Carl Richard Lepsius (see Walk II) established Berlin as the greatest centre for Egyptian art in the Western world and began a Prussian craze for archaeological and ethnological expeditions to the four corners of the world. During the Second World War, the most prized pieces of the Egyptian collection were stashed in a bunker beneath Bahnhof Zoo for safekeeping, while much of the rest stayed in East Berlin. The pieces from the bunker form the basis of this museum. With the Cold War now over, the plan is to move everything back to a single location, probably the Neues Museum in East Berlin, by the year 2000.

The Museum of Antiquity opposite (Antikenmuseum, same hours, free) also has a well-preserved collection, this time of ancient Greek and Roman artefacts, beautifully presented in spacious, light rooms. The exhibition spans the Mediterranean from Sparta to Etruscan Italy. But there is nothing to match the scale or importance of the Egyptian Museum. The Bröhan Museum (Tues–Sun, 10–6, adm) next door has a rather more general appeal, offering a taste of drawing-room Berlin in the 1920s.

The cultural explosion that hit Berlin after the First World War was not confined to smoky jazz clubs and cabarets; it made its way into middle-class homes too. Even before the Bauhaus school revolutionized basic household items from chairs to cutlery, Berlin's porcelain, glass and furniture industries had shaken off the staid old styles and experimented with *Jugendstil* (literally, the style of youth) and Art Deco. The formal, simple lines of Biedermeier and the heavy ornateness of Wilhelmine styles were ditched in favour of freer-flowing shapes and designs. The first signs of this new movement came in the 1880s, when porcelain factories were struggling for survival in an economic depression affecting all of Europe. Berlin's state-owned Kaiserliche Porzellanmanufaktur (KPM for short, literally imperial porcelain manufacture), along with similar enterprises in Meissen and Nymphenburg, developed new burnishing and glazing techniques which put them in the forefront of their industry and heralded a new era in china production. KPM no longer relied on basic pre-prepared moulds; it could create any shape or pattern it wanted, from lattice work to petals to any kind of animal. The glass industry, mostly concentrated in France and the United States, underwent a similar revolution, extending the use of coloured glass further than in any previous era.

The museum is made up of a series of mock drawing rooms, or salons, displaying outstanding examples of these new production techniques. Each one is named after a leading designer or furniture manufacturer from the first 30 years of the 20th century, including Hector Guimard, Louis Majorelle and Edgar Brandt. Included in the museum's collection are some fine paintings by Expressionists Hans Baluschek and Willy Jaeckel, and a sensual burnished bronze sculpture by Jean Lambert-Rucki entitled *Der Kuss* (the kiss).

The last museum in the complex is the **Charlottenburg Heimat Museum** *(Charlottenburg district museum, open daily, free), which explains the development of the district in three small rooms through maps, photographs and scale models of key buildings such as the Kaiser Wilhelm Memorial Church (see Walk VII). It charts how a country village turned into a booming industrial and residential centre (the area's population increased tenfold to 300,000 in just 30 years at the turn of the 20th century).*

That concludes the tour of Schloss Charlottenburg and its museums; from here there are some wonderful **canal walks** *back towards the Tiergarten. Return to the palace entrance, then follow Spandauer Damm round to the right, then left into Luisenplatz towards an iron bridge across the Spree. Just before the bridge take the path to the right. This continues for about 2.5 km, along the banks of first the river and then the Landwehrkanal. To the right are well-to-do apartment blocks in quiet residential streets, while to the left across the water is the heart of Berlin's industry, including factories belonging to engineering giant Siemens and BMW. Between these two contrasting views are intelligently landscaped grassy verges, shrubs and trees. It sounds a strange mixture but it works. Towards the end of the walk to the right looms the glass and concrete of West Berlin's ultra-modern Technische Universität (Technical University, or TU), one of two main further education centres in the city (the other, the Freie Universität, Free University or FU, is in the* *south-western suburb of Dahlem). Shortly afterwards the path comes out on Strasse des 17. Juni, right by the* **Charlottenburg Gate** *(Charlottenburger Tor).*

This grand entrance to the district of Charlottenburg from the Tiergarten was built in 1905 to mark the 200th anniversary of Sophie Charlotte's death and the first mention of the area's modern name. Arched columns stand on either side of the road, flanked by statues of Friedrich I and his Queen. This is, however, a reduced version of the original gate. The pillars were thicker and grander until 1937, when Hitler broadened the avenue towards the Brandenburg Gate to make room for huge Nazi parades, changing its name from the Charlottenburger Chaussee to the Ost–West Axis. The current name, Strasse des 17. Juni, celebrates the spirit of the 1953 workers' uprising in East Berlin, which was put down by East German and Soviet soldiers.

The bright blue tank with pink tubing to the right has a surprisingly mundane function given its startling appearance. It is a hydraulics research centre belonging to the Technical University. From here you can return to Tiergarten S-Bahn along Strasse des 17. Juni, or head right down Müller-Breslau-Strasse and Fasanenstrasse towards Bahnhof Zoo and the Ku'damm.

Walk IX

Wannsee

Pfaueninsel

Wannsee—Kleist's grave—Kohlhasenbrück—Steinstücken—Schloss Babelsberg—Glienicker Bridge—Nikolskoe—Pfaueninsel—Wannsee Villa

Despite his many far-flung travels, the 19th-century Berlin explorer and adventurer Alexander von Humboldt always claimed that the view from the Glienicker Bridge across the Havel was one of the seven wonders of the world. The woods, lakes, fairy-tale castles and lovers' nests of the Wannsee area are indeed hauntingly beautiful, an idyllic hide-away on the edge of the big city.

But even this bejewelled corner of Berlin has its darker side. While summer sunsets over the Glienecker Bridge have inspired romantic dreams, swirling winter mists have made it the altogether more spooky scene of countless Cold War spy swaps. The Nazis chose the tranquility of the tall pines around the Wannsee Villa to plot the extermination of Europe's Jewry in 1942. And, more than a century earlier, the playwright Heinrich von Kleist sent a frisson of alarm through the souls of his contemporaries when he and his friend Henriette Vogel carried out a stunningly melodramatic double suicide at the lakeside.

Pick a clear day to appreciate the understated, limpid beauty of this area and bring a solid pair of walking shoes. During the Cold War this used to be the only bit of countryside West Berliners had easy access to.

The weekends are still very crowded, especially in the summer, but on weekdays you are left virtually alone.

Walking Time: This a long tour which requires some intelligent planning to cover in one day. The best way might be to take a boat round its main attractions. Pleasure craft leave from a mooring just by Wannsee S-Bahn station and there are stops at Kohlhasenbrück, Babelsberg, the Glienicker Bridge and Pfaueninsel. A day ticket costs DM 15 (April–November only, tel (W) 8100040). You can rent a bicycle at Grunewald S-Bahn station on your way down from the centre of town, or else rent a car for the day (see Travel section for details). This text gives details on how to reach sights by bus and on foot; however, not everything is equally accessible since transport is rural rather than metropolitan. Don't be too surprised if you can't quite see everything, especially if you idle in the sunshine over a picnic, or gaze lingeringly across the water at Pfaueninsel, or take a long walk in the woods.

Start: The walk starts and ends at Wannsee, terminus of the S-1 railway from Bahnhof Zoo and Alexanderplatz.

LUNCH/CAFÉS
Apart from obvious picnicking possibilities, this area is a mine of smart Sunday-lunchish restaurants, serving fresh game, meat and fish with salads and fine vegetables:
Blockhaus Nikolskoe, Nikolskoer Weg (closed Thurs). A log cabin that Friedrich Wilhelm III had built for his daughter. Delicious seasonal vegetables with large steaks and chops. DM 40.
Seehaase, Am Grossen Wannsee 58 (closed Thurs). Traditional German cooking with a terrace on a yacht harbour. DM 40.
Bolles Bootshaus, Am Grossen Wannsee 60 (closed Tues). A favourite with weekend sailors, serving French and German food. DM 35.
Café Schloss Glienicke, Königstr. The last stop before Potsdam, a crowded café with decent coffee and cakes.
Wirtshaus Pfaueninsel, Pfaueninselchaussee. An inn with a rambling terrace, usually full of ferry passengers going to and from Pfaueninsel.

☆   ☆   ☆   ☆   ☆

There are plenty of distractions on the way to Wannsee terminus (where our walk begins), should you find time for them, starting with the Grunewald forest. This vast forest was established in the Middle Ages to help drain the disease-ridden boggy landscape of the Havel and almost completely replanted with pines and other deciduous trees after the Second World War. The **Teufelsberg** *(devil's mountain) at the north end—most easily accessible by car or bicycle—was created out of wartime rubble and is popular for tobogganing in winter. If you have a car you will probably shoot down the* **Avus**, *which during the Cold War was the only stretch of road in West Berlin without a speed limit. Now there is talk of restricting cars to 100 kph, as in the rest of eastern Germany, but with traffic now vastly increased the issue is probably academic. From Nikolassee S-Bahn station you can take a special bus (E) to* **Wannsee beach** *(Strandbad Wannsee), a stretch of sand and shingle on the Havel. Just north of the beach is* **Schwanenwerder Island**, *an exclusive private estate connected by bridge to the mainland with, seemingly, at least one yacht and one Porsche per household. Back in the 1930s Goebbels and other senior Nazis cornered the island to build their*

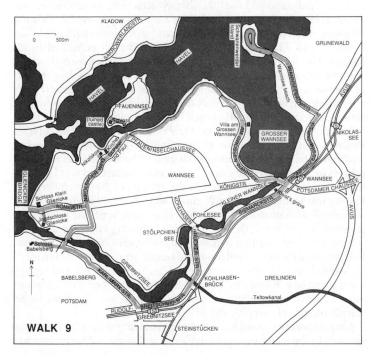

*private homes, since destroyed. From Wannsee S-Bahn you can take
cruises round the whole of the Havel, including Kladow (home to the
British armed forces in Berlin) and Spandau to the north.*

*For the first stop of the tour proper, turn left outside Wannsee
S-Bahn station and follow the railway tracks over Potsdamer
Chaussee and onto Bismarckstrasse. At house no. 3 on the right-
hand side is a narrow path leading downhill to the* **Kleistgrab***, the
grave of the great 19th-century playwright and short-story writer
Heinrich von Kleist.*

The reddish tombstone inscribed with Kleist's name, dates and a simple
quotation gives no indication that this was the site of one of the most
spectacular deaths in literary history. Born in 1777 into an aristocratic
Prussian soldiering family, Kleist had led a passionate life, travelling
around Europe in a tortured search for higher philosophical truths and
dreaming that he could rival the literary achievements of Goethe and
Schiller. His clutch of plays, including *The Broken Jug* and *The Prince of
Homburg*, received little acclaim at first, and short stories such as *Michael
Kohlhaas* and *The Marquise of O...* were not even published in his
lifetime. His work, shot through with a fatalistic irony, explores the chaos
of human life and the troubling complexity of accepted social tenets such
as honour and propriety. Kleist only received full recognition 50 years
after his death; while alive he was deemed dangerous or incomprehen-
sible. Friedrich Wilhelm III viewed him as a traitor, taking offence on
behalf of his army at scenes in *The Prince of Homburg* that depict a
Prussian officer hallucinating and fainting. By 1811 Kleist was an im-
poverished failure in the depths of despair. 'I have thrown everything I
possess into the great dice game ... and must understand that I lost,' he
wrote in one of his last poems. On the evening of 20 November 1811
Kleist came to this spot by the Wannsee with his friend Henriette Vogel,
a married woman dying of cancer. They took separate rooms at a
guesthouse and spent the night talking, drinking coffee and writing
letters. The next morning they ate breakfast quite normally. The land-
lord later said they displayed no sign of fear or depression and even joked
and fooled around in the courtyard. They paid their bill and walked
towards the lake. Kleist shot Vogel in the breast and then blew his brains
out. 'The truth is, nothing on earth could help me,' he wrote in his
suicide papers. He was 34, she 31.

Contemporaries found Kleist's death as baffling as his life. They were
shocked by the macabre double suicide, scandalized that his partner was

a woman married to someone else, and troubled by the calculation of their actions. But death brought Kleist fame, recognition and the sometimes wayward admiration of Romantic poets. Friedrich de la Motte Fouqué called Kleist's death 'one of the most marvellous suicides of all time'. In 1861 a plain marker at the grave was replaced by a white marble slab with a tribute by Jewish author Max Ring: 'He lived, sang and suffered in dark and difficult times. He sought death here but found immortality.' The Nazis saw fit to remove such a 'non-Aryan' memorial and replaced it in 1936 with the present-day stone. Vogel appears not to warrant a mention. The quotation is from *The Prince of Homburg: 'Nun, O Unsterblichkeit, bist Du ganz mein!'* (Now, oh immortality, you are wholly mine!).

It is a dark, eerily atmospheric 2-km walk beneath the pine trees to **Kohlhasenbrück**, *following the bank of the lake which starts out as Kleiner Wannsee, then changes its name to Pohlesee and Stölpchensee. You might prefer to save your energy and take the 18 bus, which leaves from the corner of Bismarckstrasse and Königstrasse. Kohlhasenbrück is not so much a sight as a starting point for walks along the shady Griebnitzsee (towards Babelsberg) or the Teltowkanal (towards Dreilinden). But the affluent residential village, its harbour packed with weekend yachts, gained its name from an incident in one of the most potent legends in German history recounted by Kleist in his novella* Michael Kohlhaas.

Kohlhaas was a hotheaded, high-principled 16th-century Berlin horse dealer cheated out of his two best animals by a Saxon *Junker* (aristocrat) who had offered his 'protection'. Infuriated by the Junker's abuse of his social position, Kohlhaas first appealed unsuccessfully to the Elector of Saxony and then, realizing that the only justice he would get was his own, plotted his revenge. He organized raiding parties on the Junker's castle and chased him to Wittenberg, Luther's home city, which he half burned to the ground. The Elector of Saxony persuaded Luther to intervene, and a deal was struck: if Kohlhaas returned home quietly he would get his horses back and the episode would be forgotten. Kohlhaas went meekly on his way but never saw the horses. In redoubled rage, he ambushed a wagon-load of gold bullion belonging to the Elector of Saxony and sank the lot under a bridge south-west of Berlin—later named Kohlhasenbrück after him. Once again he was assured he would get his horses back. But when Kohlhaas returned to Berlin he walked into a trap and was publicly executed.

This tale about the meaning of justice was a natural for Kleist, but it is also telling about the nature of German society. Conviction of mind and independence of spirit were always troubling personal qualities, especially in the rigid order of royal Prussia. The strictness of the kings and the cowed obedience of their subjects often made the nation as a whole blind to its own corruption and injustice, a failing that had reverberations long after the demise of the house of Hohenzollern in 1918. In smug modern Germany, the passionate rebel is still a figure that both fascinates and disturbs.

Continue south on the 18 bus (from anywhere on Kohlhasenbrücker Strasse). The road suddenly turns into a dual carriageway with wide, empty fields on either side. Then, just as suddenly, the road narrows as it enters a hamlet, the speed limit falls to 20 kph, and the bus reaches a dead end. All around are more empty fields. Until the opening of the Wall this was one of the world's strangest villages, **Steinstücken**.

Steinstücken was a piece of Berlin that went astray and nearly came unstuck. Although incorporated into Greater Berlin in 1920, it was 500 m outside the city boundary. What started as a bureaucratic anomaly turned into a raging argument after the Second World War between the US occupying forces in West Berlin and the Soviet army in surrounding East Germany. Steinstücken was just a sleepy village of no strategic importance, but also an irritating mini-enclave that both sides in the Cold War could have done without. In 1951, in a test of US will, the East Germans tried to claim it for themselves, blocking the approach road and banning Westerners from going there unless they could prove they were residents. The Americans responded with a mini-airlift of supplies by helicopter and even considered reopening the road by force. But the stakes were too high and they backed down. When the Berlin Wall went up a decade later, it shrouded Steinstücken in concrete on all sides. After protracted negotiations the approach road was reopened but the special travel restrictions remained in force until the normalization of German–German relations in 1972. Residents will still tell you of the uncertainty and maddening claustrophobia of the Cold War period. Slabs of concrete from the Wall still lie in the surrounding fields waiting to be taken away.

The next destination, Schloss Babelsberg, is outside the Berlin city boundary and not linked to Steinstücken by public transport. By car, heading back from Steinstücken to Kohlhasenbrück, turn left onto Rudolf-Breitscheid-Strasse and then take the first right onto Karl-Marx-Strasse which leads to Babelsberg park (about 2 km). Without a car, the best way to proceed is to take the 18 bus back to Kohl-hasenbrück ferry port and cruise round. Otherwise you can walk it, or ditch Babelsberg for now and approach it from the other side later.

But above all don't give up. **Schloss Babelsberg** is the least visited, most unspoilt sight on this tour, a neglected jewel. Its glorious forest and informal garden are on a hill overlooking the Havel with views of Potsdam, Schloss Klein Glienicke and the Glienicker Bridge. The castle itself is an extravagant folly in English neo-Gothic style, with slitted windows, turrets and crenellated parapets. The site was developed by garden architects Peter Josef Lenné and Fürst Pückler-Muskau in 1833–35 for Prince Wilhelm, later Kaiser Wilhelm I, who used the castle as his summer residence. Inside there is an eminently missable prehistory museum (open Tues–Sun 9–5, summer only, adm). Nature is the real attraction here—a thriving, ever-colourful forest of beeches, oaks, birches, poplars, maples and alders which gradually thins and gives way to a rolling grassy descent towards the waterfront of the Havel. The lakeside marks the old border. One reason why the park is so unspoilt is that all easy approaches from West Berlin were sealed with thick wire fencing on the shore and patrolled by armed guards on riverboats.

The car park and ferry port are by the Griebnitzsee at the north-east corner of the park. Cross the water on the narrow wooden bridge and follow the road up the hill to the right. Königstrasse, the main thoroughfare from Wannsee to Potsdam, is 10 minutes away on foot. Turn left, and another 10 minutes away is the **Glienicker Bridge** *(Glienicker Brücke).*

On a misty February morning in 1962, two stretched limousines drew up nose to nose on the Glienicker Bridge. One bore the US flag and State Department insignia, the other had Soviet army plates. A group of men got out of each car, their breath condensing in the cold air. They shook hands, exchanged what looked like one prisoner for another, returned to their cars and drove back where they had come from. This was the first East–West spy swap after the building of the Berlin Wall. Gary Powers, who had been shot down over the Soviet Union in a U-2 spy plane, was handed over in exchange for suspected Soviet agent Rudolf Ivanovich Abel. In the following years the Glienicker Bridge became a familiar backdrop for such swaps, both in reality and in countless thriller novels and films. The prominent Soviet Jewish dissident Natan Scharansky arrived in the West after his release from jail in 1986 at this crossing between West Berlin and Potsdam.

The bridge had acted as a barrier to eastbound traffic before. In the 1730s, the soldier-king Friedrich Wilhelm I posted guards here to stop his Potsdam conscripts escaping to Berlin; the Prussian capital itself had such an appalling record of desertion that he had had to make the city exempt from military service. (In a curious repetition of history, West Berliners were again exempted from military service during the Cold War, to draw young people to the enclave city.) The Soviet Red Army blew up the bridge in 1945 as its forces closed in on the city at the end of the Second World War. The East Germans rebuilt it and, in another twist of historical irony, renamed it the Bridge of Unity (Brücke der Einheit).

Nowadays the iron bridge almost looks like a landscaped part of **Schloss Klein Glienicke**, *the villa on the north side of König-strasse whose gardens stretch all the way to the waterfront. The entrance to the Schloss is five minutes' walk to the east.*

This graceful ensemble of perfectly manicured lawns and eccentric classical follies was designed in the early 19th century as an oasis of enchantment for aristocrats who had come to hunt in the forest. Harden-berg, the Prussian Chancellor, had begun work on the site when Prince Karl August bought it in 1822. Lenné and Pückler-Muskau developed the garden, while Karl Friedrich Schinkel was responsible for the mock Greek ruins, pergolas, temples and gilded unicorns. This kitschy mish-mash of styles was intended to ape the summer villas of Renaissance Italy. For instance, the fountain near the entrance, which depicts golden lions on high white pillars spewing water into a shallow basin while their front paws rest on ornamental balls, is a copy from the Villa Medici in Rome. But once again nature proves more alluring than the artifices of Prussia's most celebrated architects. A sunset glinting over the water and through the trees is simply in a different league from a hundred mock pieces from the Temple of Poseidon at Sounion sitting in the middle of the lawn. The squat sandstone Schloss itself is now a sanatorium.

The **hunting lodge** *(Jagdschloss Glienicke) on the other side of Königstrasse is a rambling summer house begun in the 17th century but extensively rebuilt 200 years later. Used for conferences, it is*

172

closed to the public and only just visible from the wire fencing at the road. Walk back east to the junction with Nikolskoer Weg, a narrow lane through the forest plied by the 66 bus. Three stops along is the **Nikolskoe**.

Get in the mood for love because this corner of Berlin is where the Prussian aristocracy used to indulge its softer side. The Nikolskoe is a log cabin which Friedrich Wilhelm III had built in six weeks flat in 1819 as a lovers' retreat for his daughter Charlotte and her fiancé, Crown Prince Nicholas of Russia (later Tsar Nicholas I). The dacha-like building was in fact a little piece of one-upmanship, an attempt by Friedrich Wilhelm to outdesign a similar log cabin where he had been entertained by the Russian royal family near St Petersburg. The Nikolskoe burned down in 1984, as log cabins are apt to, but has been rebuilt and is a popular restaurant (see lunch listing).

Just behind the Nikolskoe, and continuing the Russian theme, is the **Church of Peter and Paul** (Kirche St. Peter und Paul). This was an 1834 design by August Stüler, who in a tip of the hat to the Russian Orthodox Church endowed the plain red-brick building with onion domes and a narrow tower. Every hour the bells ring out the tunes of familiar hymns. The mosaics of St Peter and St Paul at the chancel were a gift from Pope Clement XIII to Frederick the Great.

From here it is a short walk along the bus route to the landing point for ferries to Pfaueninsel. Boats run regularly during daylight hours, cost DM 4 per person, and take about two minutes to cross the water.

Perhaps nobody has captured the magic of **Pfaueninsel** (peacock island) as well as the 19th-century novelist Theodor Fontane, who in a book of walks around Berlin enthused:

A picture from childhood comes to me like a fairy tale: a castle, palm trees and kangaroos; parrots squawking; peacocks idling on high branches or displaying their feathers; aviaries, fountains, shadows over the meadows; winding paths that lead everywhere and nowhere; an island full of riddles, an oasis, a carpet of flowers.

Little has changed since Fontane's day, although the kangaroos have been packed off to the zoo and the palm trees have never quite been the same since their glasshouse burned down in 1880. Pfaueninsel is a 1-sq km nature reserve for all manner of beasts, trees and plants, virtually untouched by the 20th century. No cars, no restaurants. Picnicking is forbidden, as is treading on the grass (except on one specially designated *Liegewiese*, or lying area).

Friedrich Wilhelm II bought the island, previously used for cattle and sheep grazing, from a Potsdam orphanage in 1793 as a hideaway for himself and his mistress Wilhelmine von Encke, the daughter of a trumpeter, whom he elevated to the title of Countess Lichtenau. He barely had time to enjoy this retreat before his sudden death two years later (he was knocked out by a flying champagne cork and never recovered). His son and successor Friedrich Wilhelm III took care of Pfaueninsel, overseeing the building of its many follies and hidden niches and populating it with wild animals and birds, including at one point lions, bears, buffalo and llamas. A local carpenter made the **ruined castle** at the western end of the island—a fragment of mock English Gothic with bright white brick turrets and a gate with portcullis. Inside (open Tues–Sun 10–5, summer only) is a very narrow room stuffed with Biedermeier furniture on a sparklingly polished wooden floor.

Prince Wilhelm, later to become something of a peacock himself as Kaiser Wilhelm I of a united Germany, hid on Pfaueninsel during the 1848 revolution before fleeing to England. In 1924 the island was declared a special protection area. The only person to flout that ruling has been the Nazi Propaganda Minister Joseph Goebbels, who threw a huge party here during the 1936 Berlin Olympic Games.

Back at the landing stage on the mainland, the 66 bus continues all the way to Wannsee S-Bahn station through the woods. Alternatively, you can go on a magnificent walk around the shore of the Havel and the Grosser Wannsee (allow an hour and a half), which joins up with the no. 3 bus on the road Am Grossen Wannsee. (The 3 goes to Wannsee S-Bahn station.) This corner of the forest is worth visiting for its lakeside restaurants (see listing, p. 166), and to see the building in which the Final Solution was conceived, the **Villa am Grossen Wannsee** *(house no. 56–58).*

The Nazis convened the secret Wannsee Conference on 20 January 1942 to draw up plans for the Holocaust. The gathering, chaired by the ruthless head of the security service Reinhard Heydrich, did not have to discuss the establishment of concentration camps—these had existed since the previous year. Instead the Wannsee Conference was about turning the camps into mercilessly efficient killing machines through slave labour, torture and gas chambers. The minutes of the meeting make hair-raising reading, not least for their sinister avoidance of any 'unpleasant' word or phrase. The language is cold, calculating and bureaucratic. Instead of using terms like 'killing' or 'gassing', the report talks of 'evacuation' and 'treatment'. The phrase 'Final Solution' (Endlösung) is surely one of the most chilling euphemisms in history.

The building, then known as Villa Minoux, was the German head-quarters of Interpol, a grey administrative building chosen for its seclusion. After the war it became a school for problem children (it is marked on maps as Jugenderholungsheim). There is talk of turning it into a museum, but the prospect seems a distant one. Sensitivities naturally run extremely high. When a plaque displayed on the front gate was daubed with neo-Nazi slogans in the early 1980s, the city authorities removed it and put up a new one on the façade of the building itself, out of reach (and out of sight) of the passing visitor.

Additional Sights

Wrought-iron work, Sanssouci, Potsdam

Dahlem Museums—Brücke Museum—Weissensee Jewish Cemetery—former Stasi headquarters—Potsdam

A few major sights did not fit into the Walks but it would be a shame to miss them. The Dahlem museum complex in the West displays the astonishing range and depth of Berlin's artistic wealth, with a dazzling array of Dutch and Italian Renaissance artists in its picture gallery. The Brücke museum is an out-of-the-way jewel on the edge of the Grunewald forest devoted to the leading exponents of German Expressionist painting. In the East, the Weissensee Cemetery is the largest Jewish burial ground in Europe and a poignant memorial to the fate of Germany's Jews. The sprawling former headquarters of the Stasi security police provides a unique glimpse into the paranoia and random cruelty of the East German Communist system. Finally Potsdam—a city in its own right just outside Berlin—features Frederick the Great's pleasure palace, Sanssouci, and the mock-tudor Cecilienhof mansion where Stalin, Truman and Churchill sealed the fate of post-war Germany in 1945.

The Dahlem Museums

The easiest way to reach the museums is to take U-Bahn line 2 to Dahlem-Dorf, then follow the signposts (about 5 minutes on foot).

The main entrance is at Arnimallee 23. The museums are open Tues–Fri 9–5 and Sat–Sun 10–5, tel (W) 83011. Admission is free.

The reason why such a stunning collection of painting, sculpture and popular art from around the world—the very cream of Berlin's collections—ended up in an unassuming leafy suburb is, like most stories about this city, a tale of Prussian opportunism, foreign intervention and Cold War one-upmanship. Down the centuries Berlin's ruling Hohenzollern family was notoriously bad at recognizing a good painting when it saw one. Thanks to the Great Elector's marriage to Princess Dorothea of Orange, however, the state inherited a rich chunk of Dutch and Flemish art including the work of Bruegel, van Eyck and Rembrandt. Further good fortune followed in the 1820s when a collection of some 3000 Italian masters fell into the lap of the state. Their owner, an English dealer called Edward Solly, had fallen on hard times and was forced to sell to pay off his debts. In the mid-19th century the Prussian aristocracy became more discerning and dispatched archaeologists and ethnologists to the further reaches of Europe's imperial territories, and they returned with treasures of all kinds from the Middle East, the Indian subcontinent and the South Seas.

Until the Second World War these treasures were dispersed in several museums, palaces and private collections, many of them in what is now East Berlin. When British and US bombing raids on the city began in earnest in 1943, the best pieces were whisked off to the disused saltmines of Thuringia in central Germany, while others either stayed put or were stored in bunkers beneath Bahnhof Zoo. When US ground forces occupied Thuringia in 1945, they exhumed everything and sent it home to the National Gallery in Washington DC. The decision proved a far-sighted one. Both East Berlin and Thuringia fell into the Soviet occupation zone. After Germany formally divided into separate states in 1949, the East found that much of its cultural heritage had slipped away.

The Dahlem Museums and the adjacent Free University were built in a bomb-strafed residential area in the early 1960s in an overt bid to rival East Berlin's Museum Island and Humboldt University. The gleaming complex of glass and concrete is constructed around a somewhat bald neo-classical façade (the main entrance on Arnimallee) which had been designed in the early years of the 20th century to house an Asiatic museum.

177

The highlight of the museums, the **Gemäldegalerie** (picture gallery), is something of a greatest hits of European painting. Its medieval religious art includes a series of 13th-century German triptychs depicting scenes from the life of Christ, and Jan van Eyck's early 15th-century *Madonna in a Church* showing a towering golden-tressed Virgin cloaked in red and black in front of the polished wooden carvings of a romanesque cathedral. Dutch secular work includes Holbein the Younger's 1532 portrait of the sour-faced merchant *Georg Gisze* surrounded by his money, weighing scales, papers and correspondence. There is a wonderfully playful fantasy by Cranach the Elder of a *Fountain of Youth* (1546), where old women become rejuvenated under the watchful eye of countless male attendants, and the similarly tongue-in-cheek *Dutch Sayings* (1559) by Pieter Bruegel the Elder, a picture of a village composed around popular expressions. You don't need to be conversant with the 16th-century Dutch equivalent of 'a bird in the hand is worth two in the bush' to appreciate the chaotic scenes of pies on roofs and wild animals roaming the streets. Later Dutch painting includes Ruisdael, Rubens, Frans Hals, Rembrandt (a dramatic picture of Moses breaking the tablets from 1659) and Vermeer (with a delicate study of newly-weds centring on a fragile-looking *Glass of Wine*).

The Italian collection is no less stunning. There is a serenely beautiful *Mary Honouring her Child* by Filippo Lippi, and a Botticelli portrait of a throned Madonna and child with the two Johns—a wild, tousled Baptist and a learned, white-haired Evangelist. The list of great artists goes on: Raphael, Titian with a *Reclining Venus*, a Canaletto view of the *Campo di Rialto* in Venice, and Caravaggio's *Love as Victor*, depicting a cherubic Eros clambering over the spoils of war.

The 18th-century rooms include works by Watteau, Gainsborough and Boucher, whose sensual depictions of creamy-skinned women and fine landscapes were much admired by Frederick the Great; and a more violent and dramatic Tiepolo of St Agatha being dragged to her martyrdom.

The **Kupferstichkabinett** (collection of drawings, sketches, etchings and engravings) offers an equally broad sweep through European civilization. Dürer, already represented in the picture gallery with a striking portrait of Hieronymus Holzschuher, is at his most personal in his charcoal drawing of *The Mother of the Artist*. Bruegel also reappears with a line drawing of bee-keepers, whose wicker face-masks make them look like walking treetrunks. There is a Botticelli illustration of Dante and Virgil walking round the distorted bodies of the flatterers and seducers in the Inferno, and a Michelangelo brown crayon sketch of a Madonna and child drawn with characteristically easy warmth and simplicity. There are exquisite portrait sketches by Rubens and Rembrandt, experiments with light and human forms by Goya and, bringing the collection into the 20th century, some sketches by Kandinsky and Picasso and a powerful woodcut by Otto Dix of a beggar selling matchboxes on the street.

The German contribution to the collections, so far rather thin, comes to the fore in the **Skulpturengalerie** (Sculpture Gallery). The highlight is the *Four Evangelists* by the 15th-century Würzburg master Tilman Riemenschneider. The warm reddish limewood gives a very human insight into the Apostles' struggle to write the Gospels, which lie unfinished before them. Later German sculpture verges on kitsch—yards and yards of poor imitations of High Renaissance art.

The next three collections, the **Museum für Indische Kunst**, the **Museum für Islamische Kunst** and the **Museum für Ostasiatische Kunst** (Museums of Indian, Islamic and East Asian Art), transport the visitor to a completely different world. These are an extension of similar collections in the Bodemuseum on Museum Island (see Walk II). Ordered according to religion, they could do with some background explanation for the uninitiated, but nonetheless contain some striking individual pieces. The Indian section is full of magical scenes from mythology featuring multi-headed gods, sparkling rivers and brightly coloured animals. The Islamic section has some stunningly intricate Persian carpets with animals and abstract symbols emblazoned in flaming reds, yellows and golds, and some wonderful carved wooden candlesticks and boxes. The East Asian collection is the tamest but has some fine woodcuts of woodland and mountain scenery.

The final section in the Dahlem complex, the **Museum für Völkerkunde** (Ethnological Museum), is much loved locally for its bizarre, ingenious, even horrific artefacts from around the world. From Africa there are carved figures of gods and grimacing painted masks to ward off evil spirits. The American department includes Aztec stone figures and some brightly coloured Brazilian ceremonial dancing hats made from parrot and kingfisher feathers. The exhibits from the South Seas are probably the most impressive, including a giant hall filled with wooden boats and ships from the Pacific islands adorned with carved animals and other symbols for good luck. Masks from Papua New Guinea depict human faces made entirely out of sea-shells or entwined reeds.

179

A good complement to the Dahlem Museums are the nearby **Botanical Gardens**, *which you can reach on foot in 10 minutes by walking east along Arnimallee until it broadens into Königin-Luise-Strasse. The entrance is a little further on the right at no. 6–8 (open 9–dusk daily, adm).*

Covering some 42 hectares, the gardens are set in a vast park with thousands upon thousands of tidily arranged and clearly marked tree and plant types. The tropical glasshouses, the largest of which is the size of an aircraft hangar, contain ferns, cacti, palm trees, orchids and a panoply of exotic plants for every season. Near the entrance is a rather academic **Botanical Museum** (Botanisches Museum, Tues–Sat 10–5, free), most popular with students for its 60,000-book library.

The Brücke Museum

The Brücke Museum is in a magical isolated corner of the Grunewald forest which amply rewards the effort of getting there. The 50 bus passes nearby on Clayallee (ask for the Pücklerstrasse stop). You can take the 50 northwards from U-Bahn station Oskar-Helene-Heim (two stops after Dahlem-Dorf on line 2) or southwards from Spichernstrasse U-Bahn station near the Ku'Damm (on lines 2 and 9). From the Clayallee bus stop walk west down Pücklerstrasse into the Grunewald forest, then take the first left, Fohlenweg. The first right after that is Bussardsteig, a wooded cul-de-sac which houses the museum (open Wed–Mon 11–5, adm).

The Brücke school was the founding movement of Expressionism, perhaps the most original development in German art and a lasting influence on 20th-century painting. *Die Brücke* means bridge: the Dresden artists who founded the group in 1905 intended the name to symbolize a crossing from old realist styles to freer, more abstract techniques. At first they lived and worked communally, exploring a variety of artistic possibilities. The members who gave the movement its individual stamp, such as Emil Nolde and Ludwig Kirchner, joined later, moving the school to Berlin where it developed alongside the *Blaue Reiter* movement from Munich. Expressionism is essentially a cry of anguish on canvas, a stark revelation of emotion employing warped shapes and graphic, gaudy, disturbing colours. The label first appeared in 1913—shortly before the Brücke artists split up as a formal group—in the art journal *Der Sturm*. An article contrasted the external observations of Impressionism with the internal preoccupations of the new style.

The influence of Post-Impressionists is evident in the earlier pieces in this collection: Cézanne's use of line and colour in Otto Müller's *Two Girls Bathing*, or Van Gogh's bold brushstrokes in Erich Heckel's contemplative portrait, *Man in his Younger Years*. But the originality of the movement is soon evident in Nolde's blotchy-faced *Holiday Guests* (1911), whose lazy picnic is overshadowed by a claustrophobic green background; or in Kirchner's study of snooty plumed ladies and blue-coated gentlemen in *Berlin Street Scene* (1913).

A handful of the pictures in this compelling museum are the work of its founder, Brücke member Karl Schmidt-Rottluff. He donated 74 paintings from his private collection, oversaw construction of the building (completed in 1967 when Schmidt-Rottluff was 83) and helped organize a city-wide lottery for funds to wrest some 70 paintings from private collectors. Particularly striking are his portrait of a determined *Rosa Schapire* (1911), and his bleak study of workmen hanging about on a day off, *Fischersonntag* (1923).

Weissensee Jewish Cemetery

A change of scene to quite the other side of town: catch the S-Bahn to Ernst-Thälmann-Park in East Berlin, then take the 28 tram three stops north on Greifswalder Strasse (you can also hop on the 28 at its terminus on Oranienburger Strasse near Marx-Engels-Platz S-Bahn). Walk one block further and turn right on Herbert-Baum-Strasse. The cemetery entrance is at the end of the street (open with seasonal variations Sun–Fri 8–4; men should wear a hat or borrow a skullcap from the caretaker).

After all the horrors the Jews suffered in Berlin, it is perhaps fitting that there is one memorial to them in the city that exudes perfect peace. This 40-hectare park of rambling paths and large oak and beech trees contains some 115,000 graves, from simple slabs of stone to mausoleums for several generations of a single family. The memory of the Holocaust is of course very strong—one only needs to examine the graves to see how many people, and particularly young people, died between 1933 and 1945, and to appreciate how many families were torn apart, some going into exile while others, especially the elderly, stayed behind to witness the destruction of their community. But there is an uplifting feel to the place, a sense that even the most tortured souls can find rest.

The tone is set at the entrance. A memorial temple in pale brick has the pure, clean lines of Italian Renaissance architecture. Something of the peace (and certainly the design) of Brunelleschi's cloister in Santa Croce in Florence is evoked. In the forecourt stands a simple, sober memorial stone 'dedicated to the memory of our murdered brothers and sisters of 1933–1945, and to the living who should fulfil the legacy of the dead'.

The cemetery was founded in 1880 and quickly filled with the dead of working and lower-middle class families. Traditionally, more eminent Jews were buried in the smaller cemetery on Schönhauser Allee (see Walk III). The few celebrities to be found here include the 19th-century painter Lesser Ury; Emil Rathenau, the founder of AEG; and Hermann Tietz, the father of the German department store. But the Weissensee cemetery's most fêted name is Herbert Baum, a Jewish resistance fighter who stayed in the city throughout the early years of the Second World War. In 1942 he organized an arson attack on an exhibition of anti-Soviet propaganda in the Lustgarten. Baum was tortured and killed in custody a month later, while his friends were sentenced to death and hanged. Largely because of Baum's left-wing credentials, the East German Communists always took reasonably good care of Weissensee. It became somewhat neglected in the 1980s for lack of funds, but since unification German government funds have helped to spruce it up again.

The Former Stasi Headquarters

Time was when you wouldn't have wanted to go near this sprawling concrete palace, where tens of thousands of East German security police agents operated spy networks to keep tabs on the population and meticulously logged their findings in miles and miles of archives. Now it has a unique, almost morbid fascination—well worth the trip to the dingier suburbs of East Berlin.

> *From Alexanderplatz, take the Hönow U-Bahn seven stops to Magdalenenstrasse. Head west on Frankfurter Allee and take the first right onto Ruschestrasse. The entrance to the Stasi headquarters is on the right. Check with the tourist office (tel (W) 2626031) for opening times of the exhibition rooms—once the offices and private apartments of Stasi chief Erich Mielke—which opened in November 1990.*

If you've ever sought a real-life model for the Ministry of Love in Orwell's *1984*, this is surely it. Faceless grey office blocks seem to stretch for hundreds of metres in each direction. The State Security Ministry (Ministerium für Staatsicherheit), or Stasi, was the 'Sword and Shield' of the East German Communist system, the glue that held the precarious mess together for 40 years. Its 85,000 full-time staff worked or took their orders from here, systematically opening mail, eavesdropping on telephone calls, recording, filming, burgling and blackmailing in a frenzied hunt for enemies of the Communist Party. Suspects were rated in a 101-point personality profile including assessments of body language and sexual tastes. The ministry also built up and controlled a network of at least 100,000 part-time informers who sneaked on their workmates and friends and betrayed their families, creating a poisonous atmosphere of mistrust throughout East German society. With 2000 buildings across the country fitted with state-of-the-art surveillance equipment, the organization could place human or electronic eyes and ears almost anywhere. Recent investigations suggest the Stasi could tune into conversations at NATO High Command in Brussels. Several 'sleepers' worked their way into the upper echelons of the West German security service. One, Günter Guillaume, was even appointed private secretary to Chancellor Willy Brandt; his exposure in 1974 forced Brandt's resignation. At home operatives posed as waiters, mechanics, Jehovah's Witnesses—whatever helped them to watch, listen and report.

The surveillance, carried out with typical German thoroughness grew obsessive as discontent rose through the 1980s. Rooms where agents steamed open, read and resealed mail had to be repapered every six months because of damp. Warehouses bulged with gifts plundered from Western parcels that never reached their destinations. If a telephone did not work there was no need to call the repairman; he simply showed up, as if clairvoyant. The files became stuffed full of manically precise detail about suspects: what time they entered and left buildings, what they ate for breakfast or lunch, whether they stood by the window or the basin when they cleaned their teeth. The Stasi choked on information, and stuffed it , unprocessed and undigested, into file upon file upon file.

The whole system came crashing down as fast as the Berlin Wall itself. Street demonstrators forced the Stasi's abolition within a month of the borders opening. Erich Mielke, the octogenarian state security minister who once told parliament that his work was motivated by love for all East Germans, was slapped into custody pending investigations into corruption and misrule. Doctors later said he had gone senile. The reformist

Communist government briefly attempted to resurrect the Stasi in reduced form in January 1990, but was rebuffed when thousands of angry protesters stormed this building, smashing windows, defacing walls, bashing down doors, ripping up files and flinging them to the four winds. The outburst was brief and in the end did little damage. Many of those who took part were mildly surprised to find grey corridors and spartan offices inside the building instead of wild fleshpots. Stasi self-indulgence only extended to an in-house shop for rare consumer goods, a special recreation and exercise room and a discount hairdresser.

Like the rest of the building, Mielke's offices and private rooms do not emphasize the Stasi's corruption so much as its perverted sense of duty. One visitor has written in the exhibition guest book: 'These rooms express the tastelessness, boredom and profanity of abused power.' The sparse furniture is functional and dates back to 1957 when Mielke took the job as Stasi chief. Paintings and statuettes of Felix Dzerzhinsky, the founder of Stalin's Cheka secret police, are everywhere. In the conference room is a vast canvas showing children playing and laughing with border guards at the Wall. Mielke's bedroom is dominated by another revealing painting, this time of a hunter emerging from a wood to shoot a fleeing deer. On his bedside table are Plasticine models of ducks and bananas made by children from a Stasi-run kindergarten.

It is hard to assess how much damage the Stasi did. Unlike the Nazi Gestapo or Dzerzhinsky's Cheka it did not torture or murder on any sizeable scale. Political prisoners were usually released to the West after a couple of years. As repressive machines go, it was outwardly quite mild. Its most destructive tool was its insidiousness. As often as not the Stasi intimidated people simply by letting them know it was there. Car tyres would suddenly be slashed, television aerials would disappear from the roof. Above all, the Stasi created an atmosphere of mistrust that has continued to plague German society. Its six million files, kept under lock and key with only limited access for a few officials, probably contain enough material to compromise every public figure in the country. Much of the so-called information is uncorroborated or even malicious. But former Stasi officers can still use it as a potent weapon, especially to discredit politicians. One after another, parliamentary deputies and even party leaders have stepped down under pressure of public opinion. In December 1990 East Germany's first and last democratic prime minister Lothar de Maiziere was forced to resign his Bonn cabinet post because of accusations that he had been a part-time Stasi informer. There was no proof that de Maiziere had had any more than routine contacts with the

Stasi in his capacity as a lawyer defending dissidents. Even his political rivals found it hard to believe that the allegations were true. But the mere doubt was enough to destroy him. Now nobody knows what to do with the Stasi files. Destroying them might enable former Stasi agents to evade justice for their misdemeanours and deny alleged informers a chance to clear their name. But opening them to the public could prove even more disastrous. East Germany's 'Sword and Shield' has plenty of fighting power left.

Potsdam

Potsdam is the Prussian equivalent of Versailles: a city just outside the capital converted into a royal summer residence, displaying all the excesses, fancies and eccentricities of the monarch—in this case Frederick the Great—who commissioned its palaces and parks. Frederick's Schloss Sanssouci does not match the scale or originality of Louis XIV's Versailles, but it is nonetheless a quirky and telling monument to its vain, irascible and ambitious patron. The Cecilienhof mansion, on the other side of the city, is best known as the site of the 1945 Potsdam Conference; it is an architectural curiosity as well as a historical landmark and boasts a beautiful English garden laid out between two lakes. The centre of Potsdam itself, once one of Prussia's most forbidding garrison towns, was largely destroyed by British bombers in 1945. However, it bears some colourful traces of the past, including a 'Dutch quarter' of 18th-century gabled houses and its very own Brandenburg Gate.

A trip to Potsdam makes an ideal day out. The city borders on the south-western edge of Berlin. The built-up area is more or less continuous, but the two cities are administratively quite distinct: Potsdam, with a population of 130,000, is the capital of the federal state of Brandenburg, while Berlin is a federal state all of its own. During the Cold War the two were separated by the Wall.

Although there has been a rail link since the early days of the industrial revolution, transport between Berlin and Potsdam has not got back to normal following unification. If you take S-Bahn line 1 to Wannsee, there is a connecting train to Potsdam every half-hour (get out at Potsdam Stadt, not Potsdam West or Potsdam Hauptbahnhof). Phone the Berlin tourist office (tel (W) 2616031) for latest details of bus and coach links, which are improving all the time. Otherwise commercial companies like Severin und Kühn (tel (W) 8831015) or Berolina (tel (W) 8833131) organize daily sightseeing tours. Transport in Potsdam itself is also confusing. Each of the city's 15 bus lines (numbered 1–8 and lettered A–G) covers several different routes; the only way of being sure where any of them is going is to ask. The Potsdam tourist office is at Friedrich-Ebert Strasse 5, tel 211000 (don't try getting through from West Berlin before 1995). Bus F is the most useful, plying (at least some of the time) between Sanssouci and Cecilienhof via the city centre. Avoid Potsdam at weekends as it is extremely crowded.

Potsdam goes back further in history than its big brother Berlin; it is first mentioned as 'Potzupimi', one of a cluster of swampy villages given by Holy Roman Emperor Otto III to his aunt in AD 993. But the place only gained any significance in 1660 when the Great Elector Friedrich Wilhelm picked it for his country residence. Succeeding generations of the Hohenzollern family grew ever more attached to Potsdam. Not only was the hunting good, but the town was a safe distance away from Berlin's more radical political elements, always a vague threat to the strict Prussian ruling order. When Berlin soldiers began deserting *en masse* in the 1720s under the iron rule of King Friedrich Wilhelm I, Potsdam presented itself as an ideal alternative centre for the Prussian military. When Frederick the Great inherited the throne in 1740, he decided not to take advantage of his grandfather's pleasure palace, Schloss Charlottenburg, but resolved to build his own. Potsdam was the ideal location. With the army command on his doorstep, he could direct his campaigns against Austria, Silesia and Russia in the morning; then nap, stroll, write poetry and entertain in the afternoon and evening without moving more than a few hundred metres.

Frederick picked a vacant piece of land at the western end of the town and in 1744 commissioned his favourite architect, Georg Wenzeslaus von Knobelsdorff, to execute a design of his own, a long low rococo palace called **Schloss Sanssouci**, French for 'without a care'.

The Schloss (open daily 9–5, adm only for buildings) is at the eastern end of Park Sanssouci, a rambling expanse of landscaped gardens, woods and palaces some 2.5 km long and 1.5 km wide. The buses and coaches stop behind the palace on the street Zur Histor-ischen Mühle—literally 'by the historic mill'—a reference to the granary which Frederick initially left standing for charm value but later insisted on removing because the grinding noises kept him awake at night. The windmill has been replaced by a restaurant. There is a gravelled driveway leading to the palace.

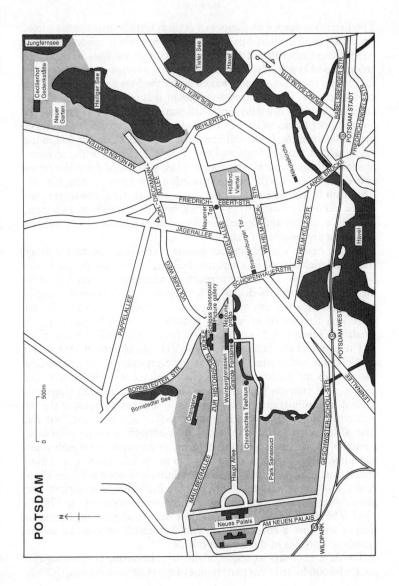

The French influence on Sanssouci extends further than just the name. Frederick liked to think himself immersed in French culture, insisting on speaking and writing in the language, although less than perfectly. He entertained French intellectuals and aspired to achieve the same glory for Prussia that France had attained under the Sun King, Louis XIV, a century earlier. It is perhaps no accident that one of Potsdam's most enduring symbols is a gold-embossed sun adorning one of the arbours on this upper terrace of the Schloss. Anyone who has visited Versailles or the châteaux of the Loire will immediately detect a familiar feel in the easy grace of the buildings and the classical elegance of the terraces, planted with vines, peach and apricot trees, which lead down in a series of five staircases from the Schloss towards a giant fountain at the bottom. The truth is that Sanssouci is derivative and, in parts, downright mediocre. After Knobelsdorff, Frederick employed armies of architects, painters, sculptors and decorators, few of them famous names and few displaying any original talent.

A good example of this indiscriminate excess is the **picture gallery** (Bildergalerie) housed in a separate building at the eastern end of the Schloss. The sheer blandness of much of the exhibition—not helped by the traditional crammed display with barely an inch of plaster showing—makes one think that any merit in a picture is pure coincidence. (In fact there is a handful of worthwhile canvases—don't miss Caravaggio's *Doubting Thomas* (no. 17) and Rubens' *Holy Family with Crib* (no. 57).)

The inside of the Schloss itself is an example of French *appartement double* layout, with a small back room for every main apartment looking out towards the garden. The décor is Bacchanalian, with frescos and paintings of cherubs blowing horns, nymphs dancing and langorous women fingering grapes. Frederick's study and bedroom are at the far (eastern) end and feature portraits of himself on all sides, most from the time of his reign. Clearly he couldn't get enough of his own likeness: paintings depict him inspecting his army or posing in royal garb while statuettes reveal him in pensive mood to fit his self-image as a philosopher king. The back room next to Frederick's suites was where Potsdam's most famous guest, the French Enlightenment satirist and philosopher Voltaire, slept during his three-year-long stay from 1750 to 1753. The room is comparatively modest, with wood panelling instead of frescos and just a small bust of Voltaire himself in contrast to the grandiose portraits of the King next door.

The difference says something about the relationship between the two men, who conducted what must be one of the most acrimonious, childish and bizarre slanging matches in history. At the beginning Frederick thought that friendship with a towering intellect like Voltaire could give credence to his own pretensions to artistic genius. Voltaire initially hoped that Frederick's commitment to freedoms of speech and artistic expression signalled the start of a new enlightened chapter in European history. Both ended up bitterly disappointed.

Voltaire disapproved of Frederick's soldiering and wrote of Potsdam to his fellow philosopher d'Alembert: 'There are an extraordinary number of bayonets but very few books. The King has made Sparta very beautiful but has brought Athens only into his private study.' Frederick's bad flute playing, French doggerel verse (which Voltaire was asked to correct) and sweeping literary judgements (he called Shakespeare a 'northern savage') drove Voltaire slowly mad. He amused himself by trying to wheedle state secrets out of Frederick over dinner. The king did not find it funny and suggested that Voltaire's visit might have outlived its usefulness: 'When you have sucked an orange, you throw away the peel.' Voltaire, fed up with having to flatter Frederick's ego, retorted: 'Does the man expect me to go on washing his dirty linen forever?'

The final bust-up was sparked by a dispute over the appointment of a new president of the Academy of Sciences. Voltaire stormed out in a fit of pique after his favoured candidate failed to get the job, but Frederick did not let him get off lightly. When Voltaire reached Frankfurt on his way back to France, Frederick had his governor there arrest him and hold him prisoner for a month because he had not returned a bound copy of the king's philosophical musings. Acrimony between the two bubbled on for the rest of their lives. Voltaire wrote to his niece about his Potsdam experience: 'I'm going to put together a dictionary for kings. "My friend" means "my slave". "My dear friend" means "I couldn't give a fig about you". "I will make you happy" means "I will put up with you as long as I need you".' Frederick responded in kind, calling Voltaire 'the worst scoundrel in the world. He has the slyness and ill will of an ape.'

That ape image has been immortalized in Sanssouci. Walking west from the Schloss towards the Neues Palais, you come across a round **Chinese Teahouse** (Chinesisches Teehaus) about 500 m along on the right. Among the golden animal figures adorning its eaves is a large monkey bearing Voltaire's features. The teahouse was begun in 1754, the year after the French philosopher left Potsdam.

The **Neues Palais** (New Palace), another 1500 m along the same path, is the most ambitious of the other buildings in the park. Built in 1765–69 by Carl Gontard, it is a much larger, more imposing edifice than Schloss Sanssouci, with two storeys and a copper dome topped by a statue of the three Graces holding up Frederick's royal crown. But inside there is a feeling of terrible emptiness. Room after sparsely furnished room drowns in the opulence of marble floors and columns. The painting is plentiful but thoroughly forgettable: one ceiling after another is painted with scenes from mythology featuring jolly goddesses and puffy-cheeked putti. Frederick only ever spent time in the west wing of the Neues Palais. He became increasingly isolated and embittered in his old age and received few visitors. When he died in 1786, Mirabeau wrote: 'Everything is gloomy, but nobody is sad. It's business as usual . . . This is the end of all those victorious battles, all that fame, a reign of almost half a century filled with so many great deeds! Everyone is glad it's over.'

Frederick even suffered the indignity of having his last wish spurned. He wrote in his will that he wished to be buried on the right-hand side of the terrace of Schloss Sanssouci. Whether out of malice or, as some reports have suggested, because dogs had been buried on the same site, contemporaries chose instead to place him next to his father Friedrich Wilhelm I in Potsdam's Garrison Church. There he stayed until the final stages of the Second World War, when his coffin was removed for safety and taken to a Hohenzollern family palace in Hechingen near Stuttgart. With the unification of East and West Germany, Frederick's descendants made plans to bring the body back. At the time of writing it is due to be reburied where Frederick wished on the 205th anniversary of his death—17 August 1991.

With Frederick gone, Potsdam went into decline. It was only some 50 years later that the Hohenzollerns resumed building here. Berlin's master architect Karl Friedrich Schinkel turned his hand to some imitation **Roman Baths** (Römische Bäder) in green marble and the Greek temple façade of **Schloss Charlottenhof** at the south end of the park. Both were used by Friedrich Wilhelm IV. A generation later Schinkel's pupil August Stüler undertook the **Orangerie** just to the west of Schloss Sanssouci. The warm sandstone building, at the top of a formal terraced garden leading down to a grotto, was used to entertain foreign dignitaries including the Russian Tsars. It boasts a Raffaelsaal, or Raphael hall, filled with copies of Italian Renaissance masterpieces. There is also a city archive open only to researchers, and a hothouse currently bereft of plants.

Catch bus F either from the Neues Palais or from the entrance to Schloss Sanssouci. On its way back into town it passes Platz der

*Nationen, the site of Potsdam's own Brandenburg Gate (Branden-burger Tor), built as an ornate entrance to the city by Gontard in 1770. It has four double columns against the six of the Berlin version and is altogether a squatter, less streamlined monument. From here the F skirts the centre and heads up to the **Neuer Garten**, a magnificently landscaped park at the end of which is the **Cecilien-hof** mansion (open daily 8–5, adm). The bus terminates here.*

Berlin's most prominent landscape architect, Peter Josef Lenné, who touched up the grounds of Sanssouci in the 1830s, also turned his hand to the Neuer Garten, a stretch of land between the small Heiliger See to the east and the Havel lake facing Berlin to the north. The greatest pleasures of the garden are its gracious perspectives across the two stretches of water and its well-tended woodland and beds of flowering plants. However, it is also filled with the follies much beloved of Prussian aristocracy, including a pyramid and a marble palace designed by Gontard.

The most famous building in the park is the most recent, the mock-Tudor Cecilienhof used to host the 1945 Potsdam Conference. The mansion, with its typically English thatched roof, clipped lawns and topiaries, looks curiously out of place in the German context. It was built during the First World War for Crown Prince Wilhelm, the son of Germany's last Kaiser, Wilhelm II, who had been educated in England, and his wife Cecilie. They had little chance to use it before the abolition of the monarchy in 1918. In July 1945, with most of Berlin and the surrounding area in ruins, it was an ideal island of tranquility for the three great powers—the United States, Britain and the Soviet Union—to sit down and decide the future of the defeated German nation. The sunny weather, plush parkland and glorious views over the Havel did not, however, stop the occasion being a shambles which, along with earlier conferences before the end of the war in London, Tehran and Yalta, established the Cold War polarities of East and West and led to the division of Germany. The conference began inauspiciously: the United States' long-serving president Franklin D. Roosevelt had died six weeks earlier, leaving the delicate task of settling the peace to a newcomer, Harry S Truman; Britain's similarly experienced prime minister Winston Churchill had just lost an election and was replaced in the middle of the proceedings by Clement Attlee. With the Western allies in such disarray, Stalin had a relatively easy time refusing to relinquish any part of the Soviet occupation zone, and in particular East

191

Berlin. He capitalized on the other two powers' mistrust of him to ensure that no permanent solution was found, thus giving him time to establish a Communist power base in the east of Germany. The British general Brian Robertson summed up the mood of the occasion thus: 'Soviet methods at the Berlin conference at Potsdam were not merely obstruction. They were based on a completely clear idea of what they wanted, and a determination to get it. The British and Americans were not always quite sure what their aims were.'

The interior of Cecilienhof includes the imposing round oak table where the Potsdam Agreement was signed on 2 August 1945. The rest of the building is used as a luxury hotel—if you fancy staying here call 23141 for details. There are fine views across the Havel towards Pfaueninsel and the park of Schloss Klein-Glienicke (see Walk IX). Until mid-1990 you could see very little because the Wall ran along the shore here and border guards ensured visitors kept their distance. Take bus F back to the centre of Potsdam and make your way to the old market place (Am alten Markt), dominated by the vast dome of the Nikolaikirche.

On the night of 14 April 1945, just three weeks before the end of the war, the British armed forces put out the following bulletin: 'Potsdam no longer exists. The city was reduced to rubble on Saturday night.' Like most wartime claims the report proved to be exaggerated, but not by much. The 490 RAF bombers who attacked this largely civilian target obliterated the outskirts where the machine-tool factories and residential areas were. They were a little less brutal in the centre. The Garrison Church, built by King Friedrich Wilhelm I and notoriously used by Hitler in March 1933 to proclaim his inheritance to the Prussian militaristic tradition, was destroyed and never rebuilt. But the **Nikolaikirche**, built by Schinkel in 1837–49 following the design of Christopher Wren's St Paul's Cathedral in London, survived more or less intact. The impression made by its vast dome and swooping vaulted interior is dented somewhat for anyone who knows the London original. The inside is virtually bare apart from a fussy Biedermeier collection of wall paintings depicting scenes from the New Testament. Outside stands an obelisk erected by Knobelsdorff in 1750, its pedestal bearing relief portraits of the four Prussian rulers from the Great Elector Friedrich Wilhelm to Frederick the Great. The other major building in the square is the **old city hall**, now known as the Kulturhaus Hans Marchwitza after an obscure communist hero. This elegant circular townhouse is another copy, this time of a never-used Palladio design. On top is a statue of Atlas carrying the world on his shoulders. Humanity can be thankful that the real Atlas apparently has safer hands than this gold-plated representation: in 1776 the globe smashed to the ground and was only replaced with a new one made of light copper in 1965.

From the market square, walk north along Friedrich-Ebert-Strasse towards the **Nauener Tor** (Nauen Gate), an early example (1755) of the Prussian fondness for English neo-Gothic style. Two chunky yellow-brick towers stand on either side of the road, joined by a crenellated bridge. Just before the gate to the right, around Mittelstrasse and Benkertstrasse, is the **Dutch Quarter** (Holländisches Viertel), a remarkably unspoilt series of gabled red-brick houses built by a group of Dutchmen who settled here in 1732. The area is of course a gift for film crews seeking a period location, and they take full advantage of it.

Food and Drink

Berlin is as schizophrenic about its food as anything else. Old traditions somehow got diced up in the magimix of post-war politics, producing totally contrasting diets in the two halves of the city. East Berlin stuck rather more closely to the city's long-established pork-and-cabbage dinners, but suffered from shortages and poor quality. The West, on the other hand, broke out into new territory, importing ingredients and recipes from around the world for a gastronomic experience unrivalled in the rest of Germany. The gap has narrowed a little since the opening of the Wall, but not by much. Restaurants in the East have access to fresh vegetables now but are reluctant to serve them; so far they have shown little of the West's interest in experimenting with pasta, souvlaki, satay and couscous.

A brief history of eating in Berlin

This flat, cold part of Germany has never been noted for its good food. The staples that kept the city going for most of its history were the pig and the potato. Fish was restricted to a few eel from local rivers and lakes; peas, cabbage, onions and beans were the only vegetables to speak of. The Huguenot merchants who arrived from France in the late 17th century were the first people to attempt to enliven the local diet, importing more various foreign goodies. Their meatballs, known by the

194

French-derived name *Bouletten*, are still around today. Frederick the Great, for all his relish for the finer things in life, did not appear to include food among his priorities. However, he left his stamp on Berlin's diet by forcing the city population to buy up huge quantities of heavily taxed salt to pay for his military campaigns. The result was a profusion of salted gherkins, salted herring and salted pork.

Few restaurants of any quality serve traditional Berlin food nowadays; most people consider that a blessing. You find it in the East and in some traditional pubs like Leydicke (see below). A meal might start with a thick pèa, potato or lentil soup, or a *Pellkartoffel*, a jacket potato filled with curd cheese and linseed oil (the stuff cricketers use to oil their bats). Main courses include *Eisbein* (pickled fatty pork) traditionally served with *Erbspüree* or mushy peas, and *Kasseler Rippenspeer* (pickled pork chop) usually served with red cabbage and salted potatoes. On the fish front there is *Aal grün*, or eel in a dill and parsley sauce, and herring with onion, gherkin, or horseradish. Salads are long on potatoes, vinegar and sugar but short on lettuce, tomatoes and other vegetables. For desert there is *Brombeerbowle*, a bowl of jellied wild fruits, and heavy sponge cakes.

The building of the Wall in 1961 had a decisive effect on the city's diet. The leaders of West Berlin quickly realized that one of the best ways to attract people to their enclave city was through the stomach. While the federal government subsidized food and restaurants, the city gobbled up the most varied gastronomic influences. Waves of immigrants from Turkey, Greece, Italy, the Far East and Latin America have influenced a whole generation of Berliners. Aside from contributing hundreds of specialist restaurants, the foreigners have encouraged local cooks to dip into the multi-cultural melting pot and try innovative menus combining a little bit of everything.

East Berlin was a very different story. In the early 1970s the Communists ordained that meat was the key to physical and spiritual well-being, and started systematically turning agricultural land over to industry or giant pig factories. As a result fresh vegetables virtually disappeared. And for what? East Germany produced so much meat of such low quality that it sold half to the West as catfood. Eating out was more a test of will than a pleasure. Cooks and waiters were interested only in fulfilling work quotas, not in doing a competent job or even being polite. Tables would remain empty while crowds queued outside. The best restaurants were reserved for the élite. For Western visitors the fare was outrageously cheap. But actually enjoying a meal was a rare fluke.

Berlin Food Today

The chances are you will do most of your eating in the West. Not only is the food far superior, there are ten times as many restaurants there (6000 compared to around 600 in East Berlin). Don't dismiss the East entirely, however. There is a handful of new establishments where salads actually contain fresh vegetables, coffee is not watered down, and service comes with a smile.

Breakfast is a Berlin speciality. Although a solid meal at the start of the day is a common feature throughout Germany, in Berlin you can linger all morning—or all day—over familiar and exotic delights such as mango yoghurts, cheese platters adorned with grapes and star fruit, eggs, cornflakes, salami and fresh rolls known locally as *Schrippen*. Hotels usually include breakfast in the price of their rooms, but you might do better in one of the specialist cafés listed below.

For the rest of the day, anything goes. West Berlin is perhaps the world's most cosmopolitan culinary centre after New York and London. The Turks are so established that they import fresh vegetables and spices daily from home, with the result that the city has the best aubergines, sweet peppers and fresh figs outside the Mediterranean. Since Berlin has the largest Turkish population of any city after Istanbul, Turkish food—typically, yoghurt and aubergine starters, lamb in a spicy sauce for main course and sweet sticky cakes to finish—is a vital component in Berlin's culinary make-up. Berliners love to argue about where to find the best doner kebab, a delicious glorified sandwich of hot flat bread filled with grilled lamb, salad and a squirt of garlic sauce (available on every second street corner for around DM 3.50). Of other foreign foods, Greek, Thai and Japanese are first rate. Good Italian restaurants are slightly harder to find, and Indian food, with some exceptions, is rather iffy.

Modern German fare is much harder to define. It varies from a hefty chunk of meat in a thick sauce and a side salad to a buckwheat and celeriac roll in dill sauce. At its best Berlin food is simple, fresh and impeccably presented. And although prices have jumped since the opening of the Wall, it remains remarkably cheap.

What About the Sausages?

Despite their prevalence in the rest of Germany, sausages are not a Berlin speciality. You will most commonly find them at snack bars.

They include: *Bockwurst* (thick and chunky, boiled), *Bratwurst* (grilled), *Ketwurst* (slithery and thin, boiled) and *Currywurst* (boiled with a curry sauce). All are traditionally served with a rather dry slice of bread and a dollop of mustard.

How to Survive as a Vegetarian

This is the land of schnitzels, steaks and cold cuts and, despite some moves towards a more meat-free diet, vegetarians will be treated with suspicion most of the time. Here are a few hints:

1. Say out straight: '*Ich bin Vegetarier*' (I am a vegetarian). If this registers with the waiter, you are probably on safe ground. Otherwise order at your own risk.
2. Watch out for vegetable soups. Pea, lentil, and potato soups almost always contain bacon or pork. Sometimes they will have a whole sausage floating in them. Lentil soup in Turkish restaurants is safe.
3. Avoid East Berlin. Almost every dish, even salad, comes with meat. Even if you make it clear that you are vegetarian, the chances are you will find bits of chopped pork floating in your order. The most promising areas of town are Charlottenburg, Schöneberg and Kreuzberg (see recommendations below).

Drink

Beer is *the* Berlin drink. Old Berliners (and some younger ones) sit in cafés drinking *Molle mit Korn*, a light beer with schnaps chaser. In the summer you can order a *Berliner Weisse*, a light, foamy variety served in a bowl-like glass with a little raspberry or woodruff liqueur added. This tradition stems back to the Huguenots who found the local brew too bitter and so sweetened it with stronger stuff. Any number of lagers include the local *Schultheiss* and *Radeberger*. *Weizenbier*, made from wheat, is a refreshing alternative (light or dark) served in a tall thin glass. Other favourite tipples are kümmel (caraway seed liqueur) and vodka. Wine is less prevalent—the nearest vineyards are near Dresden. In East Berlin you might get a taste of Hungarian, Czechoslovak or even Albanian wine. Otherwise the standard French, German, Italian and Spanish varieties are widely available. Turkish red wine, also very common, is full-bodied and fruity.

Listings

There are far more good restaurants than space permits to mention. Those listed should be treating as starting points—covering a variety of cuisines and styles—for further discovery. Germany is still largely a cash society, and that is the best way to pay. Restaurants listed as expensive accept all credit cards; the rest generally accept none. Service and cover charge are usually included, although a tip never goes amiss. Places are open every day for lunch and dinner unless the listings say otherwise. Charlottenburg is the best and most varied area for eating out. Kreuzberg is the cheapest—don't dress up unless it is in black leather and a slit T-shirt. Cheap means under DM 30 per head; moderate DM 30–60 and expensive anything above that (up to about DM 150).

Charlottenburg and Ku'damm

EXPENSIVE

Kempinski-Grill, Ku'damm 27, tel 884340, closed Mon. Open your palate to the fantasies of master chef Bernhard Schambach, who serves traditional, solid German and French dishes with an added panache worthy of the poshest hotel in town.

Ciao Ciao, Ku'damm 156 (next to the Schaubühne), tel 8923612. Impeccable Neapolitan food served in a bustling and friendly atmosphere. The (better off) Italian community flocks here to meet and tuck into mouthwatering fresh fish, seafood and vegetables.

MODERATE

Reste Fidèle, Bleibtreustr. 41, tel 8811605. This corner restaurant combines French and Italian cuisine with spectacular success. Delicious fresh vegetables and salads and an ever-changing variety of main dishes. Near impossible to get an outside table in summer.

Yukiguni, Kantstr. 30, tel 3121978, closed Sun. Mouthwatering sushi and other Japanese specialities. A feast for eyes and stomach.

Mahachai, Schlüter Str. 60, tel 310879. Excellent authentic Thai restaurant with bamboo décor inside and tables on a small terrace outside. The soups and tofu dishes are especially recommended.

Cour Carrée, Savignyplatz 5, tel 3125238. A tad pretentious but unrelentingly popular, this outsize bistro serves reasonable French food and American beer. It has a large terrace for summer evenings.

Jahrmarkt, Bleibtreustr. 49 (Savigny passage), tel 3121433, evening only. Warmhearted restaurant with large wooden tables and solid German/European cooking. Try the soups and monster salads.

Istanbul, Knesebeckstr. 77, tel 8832777. The best Turkish restaurant outside Kreuzberg, and considerably smarter as a result.

Tucci, Grolmanstr. 52, tel 3139335. Excellent, authentic Italian fresh pasta and desserts in a café atmosphere. Friendly but sometimes slow service.

India Palace, Leibnizstr. 35, tel 3137575. The best Indian restaurant in town. Aromatic but mild.

Katschkol, Pestalozzistr. 84, tel 3123530, evening only. An exotic, little-known Afghan restaurant, with lots of yoghurt, spicy vegetables and ample roast meats.

CHEAP

Litfass, Sybelstr. 49, tel 3232215, evening only. Slightly off the beaten track (near Adenauerplatz), but always crowded for cheap and tasty Portuguese food.

Udagawa, Kantstr. 118, tel 3123014, closed Sun lunch. Self-service and sit-down Japanese noodle bar highly popular with the Japanese community. Watch the cook prepare mouthwatering tofu and noodle dishes through a glass front separating the seating area from the kitchen.

BREAKFAST/OTHER CAFÉS

Paris Bar, Kantstr. 152, tel 3138052, Mon–Sat noon–1 am. *The* place to be seen in Charlottenburg, attracting middle-aged lawyers who wish they were young and arty again, as well as some (well-off) true Bohemians. Best for boozing and coffee but there's French food too at around DM 50.

Shell, Knesebeckstr. 22, 9 am–2 am daily. Once a petrol station (hence the name), this is a rather self-conscious dressy bar, but has good food leaning towards the vegetarian.

Diekmann, Meinekestr. 7, Mon–Sat 11–midnight. Cellar-like wine bar with a French accent. Good for tea and cakes, a snackish meal, or late night *moules marinières* to satisfy unpredictable pangs of hunger.

Café Savigny, Grolmanstr. 53, 11–1 am, breakfast until 4 pm. One of the best breakfasts in town, with cornflakes and London newspapers for homesick Brits as well as the usual exotic trimmings. In summer the outside tables catch the evening sun beaming down Pestalozzistr.

Ganz anders, Pestalozzistr. 34, 10–1 am. Excellent for breakfast and pasta lunches, on a quiet side street near Wilmersdorfer Str. shopping centre. Friendly staff and black and pink décor.

Cafésolo, Pariser Str. 19, 8 am–2 am, early closing on weekends, breakfast until 3 pm. Watering hole in an elegant street south of the Ku'damm. Cheap food.

Café Bleibtreu, Bleibtreustr. 45, 10–1 am daily. Popular, young, stylish. Open all day but comes into its own in the evening. Great for after-dinner calvados and an intense chat about the meaning of life.

Schwarzes Café, Kantstr. 148, closed Tues 1.30 am–9 pm. A Berlin rarity—a 24-hour bar. Red and black fake leather décor, trendy crowd, eccentric theme breakfasts.

Wintergarten, Fasanenstr. 23, 10–1 am. Part of the Literaturhaus. Best to come during the day to browse, read the paper and sip good coffee in the tranquility of a smart town garden.

Irish Harp Pub, Giesebrechtstr. 15, 10–1 am. A little clichéd, perhaps, to go to an Irish pub, but this one has all the advantages (plenty of room to sit, good beer and pub food) minus all the disadvantages (tweeness, joining arms to 'traditional' music, etc).

Zwiebelfisch, Savignyplatz 7, noon–6 am. The closest thing to a dive in this part of Berlin. A chummy place to drink, with cheap, so-so food if you get peckish. Plenty of outside tables in summer.

Schöneberg and Kreuzberg

EXPENSIVE

Zum Hugenotten, in the Intercontinental Hotel, Budapester Str. 1, tel 26020. Classy French restaurant in the post-modern style of the whole hotel. The menu is shaped like a fridge and the pepper mill so huge it could be classed as an offensive weapon.

Bamberger Reiter, Regensburger Str. 7, tel 244282, evening only, closed Sun, Mon. Fine Tyrolean cooking with homemade *Knödel* dumplings, best cuts of meat and irresistible desserts. Reservations essential.

Chez Moncef, Budapester Str. 11, tel 2625123, closed Sun. Real French *nouvelle cuisine*, amongst other things, with attendant high style, high class and high prices. Superb couscous on Fridays and Saturdays.

MODERATE

Café EinStein, Kurfürstenstr. 58, tel 2615096. A Berlin institution inside the former villa of US silent film star Henny Porten. Best for evening meals including adventurous pastas. Literary readings on Tuesdays. Popular for private parties.

Holland Stübl, Martin-Luther-Str. 11, tel 248593, evenings and Sun lunch. Attractive combination of Dutch and Indonesian food in a friendly, chatty atmosphere.

Bagdad, Schlesische Str. 2, tel 6126962. Think not of Saddam Hussein but the Arabian Nights. Delicate aromas and spices waft from kebabs and aubergine starters. Has a popular garden with fish pond and, best of all, belly dancing on Friday nights.

Exil, Paul-Lincke-Ufer 44, tel 6127037, evenings only, closed Mon. So called because homesick Viennese used to gather here. The star attraction is a terrace with climbing plants looking over the canal. Middle European food (i.e. lots of meat and red cabbage), but well done.

Carib, Motzstr. 30, tel 2135381, evenings only. Great soul food and other Caribbean delights served in an unpretentious, straightforward style. Reggae music and a pool table could persuade you to make a night of it.

Merhaba, Hasenheide 39, tel 6921713, evenings only. Turkish food at its best and most imaginative—try the artichoke hearts filled with sheep's cheese—with décor a cut above the usual Kreuzberg drabness. Attractive if slightly noisy terrace.

Hyperion, Yorckstr. 90. An outstanding Greek restaurant, with no trace of the piles of raw onion and lashings of salad dressing found all too often in Mediterranean food in Germany. Simple, fresh ingredients including deliciously spiced salads and tsatsiki. Friendly staff.

CHEAP

Alte Welt, Wissmannstr. 44, tel 6226396. Simple, versatile home-style cooking. The star attraction is the huge beer garden, but in winter the wooden interior is cosy and warm.

Osteria No. 1, Kreuzbergstr. 71, tel 7869162, evenings only. Very popular, unpretentious Italian restaurant with great food and sociable atmosphere. Don't go expecting a quiet evening for two, and you'll love it.

Hasir, Adalbertstr. 15. This 24-hour Turkish community mecca has only ever shut once: when a gas explosion blew the place up (you might still see the burnt-out ruins on the corner of Oranienstr.). It moved with astonishing speed two doors down the road. Day or night, simple, cheap and good.

Thurnagel, Gneisenaustr. 57, tel 6914800, evenings only. The best vegetarian restaurant in town, with constantly changing innovative, tasty and colourful recipes. The spinach *gnocchi* are particularly good.

BREAKFAST/OTHER CAFÉS

Leydicke, Mansteinstr. 4, 4 pm–1 am, closed Wed. Berlin's most famous pub, with a huge range of beers and fruit wines, and traditional snacks.

Nolle, at the Nollendorfplatz flea market, Wed–Mon 11–7.30. Watering hole for market-goers and stall holders. Good, cheap food. Jazz on Sunday mornings.

Café Altenberg, Oppelner Str. 24, 10–1 am, breakfast until 4 pm. You can easily spend all day here with newspapers, a pool table and friendly staff to keep you company. Average breakfasts but excellent evening salads and vegetarian food. The service is sometimes slow.

Sahara, Eisenbahnstr. 46, 10–1 am. A suntrap with Mediterranean décor, otherwise little connection with the eponymous desert. Good breakfasts, especially for egg dishes and cheese platters.

Café am Ufer, Paul-Lincke-Ufer 43, 9 am–2 am daily, breakfast until 4 pm. Bar and enchanting small garden looking onto the canal. Staff are aggressive at the bar but much friendlier at the tables.

Elefant, Oranienstr. 12, 3 pm–3 am daily. The perfect pavement perch from which to observe Kreuzberg by night. Unless of course you prefer to sit next door at the...

Rote Harfe, Oranienstr. 13, 10 am–3 am. Similar, noisy crowd with music blaring out of the basement.

East Berlin

EXPENSIVE

Silhouette, in the Grand Hotel, Friedrichstr. 158–62, tel 20920. French *haute cuisine* at the top of East Berlin's premier hotel.

Rôti d'Or, in the Palast Hotel, Karl-Liebknecht-Str. 5, tel 2410, evenings only. French-oriented fine food served at discreet, small tables on the first floor of the excessively orange Palast Hotel.

MODERATE

Moskau, Karl-Marx-Allee 34, tel 2792869. Decent Russian and Ukrainian cooking just off Alexanderplatz, with two bars and private rooms. Rapidly improving in quality and service at the time of writing.

Bistro 1900, Husemannstr. 1, tel 4494052, evenings only, closed Sun. Traditional Berlin specialities in renovated *art nouveau* style.

Die Moewe, Hermann-Matern-Str. 118. Elegant 19th century rooms in a former artists' and actors' club. So popular in the past that first the SS, then the Communist trade union élite took it over for themselves. The food is only slightly above average, but the location makes it.

Ratskeller, Rathausstr., tel 2125301. The vaulted brick cellars of the city hall are an atmospheric place to pick your way through above-average East Berlin fare. Have lots of beer and the tinned vegetables will slip down, no problem.

Zur letzten Instanz, Waisenstr. 14, tel 2125528, closed weekends. The name means 'at the last minute', so called because medieval prisoners on their way to execution would stop off here for a final wish. Berlin's oldest pub, this has become quite a haunt for tourists. With good reason.

CAFÉS

Arkade, Französische Str. 25, 10–10. A former hangout for the Stasi, it's now a smart tearoom cum pub. No beer, but large ice-cream beakers instead.

Café Bauer, Friedrichstr. 158–64, 10–midnight. Living off its past reputation as one of the best bars in Berlin, it's now part of the Grand Hotel. Worth it for the outside seats beneath the arcades.

Operncafé, Unter den Linden (near Staatsoper), tel 2000256, 10–midnight. A great location in the heart of Prussian Berlin, with a garden.

Mosaik, corner of Prenzlauer Allee and Hiddenseer Str., noon–midnight. Pavement café increasingly popular with West Berlin visitors.

Wiener Café, Schönhauser Allee 68, 10–10, slightly later at weekends. The closest East Berlin gets to a cocktail bar, with martini and brandy specialities.

Vegetarian

Thurnagel, Gneisenaustr. 57, see above (p. 202).

Café Tiago, Knesebeckstr. 15, tel 3129042. More for snacks than meals, but with a wide range of salads and hot vegetable dishes.

V, Lausitzer Platz 12. Closed Tues. Run by a collective, this is as much a small community centre as a bar/restaurant. With leaflets, books and lively political chatter to help digest the wholemeal delights.

Baharat Falafel, Winterfeldtstr. 35. Middle Eastern without the meat.

Golden Temple, Rankestr. 23. Cheap, largely vegetarian Indian dishes.

After Midnight

Ça va, Pariser Str. 56, tel (W) 8833674, open till 7 am. A convincing impersonation of an all-night Paris bistro. DM 30.

Mau-Mau, Motzstr. 28. open until 10 am. Good place to fill up on starch after a night's drinking. DM 25.

Uhlwig, Uhlandstr. 49, open until 4 am. Spacious French/Tunisian. DM 25.

Society, Budapester Str. 40, open until 6 am. Desperately inauthentic Italian place but still not bad. Pasta, pizza and salads. DM 25.

Capri, Lietzenburger Str. 76, all night. Noisy, slightly chaotic Italian pavement restaurant popular after concerts, plays etc. DM 30.

Where to Stay

Berlin has such a chronic shortage of hotels that only one visitor in three gets to stay in one. The mad scramble for accommodation began the day the Wall opened in November 1989 and has never stopped. Tourist figures doubled overnight; the city simply could not cope. Agencies offering three-day lets on apartments are making their fortune. Tens of thousands of families are earning extra cash by renting out rooms. Property developers cannot snap up land for hotel development fast enough. Tourist officials say the situation should be under control by the year 2000. Until then, expect chaos.

So the message is book, and book early. You'll need to phone two or three weeks in advance to be sure of getting a room, any room. Often you will be asked to pay a deposit, either by wire or by credit card over the phone. If you are picky about the hotel, plan two or three months ahead. If you do turn up on spec, all is not necessarily lost. The tourist office (either inside Bahnhof Zoo or at the Europ-Center, tel (W) 2626031) will phone around for last-minute vacancies or else find you a room with a family. In the smarter hotels, where there are usually a few rooms kept quietly in reserve, you can bluff and protest that reception must have lost your booking. Put a little conviction in your voice and, nine times out of ten, you will be signing the register within minutes.

As it turns out, there's not much to pick and choose between Berlin's hotels. Nearly all of them—East and West—are clean, warm and comfortable, and include a slap-up buffet breakfast in the price of the room. But they are functional and efficient rather than charming or offbeat. None could really be described as honeymoon material. The one idiosyncrasy to watch for is your bed. Especially in older hotels, the sheets tend to be just too short to cover the mattress, and the duvet just too short to cover you. The phenomenon has nothing to do with the class of hotel, but harks back to the days of wartime rationing. Germans evidently got so used to linen being scarce that they never thought to change their habits. Hotels are well used to handing out extra blankets to nonplussed foreigners.

Charlottenburg is the most fertile area for accommodation in all categories. Schöneberg and Kreuzberg are cheaper and a little seedier. The East, by and large, offers five-star luxury or nothing—the legacy of the days when hotels were a major source of hard currency for the East German Communist government. Some of the surly, intransigent service of that era has survived too. If your hotel makes a booking error, fails to deliver your bar order, overcharges for room service or loses your luggage, the stock response to any complaint is the magic word *Feierabend*. *Feierabend* literally means evening off—as in, 'I'm sorry but the person you need to speak to leaves work early on Thursdays.' It is used as a catch-all for a veritable compendium of half-baked excuses. You can be as incredulous as you like, but when your waiter, receptionist, bellboy or manager utters the word *Feierabend*, it is usually a reliable signal that you should give up arguing. The good news is that newly built establishments in the East are rather more helpful than their forebears. They also offer some of the best bargains in town.

The following list orders hotels by area, starting in each case with details of places that are worth a bit of effort to get into. These are followed by a list of more run-of-the-mill establishments where, with luck, you won't freeze, starve, run out of hot water, encounter rodents, curse your lumpy mattress or wish you'd brought fortified earplugs. The price given is for a double room for one night. Single rooms are about a third cheaper. Soaring demand is pushing up hotel prices faster than inflation, so add around 10 per cent per year from 1991 on. At the end are some suggestions for other kinds of accommodation. If you are willing to be a bit independent, these can be the best option of all.

East Berlin

RECOMMENDED

*****Grand Hotel, Friedrichstr. 158–64, tel (E) 20920. Grand by name and grand by nature, this recently built hotel lovingly reconstructs the pomp of Wilhelmine Prussia, including liveried staff who beetle up and down its sweeping central staircase. Once a gathering place for spooks, Middle Eastern guerrillas and shady businessmen, the Grand is now the hotel of choice for executives sizing up the investment potential of eastern Germany. DM 250–300.

*****Dom Hotel, Mohrenstr. 30, tel (E) 20980 or (W) 2647400. East Berlin's spanking new luxury hotel avoids the tacky modernity of some of its rivals, featuring an old-fashioned beer cellar and a plant-filled winter garden. Demand a room overlooking Platz der Akademie. DM 250–300.

***Charlottenhof, Charlottenstr. 52, tel (E) 20356600. Enjoy Platz der Akademie at half the price of the Dom. Quiet, with warm, comfortable rooms and friendly service. DM 185.

***Newa, Invalidenstr. 115, tel (E) 2805173. Capture the shabby, slightly seedy atmosphere of the old city in a part of central East Berlin most visitors do not see. Despite the tumbledown appearance, the rooms are well-kept and clean. The food is good east European pork and red cabbage. DM 180–200.

ALTERNATIVES

*****Palasthotel, Karl-Liebknecht-Str. 3, tel (E) 2410. Decorated in lurid orange and brown. DM 200–250.

*****Metropol, Friedrichstr. 150–53, tel (E) 22040. A rather soulless skyscraper. It has a great swimming pool, however. DM 200–250.

****Unter den Linden, Unter den Linden 14, tel (E) 2200311. A little drab, despite the grand address. DM 200.

****Stadt Berlin, Alexanderplatz, tel (E) 2190. Clean, efficient but characterless. DM 200–250.

Charlottenburg/Tiergarten

RECOMMENDED

*****Bristol Kempinski, Kurfürstendamm 27, tel (W) 884340. By common consent the best, most exclusive hotel in Berlin. An ugly-duckling cream façade conceals period-furnished rooms, opulent chandeliers and immaculately deferential service. DM 380–430.

****Steigenberger, Los-Angeles-Platz 1, tel (W) 21080. Modern hotel with cosy rooms and foyer art exhibitions. DM 260–420.

****Grand Hotel Esplanade, Lützowufer 15, tel (W) 261011. Large rooms decked out in chrome and leather make up for a somewhat snooty atmosphere. Hotel guests can borrow bicycles free of charge. DM 285.

***Hecker's Hotel, Grolmanstr. 35, tel (W) 88900. Wood panelling and heavy bedclothes make for snug comfort a stone's throw from the bars of Savignyplatz. A smoky restaurant serves beer and sizzling roasts. DM 220.

***Curator, Grolmanstr. 41–43, tel (W) 884260. Slightly overpolished but ultra-modern. Hard beds and hi-tech toilets. DM 160–220.

***Pientka, Kurfürstendamm 12, tel (W) 884250. Perched high above the Ku'damm, the Pientka has great views of the Kaiser Wilhelm Memorial Church opposite. Solid, comfortable beds. DM 270.

***Askanischer Hof, Kurfürstendamm 53, tel (W) 88118033. Lively theatre-district hotel, favoured by visiting actors. DM 145–205.

***Hotel Ambassador Berlin, Bayreuther Str. 42–43, tel (W) 219020. Decent rooms and obliging staff on a quiet street between the Ku'damm and the Tiergarten. DM 248–288.

***Hotel Berlin, Lützowplatz 17, tel (W) 26050. Walking distance from the Tiergarten and the Bauhaus Archive. Comfortable, with a well-equipped sports centre. DM 180–225.

*Pension Knesebeck, Knesebeckstr. 86, tel (W) 317255. Modest but clean, friendly and central. Breakfast not included. DM 70.

ALTERNATIVES

*****Intercontinental, Budapester Str. 2, tel (W) 26020. Lots of post-modern pyramids but little spirit. DM 255–500.

****Hotel Schweizerhof, Budapester Str. 21–31, tel (W) 26960. Efficient but slightly antiseptic. DM 245–440.

****Savoy-Hotel, Fasanenstr. 9–10, tel (W) 311030. DM 280–420.

***Hotel am Zoo, Kurfürstendamm 25, tel (W) 884370. DM 200–295.

***Hotel Astoria, Fasanenstr. 2, tel (W) 3124067. DM 175–85.

***Berlin Excelsior, Hardenbergstr. 14, tel (W) 31991. DM 225 plus.

***Hotel Consul, Knesebeckstr. 8–9, tel (W) 3123054. DM 150–160.

***Hotel Hardenberg, Joachimstaler Str. 39–40, tel (W) 8823071. DM 130–210.

***Hotel Heinz Kardell**, Gervinusstr. 24, tel (W) 3241066. DM 160.
****Hotel Charlot**, Giesebrechtstr. 17, tel (W) 3234051. DM 85–150.
****Eremitage**, Schlüterstr. 54, tel (W) 8827151. DM 90–170.
****Panorama am Adenauerplatz**, Lewishamstr. 1, tel (W) 320940. DM 160.
****Hotel Heidelberg**, Knesebeckstr. 15, tel (W) 310103. DM 80–140.
****Hotel Westerland**, Knesebeckstr. 10, tel (W) 3121004. DM 125–45.
****Hotelpension Amirir**, Leibnizstr. 57, tel (W) 3242326. DM 75–95.
****Pension Silvia**, Knesebeckstr. 29, tel (W) 8812129. DM 80–90.
***Alpenland**, Carmerstr. 8, tel (W) 3123970. DM 90–130.
***Pension Alexis**, Carmerstr. 15, tel (W) 3125144. DM 65–75.

Schöneberg/Kreuzberg

RECOMMENDED
****Riehmers Hofgarten**, Yorckstr. 83, tel (W) 781011. A magnificent red-stone *Jugendstil* building with elegant courtyards at the tamer end of Kreuzberg. DM 145–175.
****Hotelpension Schöneberg**, Hauptstr. 135, tel (W) 7818830. Peaceful, comfortable hotel just off a lively shopping street. DM 90–150.
***Pension Kreuzberg**, Grossbeerenstr. 64, tel (W) 2513064. One of the best bargains in town, much frequented by students, with friendly communal atmosphere. DM 65.
***Hotel am Hermannplatz**, Kottbusser Damm 24, tel (W) 6912002. Charming if a little tatty hotel not far from the canal and the heart of Kreuzberg. DM 68.
***Reichspost**, Urbanstr. 84, tel (W) 6911035. Plain but friendly, in a lively neighbourhood. DM 70–80.
***Hotel Transit**, Hagelberger Str. 53–54, tel (W) 7855051. As bustling as the name implies, just behind the Viktoriapark and Kreuzberg monument. Extremely cheap dormitory beds, or doubles from DM 70.

ALTERNATIVES
****Sylter Hof**, Kurfürstenstr. 116, tel (W) 21200. DM 230.
****Galerie Rogowicz**, Hedemannstr. 25, tel (W) 2513842. DM 100–110.
****Hotel Columbia**, Dudenstr. 4, tel (W) 7851077. DM 100–110.
***Grossbeerenkeller**, Grossbeerenstr. 90, tel (W) 2513064. DM 100.
***Hotel Wendenhof**, Spreewaldplatz 8, tel (W) 6127046. DM 55–80.
***Hotel-Pension Südwest**, Yorckstr. 80, tel (W) 7858033. DM 60.

Other Accommodation

SPECIAL HOTELS

Artemisia, Brandenburgische Str. 18, tel (W) 878905. Women only. No need to resort to this for safety reasons, but you may enjoy the atmosphere, which varies from carefree to earnestly political. DM 120–180.

Gästehaus der Fürst-Donnersmarck Stiftung, Wildkanzelweg 28, tel (W) 402021. Special hotel for the severely disabled. Surrounded in greenery but a long way out of town. Rates vary according to nursing or medical requirements. Very popular, so book in good time.

CAMPING

Only recommended if you are lugging your tent anyway, or if you are very short of money—all the campsites are on the outskirts of town. The standard is, however, very high with impeccable washing facilities and several shops. The charge per night is around DM 5 per tent, plus DM 6.50 per adult and DM 2.50 per child. Under-7s get in free. Don't try camping in the Tiergarten—you will be chased away within minutes.

Zeltplatz in Kladow, Krampnitzer Weg 111–117, tel (W) 3652797. Open all year.

Campingplatz Haselhorst, Pulvermühlenweg, tel (W) 3345955. Open all year.

Campingplatz Dreilinden, Albrechts Teeroffen, tel (W) 8051201. Open April to October.

SHORT-TERM LETS

For a small commission, specialized agencies can fix you up with an apartment for a few days, or else put you up with a family. Prices depend on the size of the room or flat, but are almost invariably lower than for equivalent comfort in a hotel. Contact:

Erste Mitwohnzentrale, Sybelstr. 53, tel (W) 3243031.

Mitwohnzentrale Ku'damm-Eck, Kurfürstendamm 227–28, 2nd floor, tel (W) 8826694.

Agentur Wohnwitz, Holsteinische Str. 55, tel (W) 8618222, and Immanuelkirchstr. 11, tel (E) 4392494.

City Kontakt, Marienburger Str. 47, tel (E) 4365447.

Entertainment and Nightlife

Berlin nightlife enjoys a near-mythical status. Ever since the heady 1920s, the city has been a byword for liberal all-night entertainment and a certain seedy decadence. Films from *The Blue Angel* (1931), with Marlene Dietrich, to the 1971 musical *Cabaret*, starring Liza Minelli, have created an image of sultry elegance and risqué song and dance in smoke-filled backstreet clubs. On top of that has come West Berlin's Cold War reputation as an island of pleasures in a sea of communism; a raucous all-night city defying standard German concepts of order and sober living.

However, the myth has never quite matched the reality. For centuries Berlin was a provincial backwater with little entertainment of any kind. When the French novelist Honoré de Balzac, a noted night-owl, visited in 1843 he complained there was so little to do that he went to bed at nine every evening. 'Perhaps Berlin will one day be capital of Germany, but it will always remain the capital of boredom,' he wrote. Fortunately things turned out a little differently. The dramatic expansion of the city into a metropolis of four million people at the beginning of the 20th century transformed a backwater into a night-time paradise of theatres, clubs, bars and cabarets. But the exhilaration of the 1920s was tempered by the economic misery following the First World War. For every Sally Bowles flirting with the glamour of singing in a club, there were 10 downtrodden factory workers or destitute families or drunks or bums or slum dwellers.

The political scene, polarized by the simultaneous rise of the Commmunists and the Nazis, always teetered on the brink of anarchy. The city lived off this tension and, to some extent, thrived on it. Contemporary novelist Conrad Alberti summed up the peculiar ambiguity when he talked of 'the nervous, endlessly quivering Berlin air ... which works upon people like alcohol, morphine, cocaine, exciting, inspiring, relaxing, deadly: the air of a world city.'

Barely a trace of that world still survives. Venues boasting that they recreate the original cabaret atmosphere—such as the Europa-Center clubs in the West or the Friedrichspalast in the East—are usually tourist traps with muzak and tacky strip shows. Serious artists like Ute Lemper have recently reinterpreted the old Brecht–Weill songs, complete with husky voice and androgynous tails and make-up. But these are mere winks to the past, not the continuation of an unbroken tradition. The closest approximation to the 1920s atmosphere is in the East, where you can still go to old-fashioned ballrooms for tea and a two-step.

West Berlin's post-war nightlife reputation was built almost entirely on its status as an enclave city. The Bonn government offered generous living subsidies and exemption from military service as enticements to keep people living there, attracting an innovative crowd of artists and social and political movements who kept the free-for-all image of the past alive. German avant-garde cinema, theatre and rock music made its home here. Lou Reed and David Bowie both lived in Berlin for a time to feed off the atmosphere. The radical Kreuzberg squats of the early 1980s spawned a tradition of hole-in-the-wall venues with spontaneous musical and artistic happenings. But the Berlin *Szene*, or alternative scene, has always been small in both size and appeal, and relatively inaccessible to the casual visitor. London and New York have far more theatre and music venues, both mainstream and experimental. Berlin does not touch Paris for cinema or late-night drinking. But what it does have is a certain raw energy and exhilarating spontaneity.

These qualities have remained in Berlin despite the opening of the Wall, and have in fact spread East, notably to Prenzlauer Berg. This used to be the dissident intellectual centre of East Germany, where cultural events were announced at the last moment to avoid interference from the Stasi. Rock bands would play in churchyards, authors read from anti-establishment works in derelict tenements. While Kreuzberg now fears being taken over by property speculators and turned into just another boring neighbourhood, Prenzlauer Berg is still discovering its artistic possibilities. Many events are even now publicized only by word of mouth and are often highly bizarre. One night 40 or 50 people gathered in a back courtyard to watch two performers with blowtorches burning shapes out of a shack of painted sheet metal for an hour and a half. On another night a 10-piece jazz band might appear unannounced in an improvised bar in a deserted block of flats.

The most enduring entertainment in Berlin has been in the mainstream. The division of the city has created a profusion of artistic organizations including three opera houses, twice as many theatres as any other city its size, and a staggering seven symphony orchestras. It's hard to see how all these can survive in the reunited city. One institution sure to endure, however, is the Berlin Philharmonic, arguably the best orchestra in the world, based at a stunning modern concert hall (see Walk VI). The present chief conductor, Claudio Abbado, is the first non-German in the post but has more than lived up to the awesome reputation of his predecessor, the late Herbert von Karajan.

PRACTICAL INFORMATION

Berlin has two exhaustive listings magazines, *Tip* and *Zitty*, which both come out fortnightly but in different weeks. *Tip* is slightly clearer in layout and slightly more expensive (around DM 3.50). *Zitty* likes to think of itself as more offbeat. But both have essentially the same, often baffling critical taste. Films and shows that win rave reviews in the rest of Europe often get panned, and vice versa. Hotels will sometimes have free handouts about what's on, concentrating on major venues. Otherwise, check the plethora of posters on walls and on *Litfasssäulen*, Berlin's distinctive advertising pillars.

Roughly speaking, the higher the culture the greater the need to book tickets in advance. You can do this either direct (see addresses and telephone numbers on pp. 214–5) or through one of the following booking agencies which charge a small commission:

City Center, Kurfürstendamm 16, tel (W) 8826563
Theaterkasse im Europa-Center, Tauentzienstr. 9, tel (W) 2617051
KaDeWe, Tauentzienstr. 21, tel (W) 248039
Kiosk am Zoo, Kantstr. 3–4, tel (W) 8813603
Wertheim, Kurfürstendamm 231, tel (W) 8825354
Kant-Kasse, Kantstr. 54, tel (W) 3134554
Kasse am Quartier Latin, Potsdamer Str. 96, tel (W) 2627070
Theaterkasse im Palasthotel, Spandauer Str, tel (E) 2125258

Music

OPERA

Staatsoper, Unter den Linden 7, tel (E) 2054456. Box office Mon–Sat 12–6 pm, Sun 4–6 pm. Traditionally the best house in Berlin, attracting international stars to usually straight-laced productions of the classics.

Deutsche Oper, Bismarckstr. 34–37, tel (W) 3414449. Box office Mon–Fri 2–8 pm, Sat–Sun 10 am–2 pm. Second-best to the Staatsoper, with a similar repertoire and slightly more adventurous productions.

Komische Oper, Behrenstr. 55–57, tel (E) 2292555. Box office Tues–Sat 12–6 pm. Mostly German-language performances, with the emphasis on light opera and operetta. Offenbach and Johann Strauss are house favourites.

CLASSICAL CONCERTS

Philharmonie, Matthäikirchstr. 1, tel (W) 2614383. Box office Mon–Fri 3–6 pm, Sat–Sun 10 am–1 pm. Home to the Berlin Philharmonic and one of the world's best concert halls with near-perfect vision and acoustics from any of its 2200 seats. Book at least two weeks in advance.

Schauspielhaus, Platz der Akademie, tel (E) 2272129. Box office Mon–Sat 1–6 pm. Home to the (East) Berlin Symphony Orchestra. Most rewarding for lavish neo-classical décor, less so for its acoustics.

Staatskapelle, Unter den Linden 7, tel (E) 2054556. Box office Mon–Sat 12–6 pm. Berlin's oldest concert hall, founded in 1570, with its own orchestra and a wide-ranging repertoire of classics and moderns.

JAZZ

Berlin jazz wakes up from a rather somnolent existence twice a year: during *Jazz in July* at **Quasimodo** (Kantstr. 12a, tel (W) 3128086), which attracts some the world's best funk, fusion and bebop artists to a smoky cellar; and during the *Berlin Jazz Festival* in early November, which features bigger bands in sometimes rather impersonal venues including the Philharmonie. Home-grown German jazz tends to be somewhat derivative. Quasimodo is deemed the best club all round, with shows usually starting around 10 pm. Otherwise try **Flöz** at Nassauische Str. 37, tel (W) 8611000, for free jazz, or the **Haus der jungen Talente**, Klosterstr. 68–70, tel (E) 21030, the centre of East Berlin's jazz revival.

ROCK/POP

After a golden period in the 1970s and 1980s, Berlin has been without new performers of world standing. Real or adoptive Berliners such as Nina Hagen, Udo Lindenburg and DAF are still going in some form or other. Their 1990s successors include the thrash band Die Toten Hosen (literally Dead Trousers—Berlin slang for nothing going on) and the post-industrial ensemble Einstürzende Neubauten (literally Collapsing New Buildings—a good description of their overall sound which includes jackhammers, drills, iron girders, etc). Berlin musical preferences, wackos apart, seem desperately middle-of-the-road for British or American tastes. Even the most hard-nosed, style-conscious Berliner is likely to have a passion for Phil Collins, Lionel Ritchie or Belinda Carlisle. Big-name venues include the open air **Olympic Stadium** (Olympiastadion) and **Waldbühne** in the far west of the city, the **International Congress Centre** (ICC) on Messedamm and the **Tempodrom** tent in the Tiergarten. For details of shows here and at smaller venues, check the listings magazines.

Theatre/Cabaret

This is the city that spawned director Max Reinhardt and playwright Bertolt Brecht in the first decades of the century, and it still has perhaps the best stage entertainment in Germany. English-language theatre is a rarity and usually organized by the **British Council** (Hardenbergstr. 20, tel (W) 3110990). The **Hebbel Theater** (Stresemannstr. 29) puts on occasional productions, often Shakespeare, by touring British and American companies. Otherwise the main attraction is the **Berliner Ensemble** (Am Schiffbauerdamm, tel (E) 28880) specializing in Brecht (see Walk II). The best general house is the **Schillertheater**, Bismarckstr. 110, tel (W) 3195236. For more experimental work there is the **Schaubühne** in the West (Ku'damm 153, tel (W) 890023) and the **Volksbühne** in the East (Rosa-Luxemburg-Platz, tel (E) 2805103).

Cabaret in Berlin is not what it was (see above). German stand-up comedy is not generally noted for its spontaneity or even humour—no trace here of the renaissance enjoyed by stand-ups in Britain and North America. The only place worth spending an evening in is the **Distel** (Friedrichstr. 101, tel (E) 2071291), which became famous for its daring political satire during the Communist era and has kept its bite to comment on chaotic developments in a unified Germany.

215

Cinema

When Robert Wiene made his spooky Expressionist classic *The Cabinet of Dr Caligari* in 1919, he gave birth to German art cinema and made Berlin its home. Virtually all the great German directors—Fritz Lang, Rainer Werner Fassbinder, Wim Wenders—emerged from the UFA (Universum Film AG) studios here. The city itself became an evocative screen set in the 1980s for Fassbinder's adaptation of Döblin's *Berlin Alexanderplatz* and for Wenders' haunting elegy to life in the divided city, *Wings of Desire*. East German cinema has enjoyed a revival since unification, notably a series of long-banned 1960s social satires starring Manfred Krug.

Unfortunately the cinemas themselves do not live up to the reputation of the film makers. Except during the two glorious weeks of the Berlin Film Festival in February, most show a solid diet of Hollywood thrills, spills, blood and sex—the kind of thing you can see just as easily at home. To add insult to injury, virtually everything is dubbed into German. Art films have very short runs and generally appear in the original language for only a night or two at specialist houses. All, however, is not lost. Look for the markings OF (*Originalfassung*—films in the original language without subtitles) and OmU (*Original mit Untertiteln*—in the original with German subtitles). Occasionally obscure-language films will come with English subtitles.

The only exclusively English-language cinema is the **Studio** on Adenauerplatz, tel (W) 3245003, which shows newish releases for a week at a time. The British Council (Hardenbergstr. 20, see above) occasionally has movies from the UK.

Bar Crawls

Here are some suggestions on how to drink and dance the night away, and then get back home again. For the best watering holes, refer also to the Food and Drink section. Admission to discos and nightclubs tends to be very cheap (under DM 10) and varies depending on when you go and whether the bouncer likes your face. The lifespan of many places, especially in Kreuzberg and Prenzlauer Berg, is highly unpredictable. The U- and S-Bahn are shut from around 1–5 am. You can call a taxi on (W) 6902, 261026 or 240202, flag one down or else go to one of the ranks listed below.

CHARLOTTENBURG

Away from the gloss of the Ku'damm, this is a relaxed, eclectic area. You can dress how you like, but the snappier the better. Brightly lit, Charlottenburg is safe at night and easy for getting home.

Taxi Ranks: every third block along the Ku'damm, Savignyplatz, Wilmersdorfer Str. U-Bahn.
Night Buses: from Zoo station, in all directions.

Start at one of the bars on Savignyplatz—the raucous **Zwiebelfisch** at no. 7 or the cosier **Dicke Wirtin** on the corner of Carmerstr. The **Quasimodo** (Kantstr. 12a) has a Viennese-style bar open late as well as the jazz club downstairs (see above, p. 214). For discos, try **Linientreu und Ekstase** (Budapester Str. 40) for soul and disco music, **Far Out** on Lehniner Platz (wear white!), or the **Abraxas** (Kantstr. 134) for Latin music. The only place on the Ku'damm worth stopping for is the **Big Eden** disco at no. 202, which, like the London Hippodrome, is big, lively but impersonal. Open till 4 am. Don't confuse it with the **New Eden** at Adenauerplatz, which has upmarket strip shows and a very pricey bar. **Lipstick** (Richard-Wagner-Platz 5) is a famous women-only disco. For something completely different, try the roof garden at the Intercontinental Hotel (Budapester Str. 2) which has more sedate music, an older crowd and a great view of the city. Pricey drinks.

SCHÖNEBERG

A bit wilder than Charlottenburg, with dress varying accordingly. Wear leather and you can't go wrong.

Taxi Ranks: corner of Martin-Luther-Str. and Motzstr., every three or four blocks along Potsdamer Str.
Night Buses: 48N or 83N from Potsdamer Str. to Bahnhof Zoo.

The best streets to crawl are Motzstr. and Goltzstr. Highlights on Motzstr. are the **Cabeza Blanca**, with 1950s décor including fake cactuses and a huge variety of tequilas and mescals for serious drinkers. The **Krik** at no. 7 has a small, intimate bar and a dance floor which gets going after midnight. In Goltzstr. try **Lux** (no. 35) for cocktails, or the **Slumberland** (no. 24) near Winterfeldtplatz which has a long bar and sand-covered floor. In the parallel street, Kyffhäuserstr., is the **Fisch Büro** disco on the corner of Frankenstr, designed to make you feel literally out of this world. You can recline in spaceship-like seats and sip 'space beer' or dance under a flood of lasers and lights. At Wartburgstr. 54 is the **Pinguin Club**, a crowded bar packed with 1950s and 1960s memorabilia. The **Turbine Rosenheim** (Rosenheimstr. 4) has house and hip-hop music until dawn. Finally, on Nollendorfplatz is the giant and highly popular **Metropol** with frequent live performances as well as monster discos. Open all night.

KREUZBERG

Kreuzberg bars and clubs are filled with punks, anarchists, freaks and dropouts. It's the most colourful area of Berlin at night, but not always the most welcoming. Closing times are very flexible but generally late. Dress is strikingly uniform and revolves around the colour black. If you have a blotchy cotton neckscarf and red streak in your hair, so much the better.

Taxis: Sometimes on Mehringdamm or at Kottbusser Tor, but you do better to call one.
Night Buses: 29N from Oranienstr. or 19N from Urbanstr., both to Bahnhof Zoo.

At the tamer, western end of Kreuzberg is Yorckstr. The **Café Wirt-schaftswunder** at no. 81 is open until 4 am and has 1950s armchairs and a Wurlitzer jukebox. **Riehmers** next door at no. 83 is a punk and new-wave disco. In the summer you can sit out and dance until late on the Kreuzberg hill itself at **Golgatha** (approach from Katzbachstr.)

To get to know the wild heart of Kreuzberg, close in on Oranienstr. and its extension Wiener Str. The **O-Bar** at Oranienstr. 168 and **Cazzo** at no. 187 are both gay hangouts, the former with scrubbed tiled walls and red lighting, the latter metallic and raucous. Heinrichplatz has two great summer bars, the **Rote Harfe** and **Elefant**. For hip-hop and rap there's **Sox** at no. 40. Next door at no. 39 is **Trash**, the ultimate black leather venue which is at its bleary best after 5 am. The **F.S.K.** (Wiener Str. 20) is a select film club with a bar open till 3 am. **Madonna** at no. 22 has mock-religious décor, more mainstream music and closes around 2 am (outrageously early for Kreuzberg). The **Bronx** at no. 34 is an informal disco with a stainless steel dance floor. **Morena** at no. 60 is a cosy, chatty late bar. Next door is the **Mini Bar** which has silver cushions on the ceiling and live music until 10 pm.

218

MITTE

Bar crawling is not really possible in the centre of East Berlin: there are too few places too far apart from each other, and closing time is early. Venues still like to make people wait needlessly as they did in the bad old pre-revolution days. However, there are plenty of surprises as places develop new identities. If you're driving, remember that in East Berlin you're not allowed to drink a drop of alcohol. There are no night buses at the time of writing.

Taxi Ranks: outside the Grand Hotel on Friedrichstr. and at the back of the Palasthotel on Karl-Liebknecht-Str.

For a little old-fashioned waltzing try the **Altdeutsches Ballhaus** (Ackerstr. 114) or **Clärchens Ballhaus** (Auguststr. 24) (both open 7–1). The **Pieck Club** (Wilhelm-Pieck-Str. 153) has a large bar and small dance floor, with occasional live jazz or literary readings. **Klub Jo-Jo** (Wilhelm-Pieck-Str. 216) is a three-floor cultural centre with frequent live music and theatre as well as discos. For a sweaty bop, try **Club 29** (Rosa-Luxemburg-Str. 29). A smoky, late-opening cellar disco is **Im Eimer** (Rosenthaler Str. 68). The **Sophien Club** (Sophienstr. 6) is traditionally a favourite disco and jazz club for young East Berliners.

PRENZLAUER BERG

This is the evolving new centre of Berlin nightlife—spontaneous, easy-going and constantly changing. The most rewarding venues are ones you bump into by accident in backyards and derelict houses: they may only last a week or two. Admission is rarely more than DM 5 and often free.

Transport is terrible; no night buses and precious few taxis unless you call one (and that involves finding a phone that works...). So getting home takes a little patience, but Prenzlauer Berg is worth the trouble.

Schönhauser Allee is the main drag. The **Jugendklub Franz** at no. 39 is a vivacious live music venue concentrating on punk and new wave. The **Lotosbar** (no. 46a) serves booze until late while the **Lolott-Nachttanzbar** (no. 56) has a small dance floor and a modest cocktail bar open until dawn. Despite the name, the **Café Nord** is in a fact an extremely sweaty disco with nostalgia value because it was virtually the only all-night dance venue in East Berlin in the old days. More glossy is the **Café-Bar Capuccino** (no. 90), which has mirrors on the ceiling and shows videos. No dancing.

219

Another good area is around Kollwitzplatz. The **C.V.** and **S.O.S.** on the square itself are apparently permanent squats with loud music, food and cramped dancing which spills out onto the street, weather permitting. There are two more conventional bars on the Husemannstr. side of the square. At the end of the night it's worth walking down the hill to Greifswalder Str. where diehard dancers gather at the **Knaack Klub** (no. 224). Its slightly austere whitewashed walls are compensated by the energetic crowd and lively music.

Shopping

Turkish Market.

We came, we saw, we did a little shopping
—*erstwhile graffiti on the Berlin Wall*

West Berlin was the showcase of Western consumer culture during the Cold War, and the red-and-blue neon glow of its stores pervades the whole city. On close scrutiny this turns out to be a rather empty kind of glamour; you can spend oodles of money without finding much satisfaction. But Berlin also has a wackier, more offbeat underside. It is hard to imagine many German cities where you can buy latex body stockings and second-hand Armani suits five minutes' walk from each other.

The curse of the Berlin shopper is the *Ladenschlussgesetz*, the German law which stipulates that stores must close just when they might be most useful. Like Britain's ban on Sunday trading, the ruling claims to be rooted in Christian morality but seems incompatible with the practicalities of modern living. How are single parents or double-income couples supposed to fill their fridges each week if the shops are only trading when they are at work? Opening times are 9 am to 6.30 pm Monday to Friday and 9 am to 2 pm on Saturdays. And that's more or less it. There is a 'long Saturday' (*langer Samstag*) in the first week of each month and in the run-up to Christmas, giving consumers an extra two hours' grace before the great weekend shutdown. Some stores have negotiated a 'long Thursday' too, and stay open until 8 pm. But these extensions do

221

precious little to alleviate the crush of people who elbow each other all the way to the till on Saturday mornings to ensure the family does not starve.

East Germany used to organize things much more sensibly, with shops open from early in the morning until mid-evening. Alas, the West has seen fit to force the East to comply with its way of thinking. West German retailers have also captured the Eastern market with astonishing rapidity, dominating its shop shelves and dictating the new consumer culture. Had things turned out differently, perhaps East Berlin shops would now be full of new and innovative goods. As it is, they are so far just a pale imitation of Western stores. It is sad that scarcely any of the establishments listed below are in the East.

Sizes

Women's Shirts/Dresses

UK	10	12	14	16	18
US	8	10	12	14	16
Germany	40	42	44	46	48

Women's Sweaters

UK	10	12	14	16
USA	8	10	12	14
Germany	46	48	50	52

Women's Shoes

UK	3	4	5	6	7	8
US	4	5	6	7	8	9
Germany	36	37	38	39	40	41

Men's Shirts

UK/US	14	$14\frac{1}{2}$	15	$15\frac{1}{2}$	16	$16\frac{1}{2}$	17	$17\frac{1}{2}$
Germany	36	37	38	39	40	41	42	43

Men's Suits

UK/US	36	38	40	42	44	46
Germany	46	48	50	52	54	56

Men's Shoes

UK	2	3	4	5	6	7	8	9	10	11	12
US	5	6	7	$7\frac{1}{2}$	8	9	10	$10\frac{1}{2}$	11	12	13
Germany	34	36	37	38	39	40	41	42	43	44	45

Weights and Measures

1 kilogramme (1000 g)—2.2 lb	1 lb—0.45 kg
1 etto (100 g)—¼lb (approx)	
1 litre—1.76 pints	1 pint—0.568 litres
	1 Imperial gallon—4.546 litres
	1 US gallon—3.785 litres
1 metre—39.37 inches	1 foot—0.3048 metres
1 kilometre—0.621 miles	1 mile—1.161 kilometres

Antiques

Berlin has a plentiful selection of antique shops, where you can haggle for Biedermeier or *Jugendstil* pieces—at a price. For cheaper items, try the street markets listed below.

Seidel und Sohn, Fasanenstr. 70. Baroque and Biedermeier.
Bethmann-Hollweg, Fasanenstr. 26. Specializes in iron and wrought-iron work. Some furniture and paintings too.
Krischke, Schlüterstr. 49. Priceless jewels. Berlin's answer to Tiffany's.
Bogart's, Schlüterstr. 34. Art Deco furniture, knick-knacks and *objets d'art*.
Alternativer Kontor für antike Öfen, Pariser Str. 20. Old Berlin heaters and tile ovens. Worth visiting for curiosity value.

Art

Galerie Pels-Leusden, Villa Grisebach, Fasanenstr. 25. A magnificent *art nouveau* villa specializing in early 20th-century art. This is where to buy your Expressionist masterpiece.
Galerie Poll, Lützowplatz 7. Pop art and the avant-garde.
Galerie Bremer, Fasanenstr. 37. Closed Mondays. Come here in the evening to sip cocktails, listen to cool jazz and pore over the latest from Berlin's contemporary artists.
Galerie Anselm Dreher, Chamissoplatz 6. Political art on the site of a former bakery in Kreuzberg.

Books

Marga Schoeller, Knesebeckstr. 33–34. The best English language selection in town, with everything from pulp fiction to serious academic tomes. Extrovert, competent staff. The German half of the shop includes a good selection of books on Berlin.

The Original Version, Sesenheimer Str. 17. Small but stimulating selection of English-language books and videos.

Wordsworth Bookshop, Goethestr. 69. New and second-hand books in English.

Kiepert, Hardenbergstr. 4–5. A huge bookstore with separate entrances for each department. The most extensive travel section in town (come here for maps), plus good dictionaries and study-oriented English books.

Heinrich Heine Buchhandlung, beneath S-Bahn Zoo on Hardenbergstr. No English books, but the most interesting selection of German titles in town. Stays open late, too (until about 8 pm).

Clothes

German fashion, as far as it exists, is solid, practical and conservative. Men like wearing broadly cut checked jackets, double-breasted suits and brightly coloured ties. Women go for classically cut fabric in straight-forward colours. Shoes for both sexes tend to be chunky. In Berlin there is a little more room for manoeuvre, with leather all the rage. If you want to dress like the punks in Kreuzberg, you'll find plenty of shops selling black and white cotton neckscarves, mottled T-shirts, black drainpipe trousers and Doc Martens boots. But the bottom line is that Berliners are not especially natty dressers. Guide books commend the city for its second-hand shops—a backhanded compliment if ever there was one.

FASHION

Kramberg, Kurfürstendamm 56. If you have the figure of a fantasy princess and the bank balance to match, come here to pick out your favourites from the big names of high fashion. Men's clothes too.

Durchbruch, Schlüterstr. 54. A 1940s-style tiled shop featuring the latest in Berlin women's fashion. Look and judge for yourself.

Hotch Potch, Bleibtreustr. 17. As the name implies, a centre for cosmopolitan clothing, including some exclusive lines by Italian designers.

Schuhtick, Savignyplatz 11. Shoes.

SECOND-HAND

Garage, Ahornstr. 2. Open Mon–Sat 12–9 pm. Rumoured to be

Europe's largest second-hand clothes shop, this former underground carpark sells its glad rags by weight (currently DM 25 per kilo).

Maria Makkaroni, Bleibtreustr. 49. Party clothes you would never fork out for if they were new, from sequined cocktail dresses to Hollywood ball gowns.

Macy's, Mommsenstr. 2. Designer labels that their original owners tired of after one wearing. Some real bargains.

Glencheck, Joachim-Friedrich-Str. 34. Period fashion, from 1920s chic to 1960s kaftans and beads.

Zapato, Kolonnenstr. 61. Second-hand shoes.

Die Macke, Hagelberger Str. 17. Popular reject shop.

OFF-THE-WALL

Blue Moon, Wilmersdorfer Str. 80. Get your rubber outfits, bondage suits and Grateful Dead memorabilia here.

Kant Store, Kantstr. 13. Leather cowboy boots.

Schwarze Mode, Grunewaldstr. 91. More leather and latex.

Bale, Savignyplatz 6. Pleasures from the Indian subcontinent.

Seide Silk Soie, Oranienstr. 23. Lingerie to spoil your skin rotten.

BITS 'N' PIECES

Meyer & Co., Gneisenaustr. 19. Hats for all occasions.

Knopfpaul, Zossener Str. 10. Buttons and zips galore.

Wundertüte, Stuttgarter Platz 5. Children's clothes.

Allerlei zur Hexerei, Hauptstr. 4. Extensive range of wool and knitting needles.

Cold War Chic

You can't hack out your own piece of Berlin Wall any more, but you can still buy one from street sellers at the site of Checkpoint Charlie and outside the Reichstag. Don't believe for a minute that any of it is genuine. Check the texture of the concrete for a certain brittle, grimy feel. Don't be conned by certificates of authenticity as these are as easy to fake as the chunks of Wall themselves. If your only concern is to impress your friends back home, pick up a piece of concrete from a building site in Friedrichshain or Prenzlauer Berg and spray it with some mock graffiti. Nobody will know the difference.

If you really want to impress your friends, why don't you buy a Soviet army officer's uniform (also from Checkpoint Charlie or the Reichstag)?

Or an East German Communist Party badge? Or (at a price) an East German flag (black red and gold with a hammer and compasses in the centre)?

You won't find much trace of day-to-day East German products in the shops; they all went out after the overnight introduction of the deutschmark in July 1990. You can still find cheap Hungarian or Soviet-labelled recordings of classical music—and if you go to the record shop **Schallplatten am Alexanderplatz** you can still admire the eccentric giant earphones used to let customers sample the wares. It's not advisable to invest in a chugging East German Trabant car. They may look sweet but even if they get you home they are unlikely to pass a roadworthiness test when you get there. You can, however, buy toy model Trabis at Woolworth's, Wilmersdorfer Str. 113.

Condoms

Condomi, Kantstr. 38. Pink ones, yellow ones, striped ones, spiky ones, mottled ones, ones that pop out of champagne bottles or fit into special pockets on designer underpants. Possibly the world's first specialist condom shop, and certainly the brightest.

Department Stores

Berlin department stores are singularly unrewarding: hot, stuffy, expensive and remarkably uninteresting. The one exception is the biggest of them all, the **Kaufhaus des Westens** or **KaDeWe** at Wittenbergplatz, Berlin's answer to Harrods and Bloomingdale's complete with a mouthwatering food hall. See Walk VII, pp. 144–5, for details.

Design

Interni, Potsdamer Str. 58. Galleries filled with Bauhaus-inspired furniture within sight of Mies van der Rohe's Nationalgalerie.
Design Galerie Herbert Jakob Weinand, Wielandstr. 37. Striking for its mock smashed windows (inspired by the aftermath of a Munich bank robbery) and filled with avant-garde furniture, including concrete beds and tables. The shop has a penchant, like the whole city, for chrome and leather.

Food

Aside from the street markets (see below), the best fresh fruit and vegetables can be found at the Turkish shops in Kreuzberg. The covered market between Eisenbahnstr. and Muskauer Str. has excellent meat, sausages and bread. Supermarkets (such as Meyer, Edeka and Euromarkt) are perfunctory and generally unadventurous. Delicatessens tend to be expensive but often irresistible. Here is a selection of specialist shops:

Salumeria da Pino e Enzo, Windscheidstr. 20. After all those stodgy German sausages, rediscover the real art of eating. Fantastic wines, cheeses, meats, olives, anchovies and other Italian imports. The buffalo mozzarella scarcely tastes better in Naples.
La Provence, Nürnberger Str. 28. Herbs, jams and honey from the south of France.
Teehaus, Krumme Str. 35. Mountains of tea.
Alternative Fleischerei, Körtestr. 20. Free-range meat.
Mutter Erde, Behaimstr. 18. Health-food shop offering everything from muesli to organically grown vegetables to eco-dishwashing liquid.

Jewellery

Mimo, Holsteinische Str. 42. Designer silver earrings.
Perlenmarkt, Kantstr. 93. Pearls and beads. Buy them loose or as earrings, brooches and necklaces.
Afro Beauty Shop, Potsdamer Str. 96. African jewellery.

Markets

Turkish market on Maybachufer, Tues and Fri. A whiff of the Orient in the heart of Germany. Clothes, spices and kebabs.
Nolle, Nollendorfplatz U-Bahn station. Closed Tues. Superior antiques and assorted junk, with adjoining bar and museum.
Trödelmarkt, Strasse des 17. Juni (by Tiergarten S-Bahn station). Weekends only. Turn up early for bargain clothes, antiques and artisan bric-a-brac.

Music

Berlin is a terrible place to try to buy music. Most shops concentrate on the soft muzak featured on the city's radio stations. Beat the streets of

Kreuzberg for bootlegs, imported independents and obscure recordings of German post-industrial noise (**Der Scheissladen** on Grossbeerenstr. 50 or **Mr Dead and Mrs Free** on Bülowstr. 5 might be good starting points). **Jazzcock** at Behaimstr. 4 is the best jazz shop. **Herder** at Kurfürstendamm 69 is the mecca of classical music fans. The best general collection for classical, rock and jazz music is **Bote und Bock** in the Europa-Center. The shop has an instrument and sheet music branch around the corner at Hardenbergstr. 9a.

Perfume

Harry Lehmann, Kantstr. 106. The only shop in Germany where you can mix your own perfumes. Just don't sneeze while you are doing it.

Porcelain

Staatliche Porzellanmanufaktur, Kurfürstendamm 205. Berlin china.
Meissen, Unter den Linden (between Glinkastr. and Friedrichstr.) China from Meissen, near Dresden, one of the great manufacturing centres since the early 18th century and a lucrative hard-currency earner for Communist East Germany.

Sports Gear

Ozone, Knesebeckstr. 27. Clothes, equipment, the works.
Der 7. Grad, Kantstr. 125. Hardware for serious mountain-climbers.

Toys/Games

Das Spiel, Ludwigkirchstr. 10. Everything from Barbie dolls to Plasticine.
Berliner Zinnfiguren-Kabinett, Knesebeckstr. 88. Tin soldiers. The old Prussian capital wouldn't be complete without a shop like this.
Die Jonglerie, Hasenheide 54. Everything you might need for a circus act, from monocycles to boomerangs.

Bären Luftballons, Kurfürstenstr. 31. Party balloons galore.
Zauberkönig, Herrmannstr. 84–90. Gags, jokes and magic tricks.

After-hours Shopping

A few establishments slip through the *Ladenschlussgesetz*. They are not cheap, but oh are they welcome when it's Saturday lunchtime and all you have in the house is a three-year-old tin of sauerkraut.

FOOD
The Turkish shops around Oranienstr. in Kreuzberg often stretch the rules. Otherwise, legitimate out-of-hours food shops include:

Edeka, inside Schlossstr. U-Bahn station. Mon–Fri 3–10 pm, Sat 1–10 pm and Sun 10 am–8 pm.
Metro, inside Fehrbelliner Platz U-Bahn. Daily 11 am–10.30 pm.
Metro, inside Kurfürstendamm U-Bahn. Daily 11 am–11 pm.
Naturboutique, Leibnitzstr. 51. Emergency health-food supplies. Mon–Fri 7 am–8 pm, Sat 7 am–6 pm.

NEWSPAPERS
Paper sellers bring the next day's edition of the *tageszeitung* round most bars and restaurants during the evening. For other papers, go to:

Internationale Presse, Joachimstaler Str. 1. Open 7 am–midnight.
Internationale und Berliner Presse, Kurfürstendamm 206–9. Until 11 pm.

Sports and Activities

Berlin's sporting heyday was about two hundred years ago when Friedrich Ludwig Jahn, one of the fathers of modern gymnastics, found favour with King Friedrich Wilhelm III and became PE trainer to the Prussian army. He was largely credited with Prussia's success in defeating Napoleon in 1814 and won an Iron Cross for his pains. In 1936 the city staged the Olympics, an occasion unfondly remembered as an exercise in Nazi propaganda. Its only redeeming feature was the performance of Jesse Owens, a black US athlete who cocked a snook at Nazi theories of Aryan supremacy by carrying off four gold medals. Hitler was so incensed he refused to shake Owens' hand.

On the whole Berliners are not renowned for being particularly fit. A city cannot have a reputation for riotous nightlife and produce great athletes at the same time. For 40 years a few young East Germans were put through one of the most rigorous and successful athletics training programmes in the world, bringing their country glory on track and field with a consistent clutch of Olympic medals. But their facilities, many of them in East Berlin, were never open to a wider public and are now barely used. The West has taken over in sport as in everything else, dismissing hundreds of coaches and seconding athletes and swimmers to its own training system.

Both sides of the city have nevertheless maintained decent sports facilities. The best address for general information is the Landessport-bund Berlin, Jesse-Owens-Allee 1–2, tel (W) 300020. The best sports centre is the Sport- und Erholungszentrum at Leninallee 77, tel (E) 43283320, a fine example of public spending under the East German Communists. It has swimming pools, wave baths, a sauna, solarium, skating rink and bowling alley, volleyball, badminton, table tennis, bowls, shooting and mini-golf. There are special facilities for children and the disabled. At the time of writing all this comes free—but don't count on it staying that way.

Fishing

You can fish anywhere, but not without a licence. Apply to the Fisch-ereiamt care of the Senator für Stadtentwicklung und Umweltschutz, Havelchaussee 149–51, tel (W) 3052047.

Horse Racing and Riding

There are two race tracks, both in East Berlin: the Galopprennbahn Hoppegarten (Goethestr. 1, Dahlwitz Hoppegarten, tel (E) 5596102) and the Trabrennbahn Karlshorst, Hermann-Duncker-Str. 129, tel (E) 5090891. The latter also has stables and facilities for riding.

Ice-skating and Roller-skating

Occasionally it is cold enough to skate on Berlin's lakes—official signs will tell you whether or not it is safe. Otherwise you can skate indoors for about DM 5 at the Eissporthalle, An der Jafféstr., tel (W) 30381. There is also a Rollerskating-center on Hasenheide 108 (tel (W) 6211028); it is open every afternoon and evening except on Mondays.

Marathon

The Berlin Marathon takes place every year in early October. To take part, apply to SCC Berlin, Meinekestr. 13, tel (W) 8826405.

Sailing

The Berliners are great sailors and the Havel lake is an ideal stretch of water for them to indulge their hobby. The main moorings are just by Wannsee S-Bahn station.

231

The Havel Segelschule, Alt Pichelsdorf 19c, tel (W) 3622061 and the Segelschule Berlin, Friederikestr. 24, tel (W) 4311171, both run courses on sailing and other watersports.

Soccer

Berlin has two teams. The West's Hertha SC is languishing somewhere near the bottom of the first division of the Bundesliga. The East's FC Berlin used to be the pet team of Stasi boss Erich Mielke and is now fighting to stave off a slide into obscurity. Matches are played at a number of venues, including the Olympic Stadium in the West and the Sportplatz Friedrich-Ludwig-Jahn off Schönhauser Allee in Prenzlauer Berg. For details of matches, consult the listings magazines *Tip* and *Zitty*. Soccer hooliganism has been on the increase since the opening of the Wall.

Swimming

If it's warm enough to swim outside, go to the beach at Wannsee (bus E from Nikolassee S-Bahn station) or the Müggelsee (S-Bahn Friedrichs-hagen or Rahnsdorf). Nearer to the centre of town there are open-air pools in Kreuzberg (Gitschiner Str. 18–31) and Wilmersdorf (Forcken-beckstr. 14). For the rest of the year, the following indoor pools are good and cheap:

Wilmersdorf: Mecklenburgische Str. 80, tel (W) 8689523
Schöneberg: Sachsendamm 11, tel (W) 7833005
Kreuzberg: Wiener Str. 59h, tel (W) 25885813
Charlottenburg: Krummesstr. 9–10, tel (W) 34303241
Tiergarten: Seydlitzstr. 7, tel (W) 390554011
Friedrichshain: Leninallee 77, tel (E) 43283320

Many of these also have saunas, exercise machines, table-tennis tables and so on. For a more exclusive version of the same, try one of the four- or five-star hotels (the Metropol in East Berlin is especially rec-ommended). For around DM 25 you can spend all day toning your muscles, lying under sunbeds and splashing around in Olympic-size pools.

Tennis

This is largely confined to private clubs with limited access. There are some courts in the Freizeitpark Tegel in the north of the city; tel (W) 4346666 for booking details.

Tobogganing

At the first sign of snow head for the Teufelsberg in the Grunewald, the city's highest hill made from all the rubble of the Second World War. You can hire sleds and the slopes are long and gentle. You can even ski on the Teufelsberg, although it is not very rewarding. Contact the Skiverband Berlin, Bismarckallee 2 (tel (W) 8919798) for details.

Living in Berlin

a Berlin Water Pump

'Berlin is not a city where you can find salvation,' wrote the poet Frank Wedekind in 1918. It is still a distinctly secular place, dominated by the weight of its history and brought to life by a certain frenetic vibrancy. It is not the sort of place that immediately feels like home, but its very restlessness exerts a fascination that can become compelling. Berlin is a city obsessed with itself, obsessed with the political changes that have turned the lives of its people—in both East and West—quite literally upside down. After the euphoria of the collapse of the Wall, the two sides now have to get on with the business of living with each other. If, as a new resident, you make the effort to plant roots in both East and West—and you should—you may well find yourself leading two quite distinct lives. The wounds of division are slow to heal.

Berlin in the 1990s is becoming a magnet for the footloose, the disgruntled and the dispossessed, not only of Germany but of the whole of Eastern Europe. Newcomers of all kinds are flooding in—entrepreneurs, casual workers, students, chancers, strays and bums. The city, dizzy from its sudden return to 'normality' after the Cold War, is full to bursting point, noisy, bustling and marked by vast contrasts between the affluent West and the struggling, tumbledown East. Anyone wanting to get established here faces a lot of competition with little space to fight over.

One good starting point is the **auskunfts- und beratungscenter**

234

(abc) on Hohenzollerndamm 125, tel (W) 82008260, which provides information and advice for anyone new to Berlin. It is open Tues–Fri 4–8 and Sat 11–2. Foreigners intending to work or study have to register with the police at the *Ausländeramt* (office for foreigners) at Friedrich-Krause-Ufer 24, tel (W) 390550, and apply for a residence permit. The office is open Mon–Fri from 7.30 until lunchtime. Arrive before it opens to ensure you reach the front of the queue by closing time. It will probably take two or three visits, and bundles of patience, to sort yourself out. If you are an EC citizen, you automatically have the right to work. If not, you need the sponsorship of an employer. However, thousands of foreigners with casual jobs do not bother to register at all.

If you are looking for a stop-gap to earn some money and enjoy Berlin, **finding a job** is quite easy. Bars, restaurants and hotels are constantly on the look-out for staff, and speaking English is a real advantage (as long as you speak some German too). English teachers, with or without experience, should find plenty of enthusiastic private pupils, especially in the East where Russian was previously the most common second language. More permanent jobs are harder to come by. Rising unemployment in the East has tightened the job market. Go to the **Informations- und Beratungsdienst für zuwandernde Arbeitsnehmer** (information and advice service for immigrant workers), Kleiststr. 23–26, tel (W) 31832750; in the past the office dealt mostly with Turkish workers, but it is adapting rapidly to changing times.

Finding somewhere to live can be a real nightmare. Berlin rents, once blissfully cheap, are soaring. Finding anything central is becoming virtually impossible. The listings magazines *Tip* and *Zitty* and the Sunday edition of the *Berliner Morgenpost* newspaper have decent housing sections, but you have to grab the first copy off the newsstand to get anywhere. Another option is one of the city's *Mitwohnzentralen*, or rental agencies, which specialize in short-term accommodation. Try the Erste Mitwohnzentrale in the West (Sybelstr. 53, tel (W) 3243031) or City-Kontakt in the East (Marienburger Str. 47, tel (E) 4365447). Rents will be quoted to you either *warm* (bills included) or *kalt* (bills not included). You will usually have to put one month's rent up front, plus another month's worth as a deposit. If you are short of money, you can often find cheap flats in Kreuzberg or Prenzlauer Berg that do not have a toilet or bath (find a friend's house to wash in). Squatting is also an option, especially in the East where about 25,000 buildings have been abandoned, but the present city administration is bent on clearing as many squats as it can, seeing them as seedbeds of lawlessness and violence.

235

Below is an A–Z of other useful information and addresses:

AIDS helpline: Information and counselling day and night at Berliner AIDS-Hilfe e.V., Meinekestr. 12, tel (W) 8833017 or (W) 19411.

Alcoholism: Landesstelle Berlin gegen Suchtgefahren (Berlin city office against the dangers of addiction), Gierkezeile 39, tel (W) 3418539.

Dinner Delivered to your Door: A somewhat alien concept to Germans, but catching on. The best is Kenan's Party Service, Oppelner Str. 4, tel (W) 6186758.

Drugs: West Berlin has a rather puzzling reputation for chronic drug problems, largely based on the 1980 film *Christiane F.* A nominally true story, the movie depicts a middle-class teenager who listens to David Bowie, becomes hooked on heroin, turns to prostitution and hangs out at Bahnhof Zoo with her junky friends before mending her ways and confessing all to a sensationalist magazine. In reality, drugs engender more fear than actual problems. There *are* addicts, especially among the young drop-outs of Kreuzberg, and certainly no lack of soft drugs such as marijuana. But the situation is mild, especially compared to Italian or Spanish cities where hundreds of young people die each year and needles are left lying on every street. In emergencies there is a helpline on (W) 247033. For more general information contact the Senatsverwaltung für Frauen, Jugend und Familie (city department for women, youth and family), Am Karlsbad 8–10, tel (W) 26042573.

Environmental Berlin: Following the rise of the Greens in the 1980s, Germany is extremely environment-conscious. Berliners religiously divide their garbage into paper, glass, organic waste and the rest and dispose of it in separate containers found in every flat block. However, the city still produces more rubbish than it can cope with. The arrival of Western plastic packaging in the East caused the quantity of rubbish there to triple overnight. Gloomy eco-activists talk of a looming garbage mountain. The most active environmental organization is Greenpeace at Hannoversche Str. 1, tel (E) 2828340. Several city districts have advisory centres known as *Umweltladen* (literally, environment shops). The most colourful is in Prenzlauer Berg in the East, at Dimitroffstr. 169.

Family Planning: Pro Familia, Ansbacherstr. 11, tel (W) 2139013.

Gay and Lesbian Berlin: The free-wheeling city that attracted W.H. Auden and Christopher Isherwood in the 1920s is still remarkably liberal in its attitude to homosexuality. Same-sex couples feel free

236

enough to walk arm-in-arm, hug or kiss in the street in many areas of town. The gay scene revolves around Schöneberg and Kreuzberg in the West but not exclusively; East Berlin's gays enjoyed relative tolerance from the Communist authorities and have a reasonably well-organized network. The key starting address for contact names and numbers on both sides of town is the Kommunikations- und Beratungszentrum homosexueller Frauen und Männer (contact and advice centre for homosexual women and men) at Kulmer Str. 20a, tel (W) 215200 for women, (W) 215900 for men. Berlin's main gay bookshop, Prinz Eisenherz (Bleibtreustr. 52), has information on forthcoming gay events. There are two Berlin magazine guides for gay men, the racily named *Berlin von Hinten* (Berlin from behind) and *Siegessäule* (victory column, after the monument in the middle of the Tiergarten); *Blattgold* is a guide for lesbians.

Language Courses: German classes are available at the Goethe Institut, Hardenbergstr. 7, tel (W) 3122045, or Inlingua, Ku'damm 200, tel (W) 8812020, or Berlitz, Ku'damm 74, tel (W) 3239047.

Laundry: Laundrettes are plentiful in West Berlin (there are big ones on Mehringdamm, Uhlandstr. and Dahlmannstr.), but non-existent in the East. Dry cleaners take a week to 10 days to return your clothes and charge a fortune. Most furnished flats for rent have washing machines.

Libraries: Berlin libraries are spacious, friendly and well-stocked. Joining one is free but you have to have a police certificate of residence in Berlin. Anyone can use libraries to work in or consult books on the spot. The best are:

Staatsbibliothek, Potsdamer Str. 33, tel (W) 2661, open Mon–Fri 9–7 and Sat 9–1: Hans Scharoun's post-Bauhaus masterpiece, featured in Wim Wenders' *Wings of Desire*, is worth visiting even if you aren't looking for books. It has vast collections on most subjects, but largely in German.

Amerika Gedenkbibliothek, Blücherplatz 1, tel (W) 691011, open Mon 4–8 and Tues–Sat 11–8: This contains an exhaustive collection of books on Berlin itself. Some volumes are in English.

British Council, Hardenbergstr. 20, tel (W) 310716, open Mon–Fri 12–6; 2 hours later on Tues and Thurs: Come here if you run out of English-language reading material. Everything from 17th-century cookbooks to spy novels.

Lost Property: Contact the police, tel (W) 6990 or the transport company BVG at Potsdamer Str. 184, tel (W) 2161413 in the West.

In the East there is a special depot (*Fundbüro*) at Wilhelm-Pieck-Str. 164, tel (E) 2806235.

Moving: One reliable international removal company is Hertling, Sophie-Charlottenstr. 15, tel (W) 3209030.

Newspapers: Berlin has a lively press, viewing the world from several vantage points—from the pundit's armchair to the gutter. The Axel Springer newspaper empire has its headquarters here, publishing right-wing national dailies such as *Die Welt* and *Bild*. But Berlin also has five titles of its own. In the West, the *Tagesspiegel* is solid, thorough and somewhere in the political centre. The *tageszeitung*, or *taz* for short, is Germany's foremost 'alternative' newspaper, with a self-consciously trendy outlook; evening paper sellers bring the next day's edition round restaurants, bars and nightclubs. Springer's *Berliner Morgenpost* is the conscience of the petty bourgeoisie, with a weakness for sensational stories about communists and immigrants that on close scrutiny do not always seem quite so sensational after all. In the East, the *Berliner Zeitung* offers the city's best reporting on low life and the offbeat, while the *Berliner Kurier* tries to be even sleazier than the notorious national tabloid *Bild*. It fails, of course.

Berlin is also a good place to peruse the remnants of the East's former Communist-controlled press. *Neues Deutschland*, the party organ that used to be all newsprint and no news, is now the voice of the reformed Communists, the Party of Democratic Socialism. Despite a certain amnesia about the past, it is quite a cogent critic of the establishment.

There is no local English-language paper, but you can get the British press and the *International Herald Tribune* from most newsstands and large hotels. Several West Berlin cafés provide them along with the other newspapers they leave out for customers on distinctive long wooden holders.

Pets: You need a certificate to prove your animal has been vaccinated against rabies before taking it into Germany. Dogs travelling on trains have to wear a muzzle. If you want to leave your pet in Berlin while you are away, try the *Ferienheim Hund und Katze*, Morgensternstr. 16, tel (W) 7724027, or *Urlaub für den Hund* (dogs only) at Soltauer Str. 30a, tel (W) 4324090.

Plumbers: Day or night, call H.G. Aengst on tel (W) 7462187.

Poison Emergency Service: If you've poured detergent on your cornflakes, tel (W) 3035466.

Radio/TV: The overthrow of communism in East Germany was in many ways a media revolution. During the Cold War the West spent a great deal of time, money and energy beaming its broadcasts into the East to win hearts and minds over to the ways of Western democracy and capitalism. The relics of that era, such as the radio and TV network SFB (Sender Freies Berlin, or Free Berlin Broadcasting) and the US-backed RIAS (Radio In the American Sector), live on in the new Germany. On the other hand, East German radio and TV were largely ditched after unification, just as they were becoming really interesting and refreshingly different. They live on only as regional back-up to the main networks.

The bulwarks of West German television, ARD and ZDF, are strong on soap operas and imported detective serials, but there are few serious documentaries and next to nothing that could be described as comedy. The news tends to be pro-establishment and is more wrapped up in domestic issues than most national networks in other countries. Private channels SAT-1 and RTL-plus go for sex and violence with a titillating relish; turn them on after 10 pm and you can see housewives undressing, or crazed killers with machetes, or occasionally both at the same time. On cable you can dull your senses with 24-hours-a-day music videos on MTV (in English), or tune into one of the two armed forces' channels, SSVC from Britain or AFN from the United States. Both show a blend of material from their domestic networks. The American station also features news bulletins read by energetic blue-uniformed officers doing Walter Cronkite impersonations.

German radio seems to be addicted to *Kuschelrock*, literally cuddle rock, the kind of anodyne tinkling normally confined to airport terminals. The forces provide English-language stations: AFN (88 FM) plays macho rock-'n'-roll, while BFBS (99 FM) has a more gentle mix of phone-ins, chart countdowns and gardening programmes. You can also pick up the BBC World Service on 90.2 FM.

Rape Crisis Centre: Stresemannstr. 40, tel (W) 2512828.

Women's Berlin: Berlin provides women with a rich variety of cultural centres, bookshops, further education centres and health clinics. Bars and clubs have women-only nights. For a while there were more women than men on West Berlin's ruling council, the Senat. However the current Christian Democrat-led coalition, running the whole city, is distinctly male-dominated: it looks unlikely to maintain subsidies for women's groups in the West and even more unlikely to start them up in the East.

The *Frauenzentrum* (women's centre) at Stresemannstr. 40, tel (W) 6228127, has general information; foreign women can get further

239

advice from *Hilfe für ausländische Frauen und Kinder* (help for foreign women and children), Karolinger Platz 6a, tel (W) 3023490. The best women's bookshop is *Lilith*, Knesebeckstr. 86–87, tel (W) 3123102. For further education courses contact *Cobra*, Ahrweilerstr. 4, tel (W) 8210032. The *Theater Zentrifuge* (Boppstr. 10, tel (W) 6053202) puts on all-women shows. Advice on health including contraception and abortion is available from *Im 13. Mond* (in the 13th moon), Hagelberger Str. 52, tel (W) 7864047. The *Frauenmitfahrzentrale* organizes women-only lifts in private cars (see p. 3) at Potsdamer Str. 139, tel (W) 2153165.

Chronology

1237	First mention of Coelln; nominal date for the founding of the city
1244	First mention of Coelln's twin town Berlin on north bank of Spree
1411	The Burggraf of Nuremberg, Friedrich von Hohenzollern, becomes protector of the Mark of Brandenburg including Berlin-Coelln
1432	Berlin and Coelln formally merge
1448	Elector Friedrich II (Iron Tooth) makes Berlin his capital after quelling local revolt; builds castle and official residence
1539	Brandenburg accepts Luther's teachings and becomes Protestant
1671	The Great Elector, Friedrich Wilhelm, invites 50 wealthy Jewish families to Berlin to escape persecution in Vienna
1685	Friedrich Wilhelm issues Edict of Potsdam, allowing persecuted French Huguenots to come to Berlin
1688	Great Elector dies; succeeded by his son Friedrich III
1695	Work begins on Schloss Charlottenburg
1701	Elector crowns himself King Friedrich I of Prussia
1713	Friedrich Wilhelm I, the 'soldier king', takes power
1740	Friedrich II (Frederick the Great) takes the throne; invades and annexes Silesia
1745	Work begins on Sanssouci Palace in Potsdam
1756	Frederick marches into Saxony, starting Seven Years' War
1760	Russian troops occupy Berlin
1786	Frederick dies; succeeded by his nephew Friedrich Wilhelm II
1791	Brandenburg Gate completed
1797	Friedrich Wilhelm III takes over the throne
1806	Napoleon marches through Brandenburg Gate after defeating the Prussians at Jena; occupies the city for two years
1814	The Prussians defeat Napoleon at Leipzig
1820	Schinkel draws up plans for Museum Island and begins revamping central Berlin in neo-classical style
1838	Completion of the first Berlin–Potsdam railway
1840	Friedrich Wilhelm IV takes power
1848	Revolution in Berlin; establishment of a provisional chamber of deputies until the imposition of martial law by General Wrangel
1857	Friedrich Wilhelm forced to step down after a stroke; succeeded by his brother Wilhelm I
1862	Otto von Bismarck becomes Prime Minister of Prussia
1871	Germany unified after victory in war against France. Wilhelm I crowned Kaiser in Versailles
1879	The first trams and electric street lights in the world appear in Berlin
1888	Wilhelm II becomes Kaiser

1890	Bismarck dismissed as Chancellor
1902	The first stretch of U-Bahn built in Berlin
1914	Outbreak of the First World War
1915	Anti-war protests begin outside the Reichstag
1918	Germany surrenders; the Kaiser abdicates and flees to Holland; violent power struggle between Spartacists and Social Democrats
1919	Spartacist leaders Karl Liebknecht and Rosa Luxemburg murdered; their revolt crushed; founding of Weimar Republic
1920	Establishment of Greater Berlin
1923	Hyperinflation wipes out most Germans' savings
1924	US-inspired Dawes plan restores economic stability
1926	Goebbels arrives in Berlin to rouse support for the Nazis
1929	Wall Street Crash causes economic depression; mass unemployment in Germany
1933	Nazi stormtroopers celebrate taking power with a torchlit procession through the Brandenburg Gate; Reichstag fire; burning of Jewish and left-wing books on Opernplatz (now Bebelplatz)
1936	Berlin hosts the Olympic Games
1938	Jewish homes, businesses and synagogues destroyed on *Reichskristallnacht*
1939	The Second World War breaks out
1943	British and US planes begin carpet-bombing Berlin
1945	Hitler commits suicide; the Red Army liberates Berlin after a fierce battle; Germany surrenders; the Potsdam Conference heralds the division of Germany and of Berlin
1948	Soviet blockade of West Berlin begins; city kept going by British and US airlift; establishment of separate city administrations
1949	Stalin lifts the blockade; founding of separate German states
1953	Workers' uprising in East Berlin crushed by Soviet tanks
1961	Faced with a mounting exodus of citizens through Berlin, East Germany builds the Berlin Wall
1963	President Kennedy visits West Berlin, declares '*Ich bin ein Berliner*'; West Berliners allowed to visit the East of the city again
1969	Former West Berlin mayor Willy Brandt becomes West German Chancellor; begins policy of rapprochement to the East resulting in normalization of German–German relations three years later
1987	Rudolf Hess dies in Spandau prison

1989:

10 Sept	Hungary opens its borders to the West; thousands of East Germans cross into Austria and then West Germany
7 Oct	Hundreds of thousands of people demonstrate against the government during East Germany's 40th anniversary celebrations attended by Soviet leader Mikhail Gorbachev
18 Oct	After mounting street protests and a continuing exodus to the West, East German leader Erich Honecker steps down, succeeded by his deputy, Egon Krenz

CHRONOLOGY

4 Nov   Half a million people demonstrate on East Berlin's Alexanderplatz,
         demanding open borders and free elections
7 Nov   The politburo resigns; the government resigns the next day
9 Nov   Krenz allows free travel to the West; the Berlin Wall is open
1 Dec   The East German Communist Party renounces its monopoly of power

1990:
18 March The conservative Christian Democrats (CDU), backed by Bonn
         Chancellor Helmut Kohl, win a surprise landslide election victory in
         East Germany on promise of monetary union and swift unification
1 July   The deutschmark becomes East Germany's currency; introduction of
         the free market; all inter-German border controls scrapped
8 July   West Germany wins the World Cup
3 Oct   Germany officially reunited under Bonn constitution and government
2 Dec   Kohl re-elected as Chancellor; CDU also wins Berlin's first joint city
         election since 1946

Further Reading and Films

Most books about Berlin are out of date, but that does not devalue them. On the contrary, it only helps make sense of a city that has changed so dramatically and so fast. New books on 1989 and all that are beginning to appear, but so far none has been particularly convincing. The following list gives a broad and, I hope, rewarding cross-section of the best of the literature. Titles given in German have not been translated.

HISTORY/GENERAL

Craig, Gordon, *The Germans* (Penguin, 1983). A rich and subtle introduction to the Germans, their history, neuroses, fears and guilt; contains an excellent chapter on Berlin, the perpetual 'city in crisis'.

Garton Ash, Timothy, *The Uses of Adversity* (Granta/Penguin, 1989). A survey of dissident movements throughout Eastern Europe, including some atmospheric re-creations of Cold War East Berlin and a critical essay on the legacy of Brecht after 40 years of communism.

Gelb, Norman, *The Berlin Wall* (Michael Joseph, 1986). An engaging, detailed account of the Wall in its first 25 years. Gelb saw no reason why it should not still have been there in another 25 years, a reflection of the extraordinary pace of events rather than any shortsightedness.

Kemp, Anthony, *Escape from Berlin* (Boxtree, 1987). A chronicle of the high risks and big money involved in trying to spirit East Germans out to the West.

Knabe, Hubertus (ed.), *Aufbruch in eine andere DDR* (Rowohlt, 1989). Essays by leading East German intellectuals, written immediately after the Wall opened, on how they saw the future of their country. With hindsight, a sad commentary on the wasted ideas and wasted talent swept aside in the Western takeover of East Germany.

Masur, Gerhard, *Imperial Berlin* (RKP, 1971). A thorough, intelligent analysis of the Berlin of the Kaisers.

Mander, John, *The Eagle and the Bear*. Written in the early 1960s but long out of print, Mander's history of the city is worth hunting down in libraries for its entertaining, occasionally eccentric, love of a good story and sure eye for detail.

Simmons, Michael, *Berlin: The Depressed City* (Hamish Hamilton 1988). A colourful, fast-paced account of Berlin in the 20th century.

Walker, Ian, *Zoo Station* (Abacus, 1988). The diary of an addicted commuter between East and West in Cold War Berlin. A witty, intelligent narrative wavering between the city's restlessness and contradictions and those of the author's own life.

ARCHITECTURE/GUIDES

Baedecker, Karl, *Berlin and its Environs* (first published 1906). Nothing can teach you more about the rapid changes in the city than an out-of-date guide book, the older

244

the better. Baedecker's punctilious attention to detail makes him a must. Available in travel and second-hand bookshops.

Hegemann, Werner, *Das steinerne Berlin* (Vieweg Verlag, 1930). The definitive history of how the city got to look the way it did (at least until the war). A huge, polemical book raging with contempt for Berlin's arrogant aristocratic rulers.

Kiaulehn, Walter, *Berlin: Schicksal einer Weltstadt* (dtv, 1981). An equally encyclopaedic, but more balanced history of the city's architectural development.

FICTION

Döblin, Alfred, *Berlin Alexanderplatz* (Penguin). The epic novel of the downtrodden proletariat in 1920s Berlin.

Isherwood, Christopher, *Goodbye to Berlin* and *Mr Norris Changes Trains* (Methuen). Isherwood's stories present a kaleidoscope of characters from petty conmen to seedy aristocrats in a city on the verge of doom in the early 1930s.

Schneider, Peter, *The Wall Jumper* (Allison and Busby). A series of cameos, bordering on fantasy, about life in the divided city.

Wolf, Christa, *The Divided Heaven* (Virago). Written straight after the building of the Berlin Wall, this highly political love story brought East Germany's foremost novelist her first success.

PHOTOGRAPHS

Berliner Mauerbilder (Nicolai 1989). The best of the wild mural art from the Berlin Wall, now all gone along with the concrete and barbed wire.

Eschen, Fritz, *Photographien Berlin 1945–1950* (Nicolai 1990). Striking, and highly emotional, pictures of Berlin in the aftermath of the Second World War.

Hauswald, Harald, with text by Lutz Rathenow, *Ostberlin—die andere Seite einer Stadt* (Nicolai 1990). Rarely seen glimpses of life in East Berlin, with a satirical text by one of the half-city's best writers.

FILMS

Berlin, Symphony of a Great City (Walter Rittmann, 1927). A day in the life of Europe's (then) most modern city seen through an apparently disinterested camera but chock-full of power to dazzle and shock. One critic of the time said it 'flays our retinas, our nerves, our consciousness'.

Germany Year Zero (Roberto Rossellini, 1947). A neo-realist tale of survival and family betrayal amid the ruins of post-war Berlin.

Berlin Alexanderplatz (Rainer Werner Fassbinder, 1982). Fassbinder's dark, moody, nine-hour-long adaptation of the Döblin novel.

Wings of Desire (Wim Wenders, 1986). The story of two angels who come to the divided city in search of values to save humanity. Hauntingly set in and around the Tiergarten and Potsdamer Platz.

Language

German has come in for a hard time ever since the Holy Roman Emperor Charles V dismissed it as fit only for speaking to his horse. The narrator of Anthony Burgess's novel *Earthly Powers* describes it as 'a glottal fishboneclearing soulful sobbing sausagemachine of a language'. Certainly, it is not mellifluous like Italian or French, and its baroque sentence structure can be exasperating. But German has other advantages: it is concrete, precise and capable of presenting highly complex ideas in manageable form. Spoken by Berliners in their hard, furious-paced accent it can also be down-to-earth, playful and witty.

German presents formidable problems at first: not two genders, but three; declensions for nouns and adjectives, as well as the conjugations for verbs; and a word order that appears to turn sentences on their heads. Madame de Staël once lamented that Germans were incapable of lively debate because nobody could interrupt a speaker until he had uttered the verb at the *end* of the sentence. The one compensation for the multiplicity of rules is that they are rigidly adhered to. Unlike most languages, you will rarely come across an exception in German.

The chances are you will not have to speak a great deal of German as a visitor in Berlin unless you volunteer to do so. Most West Berliners, whether taxi drivers, waiters, shopkeepers or post office workers, speak enviably good English and are only too keen to practise it. East Berlin is a slightly different story, with English only now taking over from Russian as the primary foreign language taught at school, but most people know the basics. The list below will give beginners the chance to summon up the fundamental courtesies, read the menu and ask directions.

Some basics of pronunciation: German is a mercifully phonetic language, with each letter or combination of letters usually spoken the same way. Each syllable is given roughly equal stress.

Consonants: Final *d*s are hard like *t*s. *g* is always hard, as in *goat*. *h* is only aspirated at the beginning of words or components of compound words. Roll your *r*s from the back of the mouth, as though clearing the top of your throat. *s* tends to be hard, like the *z* in *buzz*. *j* is pronounced like a *y*. *v* is pronounced *f*. *w* is pronounced *v[w]*. Say *ch* as in a Scottish *loch*, unless it has an *s* in front of it, in which case say *sh*. An *s* followed by a single hard consonant is often pronounced *sh*. *z* is always *ts*.

Vowels: *a* is short and breathy as in the exclamation *pah*. *e* is slightly longer than in English (don't forget to articulate it at the ends of words). Say *er* as in *air* and *ee* as in *say*. *u* can be short as in *put*, or long like the double *o* in *boot*. Otherwise vowels standing alone are similar to English. *au* is like the painful *ow*. *ie* is pronounced *ee*; *ei* is pronounced *eye*.

The strangest phenomenon in German is the **umlaut** (¨), which appears as two dots above an *a*, *o* or *u*. This is sometimes replaced by an *e* after the vowel. Pronounce *ä* like the *a* in *cradle* and *ö* like the vowel sound in *fur*; *ü* is the trickiest sound as it does not exist in standard English. It is like a French *u*, if that helps; otherwise imagine a Glaswegian saying *who* or *you*.

Other Oddities: All nouns begin with a capital letter, so they are relatively easy to identify in print. Double *s* is sometimes written as ß, known as a *scharfes S*.

Try out these practice sentences:

Verstehen Sie Deutsch?—Nein, ich verstehe kein Wort
fairshtayen zee doitch?—nine, ich fairshtay-e kine vort
(Do you understand German?—No, I don't understand a word)

Waren Sie schon in Berlin?—Ja, aber vor der Öffnung der Mauer
varen zee shohn in bairleen?—ya, aaber for dare erfnoong dare mao-er
(Have you ever been to Berlin?—Yes, but before the opening of the Wall)

Useful Words and Phrases

yes/no/maybe	*ja/nein/vielleicht*
and/but	*und/aber*
with/without	*mit/ohne*
please	*bitte*
thank you (very much)	*danke (schön)*
you're (very) welcome	*bitte (schön)*
hello	*hallo; guten Tag*
goodbye	*auf Wiedersehen; tschüss*
good morning/evening	*guten Morgen/Abend*
good night	*gute Nacht*
how are you?	*wie geht's?*
I'm very well	*mir geht's gut*
what is your name?	*wie heissen Sie?*
my name is...	*mein Name ist...; ich heisse...*
I come from...	*ich komme aus...*
England	*England*
Scotland	*Schottland*
Wales	*Wales*
Ireland	*Irland*
the United States	*den Vereinigten Staaten*
Canada	*Kanada*
New Zealand	*Neuseeland*
Australia	*Australien*
I am English etc (man/woman)	*ich bin Engländer(in), Schotte (Schottin) Waliser(in), Ire (Irin), Amerikaner(in), Kanadier(in), Neuseeländer(in), Australier(in)*
I don't speak German	*ich spreche kein Deutsch*
do you speak English?	*sprechen Sie English?*
I don't know	*ich weiss nicht*
I don't understand	*ich verstehe nicht*

247

can you help me?	*können Sie mir bitte helfen?*
how do you say ...	*wie sagt man ...*
help!	*Hilfe!*
it doesn't matter	*es macht nichts*
all right	*alles klar*
excuse me	*Entschuldigung, bitte*
be careful!	*Achtung!*
nothing	*nichts*
it is urgent	*es ist dringend*
who	*wer*
what	*was*
why	*warum*
when	*wann*
where	*wo*
where is/are ...	*wo ist/sind ...; wo finde ich ...*
how	*wie*
how much	*wieviel*
how much does this cost?	*wieviel kostet das?*
I would like ...	*ich möchte ...*
I am lost	*ich weiss nicht, wo ich bin*
I am hungry	*ich habe Hunger*
I am thirsty	*ich habe Durst*
I am sorry	*es tut mir leid*
I am tired	*ich bin müde*
I am hot	*mir ist warm*
I am cold	*mir ist kalt*
I am ill	*ich bin krank*
leave me alone	*lassen Sie mich bitte in Ruhe*
good/bad	*gut/schlecht*
beautiful/ugly	*schön/hässlich*
slow/fast	*langsam/schnell*
big/small	*gross/klein*
here/there	*hier/da*
entrance	*Eingang*
(emergency) exit	*(Not)ausgang*
no entry	*Eingang verboten*
open/closed	*offen/geschlossen*
cheap/expensive	*billig/teuer*

HOTELS, BANKS, SHOPS, SIGHTSEEING

bank	*Bank*
bar/pub	*Kneipe*
bathroom	*Badezimmer*
bed	*Bett*
bill	*Rechnung*
bureau de change	*Wechselstube*

small change	*Wechselgeld; Kleingeld*
church	*Kirche*
cigarettes	*Zigaretten*
credit card	*Kreditkarte*
doctor	*Arzt*
hospital	*Krankenhaus*
lake	*See*
money	*Geld*
museum	*Museum*
newspaper	*Zeitung*
pharmacy	*Apotheke*
police (station)	*Polizei(revier)*
policeman	*Polizist*
post office	*Post*
restaurant	*Restaurant; Gaststätte*
single/double room	*Einzelzimmer, Doppelzimmer*
shop	*Laden*
telephone (box)	*Telefon (zelle)*
tip	*Trinkgeld*
toilet	*Klo, Toilette*
men's	*Herren*
women's	*Damen*
traveller's cheque	*Reisescheck*
wall	*Mauer*

DAYS/MONTHS

Monday	*Montag*
Tuesday	*Dienstag*
Wednesday	*Mittwoch*
Thursday	*Donnerstag*
Friday	*Freitag*
Saturday	*Samstag; Sonnabend*
Sunday	*Sonntag*
bank holiday	*Feiertag/Festtag*
January	*Januar*
February	*Februar*
March	*März*
April	*April*
May	*Mai*
June	*Juni*
July	*Juli*
August	*August*
September	*September*
October	*Oktober*
November	*November*
December	*Dezember*

NUMBERS

one	*eins*
two	*zwei*
three	*drei*
four	*vier*
five	*fünf*
six	*sechs*
seven	*sieben*
eight	*acht*
nine	*neun*
ten	*zehn*
eleven	*elf*
twelve	*zwölf*
thirteen	*dreizehn*
fourteen	*vierzehn*
fifteen	*fünfzehn*
sixteen	*sechszehn*
seventeen	*siebzehn*
eighteen	*achtzehn*
nineteen	*neunzehn*
twenty	*zwanzig*
twenty-one	*einundzwanzig*
twenty-two	*zweiundzwanzig*
thirty	*dreissig*
thirty-one	*einunddreissig*
forty	*vierzig*
fifty	*fünfzig*
sixty	*sechszig*
seventy	*siebzig*
eighty	*achtzig*
ninety	*neunzig*
hundred	*hundert*
hundred and one	*hunderteins*
hundred and twenty-one	*hunderteinundzwanzig*
two hundred	*zweihundert*
thousand	*tausend*
three thousand	*dreitausend*
million	*eine Million*
billion (thousand million)	*eine Milliarde*
billion (million million)	*eine Billion*
1992	*neunzehnhundertzweiundneunzig*

TIME

watch/clock/hour	*Uhr*
alarm clock	*Wecker*
what time is it?	*wie spät ist es?; wieviel Uhr ist es?*

midday	*Mittag*
midnight	*Mitternacht*
one/two/three o'clock	*eine/zwei/drei Uhr*
quarter-past two	*Viertel nach zwei*
half-past two	*halbdrei* [sic]
half-past three	*halbvier*
quarter to three	*Viertel vor drei*
birthday	*Geburtstag*
year	*Jahr*
season	*Jahreszeit*
spring	*Frühling*
summer	*Sommer*
autumn	*Herbst*
winter	*Winter*
month	*Monat*
week	*Woche*
day	*Tag*
today/yesterday/tomorrow	*heute/gestern/morgen*
this week/last week	*diese Woche/letzte Woche*
morning	*Morgen; Vormittag*
afternoon	*Nachmittag*
evening	*Abend*
night	*Nacht*

TRANSPORT

airport	*Flughafen*
customs	*Zoll*
stop	*Haltestelle*
bus/coach	*Bus*
railway station	*Bahnhof*
train	*Zug*
platform	*Gleis*
underground/city train	*U-Bahn; S-Bahn*
underground station	*U-Bahnhof* (or *S-Bahnhof*)
car	*Auto*
taxi	*Taxi*
bicycle	*Fahrrad*
ticket	*Fahrkarte*
seat	*Platz*
occupied/reserved	*besetzt*

TRAVEL DIRECTIONS

I want to go to...	*ich möchte nach...*
how can I get to...?	*wie fahre ich nach...?*
where is...?	*wo ist...?*
how far is it to...?	*wie weit ist es nach...?*
when does the next... leave?	*wann fährt der/die/das nächste...?*

how long does it take?	*wie lange dauert es?*
have a good journey	*gute Reise*
near/far	*nah/weit*
left/right/straight ahead	*links/rechts/gerade aus*
forwards/backwards	*nach vorne/nach hinten*
east/west	*ost/west*
north/south	*nord/süd*
around the corner	*um die Ecke*
junction/crossing	*Kreuzung*
street/road	*Strasse*
square	*Platz*
map/atlas	*Strassenplan/Atlas*

DRIVING

car hire	*Autovermietung*
I would like to hire a car	*Ich möchte ein Auto mieten*
petrol/diesel	*Benzin/Diesel*
leaded/unleaded	*verbleit/bleifrei*
filling station	*Tankstelle*
garage (for repairs)	*Autowerkstatt*
parking place/carpark	*Parkplatz*
no parking	*Parken verboten*
breakdown	*Panne*
crash	*Autounfall*
driver's licence	*Führerschein*
insurance	*Versicherung*
speed limit	*Höchstgeschwindigkeit*

FOOD/DRINK/RESTAURANTS

breakfast	*Frühstuck*
lunch	*Mittagessen*
dinner	*Abendessen*
menu	*Speisekarte*
waiter/waitress	*Kellner/Kellnerin*
to order	*bestellen*
bon appétit	*guten Appetit*
does it taste good?	*schmeckt's?*
it tastes good/bad	*es schmeckt gut/schlecht*
service	*Bedienung*
starter	*Vorspeise*
soup	*Suppe*
main course	*Hauptgericht*
dessert	*Nachtisch*
meat	*Fleisch*
fish	*Fisch*
poultry	*Geflügel*
game	*Wild*

252

salad	*Salat*
vegetables	*Gemüse*
fruit	*Obst*
cheese	*Käse*
milk/sugar	*Milch/Zucker*
salt/pepper	*Salz/Pfeffer*
bread/butter	*Brot/Butter*
mustard	*Senf*
oil/vinegar	*Öl/Essig*
knife/fork/spoon	*Messer/Gabel/Löffel*
plate	*Teller*
cup	*Tasse*
glass	*Glas*
home-made	*hausgemacht*
fresh	*frisch*
boiled	*gekocht*
steamed	*gedämpft*
baked	*gebacken*
roasted	*gebraten*
smoked	*geräuchert*
pickled	*eingelegt*
stuffed	*gefüllt*
casserole	*Eintopf*
kebab	*Spiess, Kebab*

Breakfast

tea/coffee	*Tee/Kaffee*
orange juice	*Orangensaft*
roll	*Brötchen, Schrippe*
jam	*Marmelade*
honey	*Honig*
yoghurt	*Joghurt*
boiled/fried/scrambled egg	*gekochtes Ei/Spiegelei/Rührei*
bacon	*Speck*

Meat

sausage	*Wurst*
ham	*Schinken*
cold cuts	*Aufschnitt*
chicken	*Huhn*
duck	*Ente*
pork	*Schweinefleisch*
beef	*Rindfleisch*
lamb	*Lammfleisch*
veal	*Kalbfleisch*
oxtail	*Ochsenschwanz*
goose	*Gans*

253

rabbit	*Kaninchen*
hare	*Hase*
meat loaf	*falscher Hase*
mincemeat	*Hackfleisch*
meat ball	*Boulette*
liver	*Leber*
steak	*Steak*
chop	*Schnitzel, Kottolett*
fricassee	*Geschnetzeltes*

Fish/Seafood

eel	*Aal*
herring	*Hering, Matjes*
salmon	*Lachs*
trout	*Forelle*
perch	*Zander*
pike	*Hecht*
sole	*Seezunge*
flounder	*Butt*
tuna	*Thunfisch*
mussels	*Muscheln*
clams	*Venusmuscheln*
prawns	*Garnelen*
squid	*Tintenfisch*

Vegetables/Side Dishes

potatoes	*Kartoffeln*
chips	*pommes frites* (pronounced *pomfrit*)
rice	*Reis*
dumplings	*Knödeln, Klösse*
tomatoes	*Tomaten*
cucumber	*Gurke*
peppers	*Paprika*
sweetcorn	*Mais*
carrots	*Karrotten/Mohrrüben*
beans	*Bohnen*
peas	*Erbsen*
onions	*Zwiebeln*
garlic	*Knoblauch*
(red) cabbage	*(Rot)kohl*
cauliflower	*Blumenkohl*
spinach	*Spinat*
mushrooms	*Champignons*
leeks	*Lauch*
lentils	*Linsen*
chickpeas	*Kichererbsen*
asparagus	*Spargel*

aubergine/eggplant	*Aubergine*
parsley	*Petersilie*
dill	*Dill*
rosemary	*Rosmarin*
chives	*Schnittlauch*

Fruit/Desserts

apple	*Apfel*
orange	*Apfelsine; Orange*
lemon	*Zitrone*
grapefruit	*Pampelmuse*
banana	*Banane*
pineapple	*Ananas*
pear	*Birne*
figs/dates	*Feigen/Datteln*
cherry	*Kirsche*
peach	*Pfirsich*
plum	*Pflaume*
grapes	*Trauben*
raisins	*Rosinen*
raspberry	*Himbeer*
strawberry	*Erdbeer*
redcurrant	*Johannisbeer*
tart/cake	*Torte/Kuchen*
ice cream	*Eis*
(whipped) cream	*(Schlag)sahne*
nuts	*Nüsse*
almonds	*Mandeln*
chocolate	*Schokolade*

Drink

drink	*Getränk*
I would like to drink...	*ich möchte... trinken*
(mineral) water	*(Mineral)wasser*
fruit juice	*Saft*
beer	*Bier*
wine	*Wein*
red/white wine	*Rotwein/Weisswein*
brandy	*Brandwein*

A FEW SIMPLE BERLIN PHRASES

good luck	*Hals und Beinbruch* (break a neck and leg)
it's all the same to me	*es ist mir wurscht* (it's all sausage to me)
nothing doing	*tote Hosen* (dead trousers)
don't be a spoil-sport	*sei doch keen Frosch* (don't be a frog)
it's draughty	*es zieht wie die Hechtsuppe* (like pike soup)

Index

Notes: *Italic* numbers indicate maps.
Bold numbers indicate main references. Museums and galleries are grouped together under M.